GOVERNANCE WITHOUT A STATE?

Governance Without a State?

POLICIES AND POLITICS IN AREAS

OF LIMITED STATEHOOD

Edited by Thomas Risse

COLUMBIA UNIVERSITY PRESS   NEW YORK

COLUMBIA UNIVERSITY PRESS

Publishers Since 1893

NEW YORK   CHICHESTER, WEST SUSSEX

Copyright © 2011 Columbia University Press
Paperback edition, 2013

Library of Congress Cataloging-in-Publication Data
   Governance without a state? : policies and politics in areas of limited statehood / edited by
   Thomas Risse.
       p. cm.
   Includes bibliographical references and index.
   ISBN 978-0-231-15120-7 (cloth : alk. paper)—ISBN 978-0-231-15121-4 (pbk. : alk. paper)—
   ISBN 978-0-231-52187-1 (e-book)
     1. Security, International.   2. Failed states.   3. Non-state actors
   (international relations)   4. Nation-building.   I. Risse-Kappen, Thomas.   II. Title.

JZ6005.G68   2011
321′.08—dc22

                                                                              2011006049

Columbia University Press books are printed on permanent and durable acid-free paper.
Printed in the United States of America

c 10 9 8 7 6 5 4 3 2 1
p 10 9 8 7 6 5 4 3 2 1

Cover designed by Jarrod Taylor

References to Internet Web sites (URLs) were accurate at the time of writing. Neither the author
nor Columbia University Press is responsible for URLs that may have expired or changed since
the manuscript was prepared.

CONTENTS

T HIS BOOK PRESENTS THE RESEARCH AGENDA AS well as empirical findings of the Collaborative Research Center (Sonderforschungsbereich), "Governance in Areas of Limited Statehood," which is funded by the German Research Foundation (Deutsche Forschungsgemeinschaft). The Research Center is located at the Freie Universität Berlin, with partners at the Social Science Center Berlin, the Hertie School of Governance, the SWP German Institute for International and Security Affairs, the University of Potsdam, and the European University Institute in Florence, Italy.

Such research centers provide a unique opportunity for joint interdisciplinary research for an extended period of time (up to twelve years divided into three funding periods of four years each, following intensive and on-site evaluations). In our case, the Research Center encompasses nineteen individual research projects of political scientists, historians, and legal scholars. More than thirty doctoral students and nine postdocs collaborate in these projects. We are very grateful to the Deutsche Forschungsgemeinschaft for providing us with this opportunity.

In addition, we thank two anonymous reviewers for their detailed comments on the draft. We also thank Ursula Lehmkuhl, former co-coordinator of the Research Center, and Gregor Walter-Drop, our managing director, for their continuous contributions and inspiration. Last but not least, special thanks go to Anne Routon at Columbia University Press for her support for this project, to Christopher Pitts for a superb copyediting job, to Alison Alexanian at Columbia University Press for her help with the production process, and, finally, to Alexandra Kuhles for proofreading.

Berlin, May 2011

GOVERNANCE WITHOUT A STATE?

Governance in Areas of Limited Statehood

Introduction and Overview

Thomas Risse

N THE TWENTY-FIRST CENTURY, IT IS BECOMING increasingly clear that conventional modes of political steering by nation-states and international regulations are not effectively dealing with global challenges such as environmental problems, humanitarian catastrophes, and new security threats.[1] This is one of the reasons governance has become such a central topic of research within the social sciences, focusing in particular on nonstate actors that participate in rule making and implementation. There is wide agreement that governance is supposed to achieve certain standards in the areas of rule and authority (*Herrschaft*), such as human rights, democracy, and the rule of law, as well as to provide common goods such as security, welfare, and a clean environment.

Yet the governance discourse remains centered on an "ideal type" of modern statehood—with full internal and external sovereignty, a legitimate monopoly on the use of force, and checks and balances that constrain political rule and authority. Similarly, the "global governance" debate in international relations, while focusing on "governance without government" and the rise of private authority in world politics (e.g., Cutler et al. 1999; O'Brien et al. 2000; Hall and Biersteker 2002; Grande and Pauly 2005), is based on the assumption that functioning states are capable of implementing and enforcing global norms and rules. Even the discourse on failed, failing, and fragile states centers on state building as the main remedy for establishing or restoring political and social order (see, e.g., Rotberg 2003; Rotberg 2004; Schneckener 2004; Beisheim and Schuppert 2007).

From a global as well as a historical perspective, however, the modern nation-state is the exception rather than the rule. Outside the developed OECD world, we find areas of "limited statehood," from developing and transition countries to failing and failed states in today's conflict zones and—historically—in colonial societies. Areas of limited statehood lack the capacity to implement and enforce central decisions and a monopoly on the use of force. While their "international sovereignty," that is, recognition by the international community, is still intact, they lack "domestic sovereignty," to use Stephen Krasner's terms (Krasner 1999).

This book starts from the assumption that "limited statehood" is not a historical accident or some deplorable deficit of most Third World and transition countries that has to be overcome by the relentless forces of economic and political modernization in an era of globalization. Rather, we suggest that "limited statehood" is here to stay—even in so-called Western and modern societies—and that governance research has to take this fundamental condition into account. The book then asks how effective and legitimate governance is possible under conditions of limited statehood and how security and other collective goods can be provided under these circumstances.

The authors of this volume investigate the governance problematic in areas of limited statehood from a variety of disciplinary perspectives, including political science, history, and law. From a theoretical perspective, the volume challenges the conventional wisdom of the governance debate as being biased toward modern developed nation-states. Moreover, if we confront the central tenets of the governance debate with the empirical reality of historical or contemporary areas of limited statehood, serious conceptual and theoretical problems arise. If one of the key concepts of modern social sciences is not applicable to two-thirds of the international community, we face not only theoretical challenges but also eminently political and practical ones.

The authors probe the following assumptions: First, governance in areas of limited statehood rests on the systematic involvement of nonstate actors and on nonhierarchical modes of political steering, including bargaining and various forms of competition (see particularly chapters by Chojnacki and Branovic, Liese and Beisheim, Börzel et al., and Enderlein et al.). Yet these modes of governance do not *complement* hierarchical steering by a well-functioning state but have to provide *functional equivalents* to developed statehood (see chapters by Schuppert and Ladwig and Rudolf). Second, governance in areas of limited statehood is "multilevel governance," which links the local with national, regional, and global levels and is based on shared sovereignty. This is fairly obvious in colonial governance as well as in modern "protectorates" where international and transnational actors provide governance services ranging from security to public authority (see chapters by Conrad and Stange, Ladwig and Rudolf, Schneckener, and Brozus). But it is also the case in many other weak states that the international community co-governs through the provision of collective goods and services (see chapters by Liese and Beisheim, and Enderlein et al.).

This chapter begins by introducing the book's key concepts such as *limited statehood* and *governance*. I then discuss some conceptual issues that arise when governance is applied to areas of limited statehood. Drawing on the contributions to this volume, the next section highlights the contribution of nonstate actors in the provision of governance in areas of limited statehood. The chapter concludes by pointing to the "multilevel" features of governance in areas of limited statehood, in particular the role of external actors in the provision of collective goods and services.

Conceptual Clarifications

What Is Limited Statehood?

Our concept of "limited statehood" requires clarification.[2] In particular, it needs to be strictly distinguished from the way in which notions of "fragile," "failing," or "failed" statehood are used in the literature. Most typologies in the literature and datasets on fragile states, "states at risk," and so on reveal a normative orientation toward highly developed and democratic statehood and, thus, toward the Western model (e.g., Rotberg 2003; Rotberg 2004). The benchmark is usually the democratic and capitalist state governed by the rule of law (Leibfried and Zürn 2005). This is problematic on both normative and analytical grounds. It is normatively questionable because it reveals Eurocentrism and a bias toward Western concepts as if statehood equals Western liberal statehood and market economy. We might find the political and economic systems of the People's Republic of China and Russia morally questionable, but they certainly constitute states. Confounding statehood with a particular Western understanding is analytically problematic, too, because it tends to confuse definitional issues and research questions. If we define states as political entities that provide all kinds of services and public goods, such as security, the rule of law, welfare, and a clean environment, many, if not most, "states" in the international system do not qualify as such. Moreover, such conceptualizations of statehood, which are more than common in the literature on failing and failed states, obscure what we consider the most relevant research question: Who governs for whom, and how are governance services provided under conditions of weak statehood?

Thus, we have deliberately opted for a rather narrow concept of statehood. We follow rather closely Max Weber's conceptualization of statehood as an institutionalized rule structure with the ability to rule authoritatively (*Herrschaftsverband*) and to legitimately control the means of violence (*Gewaltmonopol*, cf. Weber 1921/1980; on statehood in general see Benz 2001; Schuppert 2009).[3] While no state governs hierarchically all the time, states at least possess the ability to authoritatively make, implement, and enforce central decisions for a collectivity. In other words, states command what Stephen Krasner calls "domestic sovereignty," that is, "the formal organization of political authority within the state and the ability of public authorities to exercise effective control within the borders of their own polity" (1999, 4). This understanding allows us to strictly distinguish between statehood as an institutional structure of authority and the kind of governance it provides. The latter is an empirical not a definitional question—for example, control over the means of violence is part of the definition. Whether this monopoly over the use of force actually provides security for the citizens as a public good and is irrespective of one's race, gender, or kinship becomes an empirical question. Whether a state's polity is democratic and bound by human rights also concerns empirical issues that should not be confused with definitional ones.

If statehood is defined by the monopoly over the means of violence or the ability to make and enforce central political decisions, we can now define more precisely what "limited statehood" means. In short, while areas of limited statehood still belong to internationally recognized states (even the failed state Somalia still commands international sovereignty), it is their domestic sovereignty that is severely circumscribed. Areas of limited statehood concern those parts of a country in which central authorities (governments) lack the ability to implement and enforce rules and decisions or in which the legitimate monopoly over the means of violence is lacking, at least temporarily. The ability to enforce rules or to control the means of violence can be restricted along various dimensions: (1) territorial, that is, parts of a country's territorial spaces; (2) sectoral, that is, with regard to specific policy areas; (3) social, that is, with regard to specific parts of the population; and (4) temporal. It follows that the opposite of "limited statehood" is not "unlimited" but "consolidated" statehood, that is, those areas of a country in which the state enjoys the monopoly over the means of violence and the ability to make and enforce central decisions. Thinking in terms of configurations of limited statehood also implies thinking in degrees of limited statehood rather than using the term in a dichotomous sense.

This conceptualization allows distinguishing among quite different configurations of limited statehood. As argued earlier, "limited statehood" is not confined to failing and failed states that have all but lost the ability to govern and to control their territory (Rotberg 2003; Rotberg 2004; Beisheim and Schuppert 2007; Schneckener 2004). Failed states such as Somalia comprise only a small percentage of the world's areas of limited statehood. Most developing and transition states, for example, encompass areas of limited statehood as they only partially control the instruments of force and are only partially able to enforce decisions, mainly for reasons of insufficient political and administrative capacities. Brazil and Mexico, on the one hand, and Somalia and Sudan, on the other, constitute opposite ends of a continuum of states that contain areas of limited statehood. Moreover, and except for failed states, "limited statehood" usually does not obtain for a state as a whole but in "areas," that is, territorial or functional spaces within otherwise functioning states in which the latter have lost their ability to govern. While the Pakistani government, for example, enjoys a monopoly over the use of force in many parts of its territory, the so-called tribal areas in the country's northwest are beyond the control of the central government and, thus, areas of limited statehood.

It also follows that limited statehood is by no means confined to the developing world. For example, New Orleans right after Hurricane Katrina in 2005 constituted an area of limited statehood in the sense that U.S. authorities were unable to enforce decisions and to uphold the monopoly over the means of violence for a short period of time. However, this book concentrates mostly on cases in which limited statehood in an area's territorial, sectoral, or social dimension extends over sustained periods of time. For example, the chapter by Chojnacki and Branovic on markets of violence deals empirically with territorially and socially defined areas of limited statehood in mostly sub-Saharan Africa, where the state monopoly over the use of force is systematically lacking. The chapter by Liese and Beisheim focuses on areas of limited statehood in the developing world according to their territorial, sectoral, and social dimensions. The chapter on South Africa by Börzel et al. concentrates on policy sectors in which the South African state does not have the capacity to implement and enforce its own laws.

Moreover, if we conceptualize limited statehood in such a configurative way, it becomes clear that areas of limited statehood are an almost ubiquitous phenomenon in the contemporary international system and also in historical comparison (see the chapter by Conrad and Stange). After all, the state monopoly over the means of violence has only been around for a little more than 150 years. Most contemporary states contain "areas of limited statehood" in the sense that central authorities do not control the entire territory, do not completely enjoy the monopoly over the means of violence, or have limited capacities to enforce and implement decisions, at least in some policy areas or with regard to large parts of the population. This is what Somalia, Brazil, and Indonesia but also the People's Republic of China have in common and share with modern protectorates such as Afghanistan, Kosovo, or Bosnia-Herzegovina—internationally recognized states that lack "Westphalian sovereignty" in the sense that external actors rule parts of their territory or in some policy areas (Krasner 1999).

The following map presents a graphical description of the phenomenon. It uses a combination of two indicators of the Bertelsmann Transformation Index (BTI) measuring degrees of, first, the state monopoly over the means of violence, and, second, basic administrative structures.[4] The countries marked in white are fully consolidated states located in the Western world, as well as a handful of others, such as Chile. On the opposite end of the spectrum, we find twenty-nine failed (marked in black) or fragile (marked in dark gray) countries, mostly in sub-Saharan Africa. The remaining countries (marked in gray)—the vast majority of states in the contemporary international system—contain areas of limited statehood in the sense defined earlier. Note that about 80 percent of the world's population lives in or is exposed to such areas of limited statehood.

These data have serious consequences for the way in which we think about statehood in general. What if the modern, developed, and sovereign nation-state turns out to be a historical exception in the context of this diversity of areas of limited statehood? Even in Europe, the birthplace of modern statehood, nation-states were only able to fully establish the monopoly over the use of force in the nineteenth century (Reinhard 2007). And the globalization

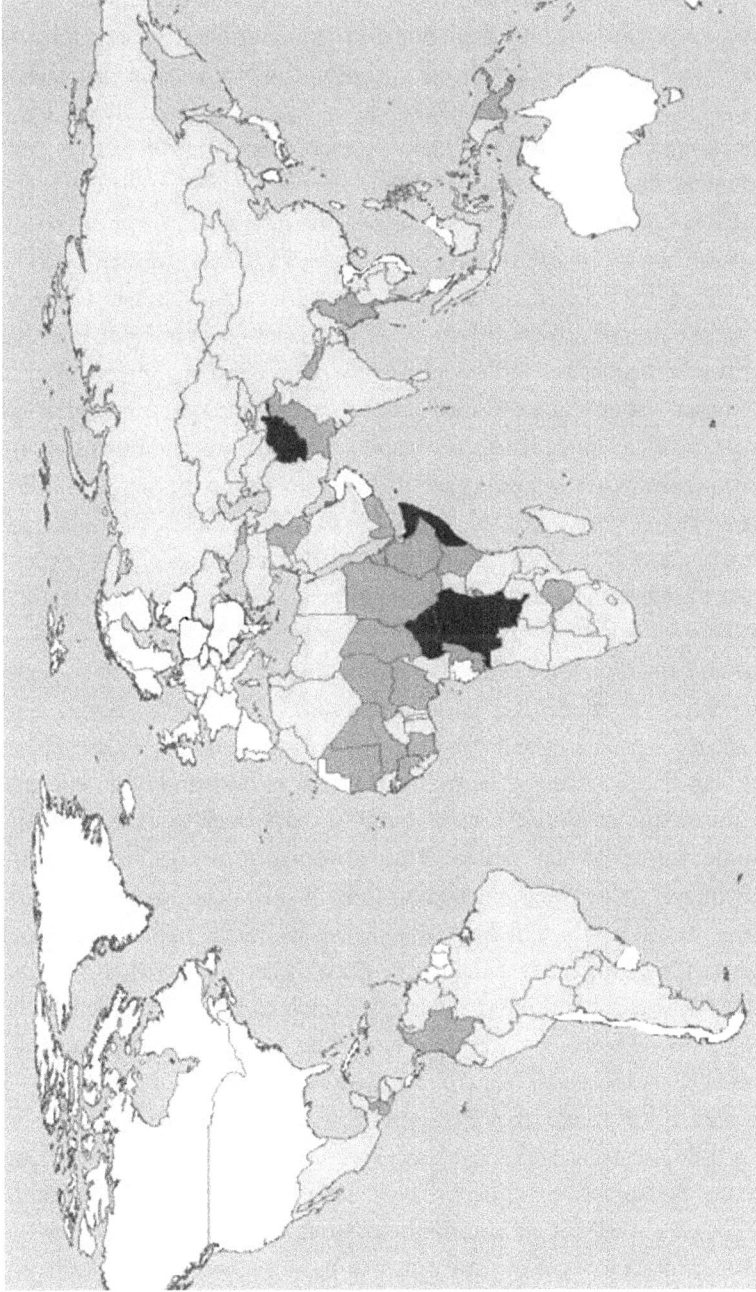

FIGURE 1.1. Degrees of limited statehood. *Source*: Bertelsmann Transformation Index 2010, www.bertelsmann-transformation-index.de/bti/ranking/.

of sovereign statehood as the dominant feature of the contemporary international order only took place in the 1960s, as a result of decolonization.

Yet the world today, as an international community of states, is largely based on the fiction that it is populated by fully consolidated states. International law embodies the idea of sovereign nation-states, which the international community assumes are functioning states that command "effective authority" over their territories (see chapters by Schuppert and Ladwig and Rudolf). The international prohibition on intervening in the internal affairs of sovereign states assumes that these states have the full capacity to conduct their own domestic affairs. Ironically, many developing countries where limited statehood constitutes part of the daily experience of the citizens firmly insist on their full rights as sovereign states and are adamantly opposed to any intervention in their internal affairs. Moreover, international law and the legalization of world politics have increasingly embedded states in a net of legal and other binding obligations in almost every policy area (Goldstein et al. 2000; Zangl and Zürn 2004; see chapter by Ladwig and Rudolf in this volume). Yet legalization assumes that states are fully capable of implementing and enforcing the law.

Most international donor agencies and most international state-building and democratization programs—from the World Bank to the European Union and the United States—also presuppose that the modern Western nation-state is the model for "good governance" (Magen et al. 2009). Underneath these programs and strategies is the assumption of modernization theory that the modern state comes as a package consisting of an effective government, the rule of law, human rights, democracy, market economy, and some degree of social welfare. This "governance package" constitutes a world cultural script (Meyer 1987) and is applied to developing and transition countries as well as to failing and failed states. "State building" is part of this governance package that the international community tries to institute in failing or failed states (see chapters by Schneckener and Brozus). But the goal of these measures is always the same: the institutionalization of fully consolidated, democratic, Western-style nation-states.

In short, this volume challenges central assumptions of both development studies and development policies, namely, that fully consolidated statehood has to be the yardstick against which most existing states are measured. Rather, we assume that areas of limited statehood constitute much of the empirical context in most existing states, both in the contemporary international system and from a historical perspective. But this volume is not about exploring the causes of limited statehood. In fact, there are multiple causes ranging from particular colonial histories, resource constraints, failures of nation building, histories of internal warfare, and the like. Exploring these root causes would require a different book. Rather, we take areas of limited statehood as our starting point and then ask how effective and legitimate governance is possible under these circumstances.

Governance and Limited Statehood

These considerations lead to the governance problems in areas of limited statehood. In this context, this book advances a major proposition, namely, that limited statehood does not equal the absence of governance, let alone political, social, or economic order. State weakness does not simply translate to the absence of political order, rule making, or the provision of basic services. Limited statehood does not mean anarchy in a Hobbesian sense. In fact, we even find failed states such as Somalia where limited statehood is all-pervasive but where governance takes place regularly and collective goods are provided (Menkhaus 2006/2007).

Before I proceed, however, the concept of governance used in this book must be clarified. In its most general version, governance refers to all modes of coordinating social action in human society. Williamson, for example, distinguished between governance by markets and governance by hierarchy (i.e., the state); later scholars added governance by networks to this list (e.g., Williamson 1975; Rhodes 1997; Kooiman 1993). However, this understanding that identifies governance with any kind of social ordering appears to be too broad.

As a result, this book employs a somewhat narrower concept that is linked to politics. By *governance*, we mean in this book the various *institutionalized modes of social coordination to produce and implement collectively binding rules, or to provide collective goods*. This conceptualization follows closely the understanding of governance that is widespread within the social sciences (e.g., Mayntz 2004, 2008; Kohler-Koch 1998; Benz 2004a; Schuppert 2005; Schuppert and Zürn 2008). Governance consists of both structural ("institutionalized") and process dimensions ("modes of social coordination"). Accordingly, governance covers steering by the state ("governance by government"), governance via cooperative networks of public and private actors ("governance with government"), as well as rule making by nonstate actors or self-regulation by civil society ("governance without government";

cf. Benz 2004a; Czempiel and Rosenau 1992; Grande and Pauly 2005; Zürn 1998). Governance is supposed to provide collectively binding rules as well as collective goods.[5]

The modern (Western) nation-state, thus, constitutes a governance structure. First, it provides a structure of rule and authority, a system of political and social institutions to generate and to implement authoritative political decisions. Today, democracy and the rule of law belong to the generally accepted norms of these institutions for authoritative rule making. Second, the Western nation-state has the task to protect the internal and external security of its citizens. The monopoly over the means of violence is supposed to do just that. Finally, the rendering of public services is part of the classical responsibilities of the state, from the creation of economic stability and the guarantee of minimal social security to public health, education, and, today, the maintenance and the creation of a clean environment. In short, the modern Western nation-state provides governance in the areas of rule making and enforcement, on the one hand, and collective goods such as security, welfare, and a clean environment, on the other. While this nation-state is undergoing a profound transformation (Leibfried and Zürn 2005; Hurrelmann et al. 2007), its ability to ultimately make, implement, and enforce decisions is beyond doubt, even if the modern state privatizes or deregulates previously public services. In other words, the modern state's "shadow of hierarchy" is never in doubt, even in the age of profound (neoliberal) privatization and deregulation (Börzel 2008).

This changes profoundly under conditions of limited statehood. Governance in areas of limited statehood requires providing these very governance services in the absence of a fully functioning state's exerting at least a "shadow of hierarchy" with the ability to enforce and implement decisions. This implies that we will have to look for functional equivalents to modern statehood (see Draude 2007 on this point)—unless we want to give up the normative proposition that human beings have a right to a decent authority structure, security, and other collective goods (for a discussion of these normative problems, see Ladwig 2007; see also chapter by Ladwig and Rudolf in this volume).

This book explores the various forms of governance emerging in the context of limited statehood. We assume that forms of governance emerge under these conditions. The contemporary social science literature discusses these as "new" modes of governance or the privatization of authority (e.g., Cutler, Haufler, and Porter 1999; Grande and Pauly 2005; Hall and Biersteker 2002). However, as the chapter by Conrad and Stange demonstrates, these "new" modes of governance are by no means specific to the contemporary international system. The colonial state, for example, constituted an area of limited statehood as we understand it in this volume, as a result of which governance took place through colonial rulers ("states"), transnational "public-private" companies (e.g., the Hudson Bay Company in North America or the East India Company in Asia), and local "private" actors such as settlers.

Governance as a process entails two dimensions: actors and modes of co-ordinating social action. Various combinations of state and nonstate actors "govern" in areas of limited statehood. These can be public-private partnerships (see Schäferhoff et al. 2009, also chapter by Liese and Beisheim in this volume) in which national governments, international (interstate) organizations, as well as (multinational) firms and (international) nongovernmental organizations co-govern. But governance can also be provided by the self-regulation of firms (chapter by Börzel et al. in this volume) and even by warlords and other violent actors (see chapter by Chojnacki and Branovic in this volume). The second part of this book explores the various contributions of nonstate actors to governance in areas of limited statehood.

The second process dimension of governance concerns modes of steering. The modern (Western) nation-state has the ability of hierarchical steering, that is, authoritatively enforcing the law, ultimately through policing and "top-down" command and control. It is precisely this ability to enforce decisions that is lacking in areas of limited statehood. To the extent that hierarchical steering and authoritative rule do take place in areas of limited statehood, we have to look for actors other than the national governments. As Chojnacki and Branovic point out in their chapter, warlords and local "big men" sometimes exert hierarchical control in war-torn areas of limited statehood. In addition, international organizations as well as—mostly Western—states often interfere authoritatively, particularly in modern protectorates such as Kosovo or Afghanistan that have all but lost their "Westphalian sovereignty" (see chapters by Schneckener and Brozus in this volume).

Much more common, however, are nonhierarchical modes of social co-ordination in areas of limited statehood (Börzel and Risse 2005; Göhler et al. 2009). Nonhierarchical steering involves creating and manipulating incentives and "benchmarking," as well as initiating communicative learning processes. Positive incentives as well as sanctions are meant to affect the cost-benefit calculations of the relevant parties and to induce the desired behavior.

Governance also includes bargaining processes and horizontal negotiation as well as nonmanipulative communication, persuasion, and learning. The latter modes of governance aim at challenging fixed interests and preferences so that actors are induced in a socialization process to internalize new rules and norms. Most chapters in the second part of this book explore the bargaining processes between state and nonstate actors involved in governance in areas of limited statehood.

When Governance Travels: The Implicit (Western) Bias of Social Science Concepts

The understanding of governance employed in this book largely follows the conceptualizations in American and European social sciences. However, applying the governance concept to areas of limited statehood reveals some implicit biases. The way in which the governance concept has been developed in the social sciences (and has become part of political practice) is strongly influenced by the experiences of Western modernity and of modern statehood as defined earlier.

The Distinction Between the "Public" and the "Private" Spheres

Defining governance and the modes of governance in terms of including state and nonstate actors in the provision of collective goods more often than not relies on the distinction between the "public" and "private" realms. This distinction, however, stems from modern statehood in its Western and Eurocentric understandings. This is problematic when we apply the governance concept to other historical contexts or other cultural experiences in the contemporary international system. Historically speaking, the modern Western notion of the "private sphere" is connected to processes of individualization and personalization that only emerged in the second half of eighteenth-century Europe leading to the separation of the public and the private (e.g., Böckenförde 1976; Keane 1988). As Conrad and Stange argue in their chapter, thinking of the "public" and the "private" spheres as binary categories is inherently problematic with regard to colonial rule. They demonstrate, for example, that the differences between state-funded administrative personnel and "private" actors among the colonizers were marginal at best—for example, the "private" East India Company exercised "public" authority on behalf of the British Empire. The same holds true for the definition of indigenous elites as "private" actors, since colonizers often gave local "chiefs" the authority to rule hierarchically.

Applying the public-private distinction to contemporary areas of limited statehood is just as difficult. Of course, we can still distinguish formally between the state and the nonstate sector including for-profit companies, on the one hand, and the nonprofit and civil society sector, on the other. But what does this mean in countries in which state institutions are so weak that government actors can easily exploit state resources for private purposes, while so-called private actors such as companies or NGOs provide much-needed collective goods with regard to education, public health, or infrastructure (e.g., Börzel et al. 2007; Fuhr et al. 2007; see chapters by Liese and Beisheim, and Börzel et al. in this volume). In other words, the implicit assumption of the public-private distinction according to which governments govern and private actors mind their own business is often turned on its head in areas of limited statehood. The distinction that comes with Western modernity, according to which "state = public" and "nonstate = private" is enormously problematic in areas of limited statehood.

Take the example of Palestine under Yasser Arafat: The Palestinian Authority was more or less corrupt at the time and the development aid provided by the international community to jump-start the Palestinian state ended up in private coffers. At the same time, the militant Islamist organization of Hamas provided crucial governance services in the social, education, and public health sectors of the Palestinian territories. So, who governed Palestine at the time? If we use the previously stated governance definition, Hamas is Janus-faced: On the one hand, it is a governance actor providing public services in Palestine. On the other hand and almost at the same time, it is a terrorist organization that undermines governance in the security realm. The same held true for the Palestinian Authority under Arafat: Its security agencies at least tried to maintain public security in the occupied territories, while Palestinian "state" actors undermined governance with regard to the provision of other collective goods.

The example of Palestine refers to widespread phenomena in areas of limited statehood: Rent-seeking governments distribute state revenues including development aid to maintain their rule via clientelistic networks (the so-called neopatrimonial state in sub-Saharan Africa, the Southern Caucasus, and elsewhere; see Erdmann 2002; Erdmann and Engel 2007). In other words, they transform public goods into club or even private goods. In a different way, the emergence of "shadow states" has to be considered here too (Koehler and Zürcher 2004; Zürcher 2007). On the one hand, formal state institutions have ceased to exist or to provide governance services in failing and failed states. On the other hand, informal governance institutions often emerge providing social and political order as well as collective goods, thereby preventing the country or the region from completely collapsing into anarchy. In some cases, such as the Southern Caucasus, shadow states survive over extended periods of time.

These examples challenge the way in which the concepts of "state" and "public" as well as "nonstate" and "private" are mostly used interchangeably in the social sciences based on the historical experience of Western modernity. They also show the implicit normative connotations of the distinction (see Ladwig et al. 2007; also chapter by Ladwig and Rudolf in this volume). We usually expect that state actors contribute to governance, that is, that they act in the public rather than the private interest. At least, they are supposed to justify their actions with regard to the common good (see Zürn 2005). While policy-makers might be power-seeking, state institutions in a consolidated state—no matter how "transformed"—are supposed to direct their practices toward governance in the common interest. And if they abuse their power, we can throw them out through democratic procedures or, in the worst case, through the judicial system. Limited statehood, however, consists of weak political institutions lacking the capacity to constrain power-maximizing actors. As a result, it becomes problematic to speak of "public" actors in such cases or to assume that state actors promote the public interest. As to private actors, we usually assume that private companies pursue their egoistic self-interest, even if their businesses practices produce positive externalities for the community (jobs, welfare, etc.). But we also assume that private actors act within the confines of the law—and if not, that the courts will take care of them.

These assumptions that come with the "public-private" distinction are missing in areas of limited statehood. At least, they can no longer be taken for granted. The conceptual problem cannot be solved easily—for example, one could speak of "hybrid" regimes or forms of governance in order to avoid the distinction between the public and private realms or between state and nonstate actors (e.g., Bendel et al. 2002). But such a solution only side-steps the problem to discern who provides governance services and who does not, and under which conditions. A possible way out would be to investigate empirically who serves as a governance actor—irrespective of a formal position in the political system or in society. In other words, one would search for functional equivalents of "public" actors (Draude 2007, 2008).

Intentionality and Normativity of Governance

These considerations lead to a second problem with regard to the applicability of the governance concept to areas of limited statehood. The governance concept as defined earlier is geared toward producing and implementing collectively binding rules and providing collective goods. In other words, governance implies intentional action toward providing public services for a given community (Mayntz 2004, 67). This does not mean that governance actors have to be necessarily motivated toward the public interest, even though motivations toward the common interest do not hurt. Policy-makers, for example, can still be egoistic power-maximizers. Yet, in a consolidated state, they are usually embedded in governance structures that institutionalize the intentionality of governance toward providing services for the community.[6]

The inherent intentionality of governance becomes problematic when applied to areas of limited statehood. First, as noted earlier, we can no longer assume that governance institutions such as the state or its "shadow of hierarchy" embody intentions toward providing collective goods. Second, we need to distinguish between the provision of some collective goods or services as the unintended consequence of "private" activities, on the one hand, and the explicit regulation of social issues and intentional provision of collective goods, on the other. Only the second understanding would qualify as governance if we stick to the earlier conceptualization.

To illustrate the point with an example: Oil companies such as BP in Angola routinely use private security firms to protect their industrial production facilities in areas of limited statehood. This transforms security into a private good. Protecting such facilities might have positive externalities for the surrounding neighborhoods insofar as the security firms might unintentionally deter armed gangs or militias from attacking nearby villages too. In this sense, the firms while primarily providing a private good for BP would also contribute to public security, albeit indirectly. But we would not call this security governance because of the lack of intentionality. This activity could be called governance only if BP explicitly instructs the security firm to protect not only the oil facilities but also the surrounding villages.

In other cases, we are faced with a continuum ranging from governance in the sense defined here to "racketeering:" The Afghan warlord who uses his militias to provide public security for the area of his rule can be regarded a governance actor. However, the more he uses the same militias to threaten the safety of the community and then resells security to clientelistic networks for a protection fee, the more he would transform public security into a club or private good. The latter would be "racketeering" (Chojnacki and Branovic 2007; Schuppert 2007, 479; see the chapter by Chojnacki and Branovic in this volume).

Thus, applying the governance concept to areas of limited statehood highlights its unavoidable intentionality and implicit normativity. If we define governance—as is common in the social sciences—as the making and implementing of collectively binding rules and the provision of collective goods, we cannot refrain from acknowledging that governance is linked normatively toward what is supposed to be in the common interest. But who are those in areas of limited statehood in whose name the "common interest" is being pronounced? What is the relevant community or collectivity for whom governance is provided? Once again, these issues are clearly decided in the ideal typical modern Western state. In most cases, governance is provided for the people or the citizens living in a given territory. While some services are only accessible to the citizens rather than the residents, even noncitizen residents enjoy some basic rights as well as access to at least some public services.

All this becomes problematic in areas of limited statehood. In many cases, it remains unclear who are the addressees of governance, who is entitled to which governance services, and who actually receives them in practice. We cannot simply assume that the collectivity for which governance is provided is clearly defined. Take border regions in sub-Saharan Africa, for example, that are beyond the control of central governments. Are those entitled to receiving governance the people living on a given territory? Or members of particular tribal or ethnic communities? And who decides who is entitled to what, particularly in cases of extremely scarce resources? Is it governance if collective goods become club goods in the sense that only particular ethnic, religious, or gendered communities are entitled to receive them? The latter constitutes a common practice in many areas of limited statehood, both historically and in the contemporary international system.

Thus, applying governance to areas of limited statehood requires taking a step back and refraining from "either everything or nothing" conceptual solutions. On the one hand, if governance is overburdened with such a strong normative orientation toward the common good or the public interest, we will not find much governance in areas of limited statehood by definition (on this point, see Schuppert 2007). In this case, governance does not travel very far outside the developed OECD world. On the other hand, if we strip the concept of governance of all normative connotations, then everything is governance and the privatization of collective goods has normative weight equal to the provision of public goods.

I suggest something in between as a way out: we should consider governance as both a process and a continuum. The more inclusive the social group for which goods are provided or regulations are formulated, the more we should consider this as governance. After all, this approximates the definition of public goods in terms of nonrivalry in consumption and nonexclusivity in access. In contrast, the more certain services are only provided for exclusive groups and the more collective goods are transformed into club or private goods accessible only to those who pay for them or who belong to specific ethnic or religious groups, the less we should conceptualize this as governance. In particular, applying the notion of collective goods to areas of limited statehood requires a more differentiated conceptualization of the collectivity for which governance is provided. In many cases, those entitled to receiving collective goods such as security are distinct from the addressees of governance services that also differ from those who factually receive governance (see the chapter by Chojnacki and Branovic in this volume; also De la Rosa et al. 2008).

It follows that the borders between governance and "racketeering" are rather fluid in areas of limited statehood. The weaker and the more fragile the state, the less it makes sense to judge governance services according to benchmarks derived from modern developed states. Rather, we should strive for minimum normative standards in these cases (Keohane 2007; Ladwig 2007; also the chapter by Ladwig and Rudolf in this volume).

Governance and the "Shadow of Hierarchy"

A third problem with regard to the application of the governance concept to areas of limited statehood concerns what has been called the "shadow of hierarchy" (Scharpf 1993). Research on modes of governance in the OECD world and on the transformation of (modern) statehood has demonstrated that public-private cooperation (such as PPPs) and private self-regulation are usually most effective under the "shadow of hierarchy." This means that state agencies supervise private regulatory efforts and that governments threaten to legislate if private actors do not get their act together or do not provide the collective goods. The liberalization of various public services—such as telecommunications, electricity, and the like—has led to ample efforts at reregulation by the modern state (e.g., Héritier 2003; Börzel 2007; 2008). Hierarchical steering or the threat to do so appears to be a precondition for the successful implementation and effectiveness of modes of governance in the modern nation-state and beyond. In other words, nonhierarchical modes of steering and including nonstate actors in governance complement rather than substitute for regulatory activities by national governments or supranational institutions such as the European Union. Moreover—and paradoxically—strong states or strong supranational organizations are required for nonhierarchical modes of steering to be effective and to enhance the problem-solving capacity of governance (Börzel 2009, 2010). Managing political authority requires effective state capacities including a strong "shadow of hierarchy."

If these findings are universally applicable, then governance in areas of limited statehood is doomed. Areas of limited statehood are by definition characterized by weak state capacities to implement and enforce decisions, that is, by weak "shadows of hierarchy." Moreover, the contribution of nonstate actors to the provision of collective goods has to substitute for governance by governments rather than to complement it. If the Bill & Melinda Gates Foundation (BMGF) decides to withdraw from providing services in the area of public health—for example, the immunization of children—in sub-Saharan Africa, these services will not be provided at all (for details see Schäferhoff, in preparation; Beisheim et al. 2008; and the chapter by Liese and Beisheim in this volume). If Daimler and other automobile manufacturers in South Africa were to withdraw from fighting HIV/AIDS at their production facilities and the surrounding areas, the fight there against the pandemic would be doomed (Börzel, Héritier, and Müller-Debus 2007; Müller-Debus et al. 2009). The same holds true for environmental protection in South Africa, as the chapter by Börzel et al. reveals. In each of these examples, the central governments are far too weak to provide the collective goods in question. As a result, private actors and the international community substitute for rather than complement governance by the state.

What explains then that we actually find governance in areas of limited statehood? The chapters in this volume suggest that there might be functional equivalents to the "shadow of hierarchy" provided by consolidated statehood (see Börzel 2010). First, in the case of the modern protectorates, the international community not only rules authoritatively in areas of limited statehood and interferes with a country's "Westphalian sovereignty," but it also provides a "shadow of hierarchy" (chapters by Schneckener and Brozus in this volume; see also Lake 2009 on hierarchy in the international order). Second, international legal standards on good governance, human rights, and the rule of law hold actors accountable in areas of limited statehood, be it governments, NGOs, firms, or even rebel groups (see chapter by Ladwig and Rudolf in this volume). While enforcement of these standards is inherently problematic, the increased legalization of these standards including the international "responsibility to protect" (R2P) casts a shadow of hierarchy in areas of limited statehood. Last but not least, there are various incentive structures available to commit nonstate actors to the provision of collective goods even under the most dire circumstances of limited statehood. As Chojnacki and Branovic argue in their chapter, even warlords, local "big men," or rebel groups sometimes provide security as a collective good in security markets if faced with an opportunity structure by which they benefit from protecting the local population rather than exploiting it. As to firms and environmental protection in South Africa, Börzel et al. show that there are several market-based mechanisms inducing companies to engage in self-regulation. If, for example, brand-name firms target high-end markets or are subjected to NGO campaigns, they are likely to provide collective goods in the framework of corporate social responsibility (CSR).

In sum, this overview suggests that there are some implicit biases in the governance concept as it has been developed in the context of Western-based social sciences and modern statehood. However, one should not throw out the baby with the bathwater. The governance concept provides a useful tool to analyze policies and politics in areas of limited statehood, precisely because it directs our attention to the role of nonstate actors, on the one hand, and nonhierarchical modes of steering, on the other. As a result, governance overcomes the state-centric bias implicit in the literature on failed and failing states as well as the modernization bias of most development studies. State building in areas of limited statehood might be futile, but "governance-shaping" certainly is not, as Brozus argues in his chapter.

I now turn to the contributions in this book in more detail to explore the role of nonstate actors in the provision of governance, on the one hand, and the contribution of the international community to governance in areas of limited statehood, on the other.

Who Governs in Areas of Limited Statehood?
The Role of Nonstate Actors

As argued earlier, areas of limited statehood are not devoid of governance. Rather, nonhierarchical modes of social interaction and nonstate actors engaged in governance abound, as the chapters in this volume demonstrate. Institutional state weakness implies that public-private partnerships or even pure nonstate forms of governance are becoming the rule rather than the exception, if governance services are supplied at all. While public-private partnerships increasingly complement classic state functions in Western developed states, they have to substitute for state weaknesses in areas of limited statehood, be it in parts of the territory, in policy sectors, or with regard to parts of the population.

To begin with, the chapter by Sebastian Conrad and Marion Stange provides a historical perspective to the discussion of governance in areas of limited statehood. In the long history of statehood, the ideal type of the "Westphalian system" frequently evoked in definitions of governance was probably the exception rather than the rule. The chapter discusses what the longer genealogy of forms of governance implies for current debates using the example of colonial states. Conrad and Stange argue that under conditions of colonialism, statehood was consistently dependent upon nonstate actors and the delegation of power and authority to them. As a result, the distinction between "public" and "private" actors that has been central for the governance concept as it has developed in political science, is inherently problematic. Moreover, the chapter suggests that we cannot start understanding the governance problematic in areas of limited statehood without taking colonial legacies into account, which is also highlighted by postcolonial studies (Conrad and Randeria 2002).

Highlighting the role of nonstate actors in governance and particularly in rule making challenges our understanding of law as wedded to the state. In the German context, for example, rule of law translates into *Rechtsstaatlichkeit* (law of the state) as a result of which human rights, predictability, and the legality of political decisions cannot even be conceptualized outside a state-centric framework. The chapter by Gunnar Folke Schuppert takes up this challenge and looks at various instances of nonstate rule making in order to explore what happens to public law in the context of the demise of the state (*Entstaatlichung*) and the deterritorialization of political rule in areas of limited statehood. He focuses on diverse examples such as the rules governing business transactions among diamond dealers in New York, the American cotton market at the Memphis Stock Exchange, the transnational sports law, and the various transnational standard-setting bodies. These examples constitute rule making by nonstate actors that are self-enforcing and do not require state regulation in order to be effective. However, as Schuppert argues, it would be misleading to analyze these forms of rule making from a perspective that treats the private and the public as polar opposites. In this sense, he agrees with the historical analysis by Conrad and Stange. Law by the state is entangled in many instances of private rule making—if only by providing a "shadow of hierarchy." At the same time, reputational concerns and the embeddedness of private rule making in social orders can make "law without a state" self-enforcing, which is exactly what Börzel et al. argue in their chapter on the conditions under which companies engage in environmental self-regulation.

The subsequent four chapters deal with the governance role of nonstate actors in areas of limited statehood from various empirical perspectives. The chapter by Sven Chojnacki and Zeljko Branovic takes on a particularly hard case by dealing with the conditions under which security as a collective rather than as a privatized good can be provided even under the most adverse conditions of fragile, failing, and failed states. State collapse and armed conflict give rise to areas where security is provided selectively by a variety of state, quasi-state or nonstate actors. In order to systematically differentiate and analyze the provision of security in areas of limited statehood, the authors trace several modes of security leading to varying forms of security governance (security as a public good, as a club good, and as a private commodity). The chapter uses the analogy of the market to argue that the emergence of different modes of security results from strategies of collective actors on hazardous markets of protection. These are characterized by areas where different public and private actors compete over territorial control, natural resources, and the recruitment of members. The emergence of security governance depends on economic and geographic opportunity structures and on the expected utility to invest in productive means instead of unproductive arming and fighting. The authors then discuss the conditions under which even violent nonstate actors such as warlords or rebel groups deem it in their interest to provide security as a public good for a given population. Chojnacki and Branovic claim, therefore, that stable security governance without a state is possible even under seemingly adverse conditions of fragile or failed statehood.

The next three chapters in this section deal with the provision of public goods in the issue areas of development, public health, social services, and macroeconomic stability in areas of limited statehood. Andrea Liese and Marianne Beisheim investigate transnational public-private partnerships (PPPs) to implement the Millennium Development Goals of the United Nations in areas of limited statehood. Transnational PPPs spread significantly in the 1990s and can be found in all policy areas. The study investigates the effectiveness of twenty-one PPPs in providing governance in the realms of public health, food, and energy for developing countries. The authors evaluate various hypotheses taking from institutionalist and compliance approaches in international relations. The chapter demonstrates that effectiveness of PPPs is highly correlated with the degree of institutionalization of these partnerships, particularly with regard to service-providing and standard-setting partnerships. This confirms arguments taken from legalization research according to which high degrees of obligation and precision of norms are conducive to compliance (e.g., Goldstein et al. 2000; Zangl 2008). In other words, institutional design matters and induces nonstate actors in PPPs to contribute to the provision of collective goods. But Liese and Beisheim also show that the process management of the PPPs influences their effectiveness too, while—interestingly enough—stakeholder participation appears to be less important.

Arguing from a strategic choice approach, Tanja Börzel, Adrienne Héritier, Nicole Kranz, and Christian Thauer reach similar conclusions as Liese and Beisheim with regard to the preparedness of multinational and other companies to enter a regulatory race to the top pushing for strict environmental regulations or even engaging in self-regulation. Their argument runs counter to the conventional wisdom that economic globalization necessarily leads to a "race to the bottom" among countries (for a similar argument see Prakash 2000; Prakash and Potoski 2006). Empirically, the chapter examines selected firms in the automotive, food and beverage, and textile industries in South Africa with regard to their propensity to engage in environmental product or process regulation. The study shows that certain factors explain why firms engage in providing environmental governance through either self-regulation or pressing for stricter state rules. These factors include the need to protect brand names and to target high-end markets, exposure to NGO campaigns, efforts to keep foreign competitors with low regulatory standards out of the home market, and, finally, strict home-country regulations in the case of multinational corporations. The chapter concludes that there are good rational reasons why firms should contribute to environmental governance, even in areas of limited statehood in which the shadow of hierarchy is weak or nonexistent.[7]

The chapter by Henrik Enderlein, Laura von Daniels, and Christoph Trebesch examines a different type of private actor, namely private creditors of developing countries. The public good under investigation here is macroeconomic stability in the face of sovereign debt crises. Many developing countries rely heavily upon financial resources provided by private creditors. Consequently, in situations of financial distress, governments and private creditors often enter a complex strategic interaction. From the perspective of governments, the key focus of this interaction is the provision of macroeconomic stability in the developing country under the constraint of servicing external debt. From the perspective of private creditors, the key interest is to limit losses from potential defaults. In other words, while the chapter by Liese and Beisheim concentrates on cooperative relations between state and nonstate actors in the provision of collective goods through PPPs, Enderlein et al. focus on much more conflictive public-private interactions. Their statistical analysis of government behavior toward private creditors shows that limited statehood—weak regulatory quality and low government effectiveness in this case—is highly correlated with aggressive government behavior toward their international creditors. The same holds true for countries with high corruption and weak rule of law. In contrast, neither democracy nor political violence or stability are correlated with aggressive government behavior toward private creditors. In some, the weaker the state, the more it drives a hard bargain toward its international and private creditors. The chapter shows that even weak and heavily indebted states are in the driver's seat when it comes to negotiations with their creditors.

In sum, these chapters yield the following conclusions with regard to the propensity of non-state actors to contribute to governance in areas of limited statehood:

1. Areas of limited statehood are not "ungoverned" or even "ungovernable." In fact, governance is sometimes provided even under rather adverse conditions of fragile or failing statehood. Under particular circumstances, nonstate actors

become governance actors in that they are systematically engaged in rule making or the provision of collective goods.

2. At the same time, governance without a state depends on particular scope conditions and on incentive structures inducing nonstate actors such as firms or even warlords and rebel groups to contribute to governance. These scope conditions appear to provide functional equivalents for a state "shadow of hierarchy," which is systematically lacking or even missing in areas of limited statehood.

3. Last but not least, the chapters also demonstrate that the state actors are not absent in areas of limited statehood. The debate is not between either governance by the state or the complete privatization of governance services. Rather, the empirical contributions to this volume show the various forms of interactions and bargaining relationships between governments and nonstate actors. In some cases (see chapter by Enderlein et al.), even hostile interactions can contribute to the provision of collective goods, in this case macroeconomic stability.

Multilevel Governance in Areas of Limited Statehood: The Role of External Actors

Governance in areas of limited statehood regularly involves international and transnational actors in providing basic services and supplying governance. This includes foreign governments, international organizations (such as the United Nations and its suborganizations), as well as transnational nonstate actors, such as multinational corporations, NGOs, or transnational PPPs. The involvement of inter- and transnational actors in governance results from necessity given the state weakness in these countries. In many cases, inter- and transnational actors directly interfere with the "Westphalian sovereignty" in areas of limited statehood, that is, they authoritatively rule in the absence of a consolidated state (see chapters by Schneckener and Brozus; Krasner 2004; Fearon and Laitin 2004). In other words, shared sovereignty is an empirical reality in many states that lack the ability to enforce central decisions.

However, shared sovereignty—the division and distribution of political authority across transnational, national, and local levels—is precisely what constitutes "multilevel governance." It prevails in areas of limited statehood in the sense that external actors directly participate in governance. It is remarkable that the enormous literature on multilevel governance that predominantly deals with the European Union (E.U.) has not yet realized that similar phenomena are all too common in the global South (on multi-level governance in the Western context see, e.g., Hooghe and Marks 2001; Hooghe and Marks 2003; Kohler-Koch and Eising 1999; Benz 2004b).

Three chapters in this book tackle the multilevel dimension of governance in areas limited statehood. Bernd Ladwig and Beate Rudolf argue that rather ambitious standards of good governance, including human rights, the rule of law, responsiveness, and public participation, are already part of positive international law and that they can also be justified by a rights-based approach of political morality. These standards interfere by definition in the "Westphalian sovereignty" of states insofar as they constitute an interest of the international community as a whole in the internal affairs of states and are preemptory norms (*ius cogens*) that are obligatory for any country in the contemporary system. At the same time, however, international law assumes fully consolidated states that are both willing and capable of complying with these norms. International law also presupposes the existence of a collectivity for which decisions can be made and the existence of a political authority that has the ultimate responsibility for such decisions. However, both elements are missing in areas of limited statehood as a result of which a completely state-centric approach to ensure compliance with international law misses the mark.

Ladwig and Rudolf then explore the question of who bears a subsidiary responsibility for guaranteeing minimum standards of good governance in areas of limited statehood. First, the international community as a whole has accepted its "responsibility to protect" in cases of severe violations of governance standards as part of its commitment to international peace and security. But this responsibility by other states is severely circumscribed by procedural considerations such as, for example, authorization by the U.N. Security Council as a result of which a discrepancy between international law and moral obligations remains (see the case of Kosovo in 1999). Second, Ladwig and Rudolf use the principle of "agency of necessity" (*negotiorum gestio*) to argue that even nonstate actors engaged in governance in areas of limited statehood are bound by international law if they exercise subsidiary responsibility. They argue, however, that this subsidiary responsibility can only be justified if the international community aims at reestablishing the material, structural, and societal preconditions for consolidated statehood. In other words, serious intrusions in the "Westphalian sovereignty" of states that lack domestic sovereignty have to engage in state building.

However, state-building efforts, particularly in postconflict situations, face their own problems, as Ulrich Schneckener argues in his chapter. He analyzes various state-building strategies, such as "liberalization first," "security first," "institutionalization first," and "civil society first." Each of these strategies inevitably produces unintended consequences. "Liberalization first" often underestimates the destabilizing effects of rapid democratization and market liberalization. In contrast, "security first" risks strengthening the status quo, including the stabilization of authoritarian rule. While an emphasis on institution building tends to empower those elites who profit from the status quo, focusing on civil society leads to the opposite pitfalls by undermining local social structures. Schneckener then argues that what all these strategies have in common is to overlook the multilevel governance character of external efforts at state building. As a result, incompatibilities between the goals and time-horizons of external actors, on the one hand, and local communities, on the other hand, are inevitable. Schneckener concludes that the key issue for external actors is not how to avoid counterproductive effects and unintended consequences of their interference in the domestic sovereignty of states, but how to cope with them. First and foremost, they have to understand that they are not external to local developments, but part of the process and its dynamics. Since external efforts at stabilizing postconflict situations result in multilevel governance structures, the "internationals" have to realize too that they are bound up with the political, social, economic, and cultural developments on the ground. "Exit strategies" amount in self-betrayal. Rather, external actors have to understand that interventions in the governance arrangements of areas of limited statehood change both those being interfered with *and* the intervenors. In other words, governance travels back.

The concluding chapter by Lars Brozus takes up these challenges and discusses the consequences of the book's findings for international foreign and security policy. Current international foreign and security policy debates picture areas of limited statehood as presenting security challenges to the so-called developed world. Most of the scenarios discussed refer to challenges resulting from international destabilization because of conflicts spilling-over from areas of limited statehood. Terrorism, organized crime, and mass movements of people are noted frequently as consequences. To confront these challenges powerful actors such as the United States or the European Union have developed security strategies with a specific focus on areas of limited statehood. International interventions differ widely with respect to their degree of intensity. While most interventions are mandated restrictively, some aim at establishing new institutions and sometimes even new forms of governance, as in Bosnia, Kosovo, Afghanistan, and Iraq. Thus, governance becomes an important part of state-building strategies.

However, the adverse implications of applying a Western governance concept to areas of limited statehood are often overlooked in these strategies. Brozus joins in Schneckener's criticism of Western efforts at state building and argues that detailed knowledge of existing modes of governance in areas of limited statehood is essential for the effectiveness of efforts by the international community. This implies that the "modernization package" that external actors try to "sell" in areas of limited statehood, is not only highly problematic, but bound to fail. Moreover, the provision of governance by external actors might actually weaken already limited statehood further and thus undermine the "state-building" goal of establishing self-supporting governance structures. Brozus concludes that the aim of the international community in areas of limited statehood should be "governance-shaping" rather than state building.

In sum, the final three chapters make the following points.

• The international legal order has established standards of good governance, which includes human rights, the rule of law, and the right to participate in governance. These standards deeply circumscribe the "Westphalian" sovereignty of states and include the subsidiary responsibility of the international community—be it states, international organizations, or nonstate actors—to help in the governance of areas of limited statehood.

• The "state-building" efforts by external actors in postconflict situations have rarely resulted in establishing fully consolidated states, but have institutionalized multilevel governance structures in which external actors become part and parcel of "local" governance and in which shared sovereignty is the rule.

At this point, however, we have come full circle: Ladwig and Rudolf argue in their chapter that the only moral and legal justification for external interventions in areas of limited statehood can be to foster effective and self-sustained governance, that is, state building. Schneckener and Brozus demonstrate in their chapters that such efforts inevitably result in the deep involvement of external actors in multilevel governance structures and that "quick impact" strategies are illusionary. If we accept their point that governance in areas of limited statehood is multilevel governance by definition that also involves nonstate actors in a systematic fashion (see the chapters in the second part of this volume), we may actually witness the emergence of new political and social orders in areas of limited statehood.

Conclusions

This book argues that the social science debate on governance implicitly or explicitly remains wedded to an ideal type of modern statehood—with full domestic sovereignty and the capacity to make, implement, and enforce decisions. From a global as well as a historical perspective, however, the modern Western nation-state constitutes the exception rather than the rule. Outside the developed OECD world, we find areas of limited statehood that lack domestic sovereignty. Under such conditions, governance requires the inclusion of nonstate as well as external actors in the provision of collective goods and the regulation of social issues.

Yet, our conceptual apparatus is ill-equipped to deal with the governance problematic in areas of limited statehood. The Western governance discourse is not only heavily influenced by modernization theory, but also assumes modern statehood and a fully functioning state as a background condition. I have tried to illustrate this point with regard to the applicability of the governance concept to areas of limited statehood. In particular, I have discussed problems with regard to the distinction between the "public" and the "private" spheres, the implicit intentionality and normativity of the governance concept, and concerning the "shadow of hierarchy."

This discussion appears to demonstrate that, on the one hand, governance still provides a useful conceptual tool to study political issues and the provision of collective goods in areas of limited statehood. In particular, it removes the state-centric bias in the study of politics and focuses our attention on the contribution of nonstate actors as well as on nonhierarchical modes of steering. So far, so good! On the other hand, the ability of the governance concept to travel to areas of limited statehood has its own limits. Discussing governance under conditions of limited statehood reveals several blind spots with regard to implicit and explicit theoretical and normative assumptions. These assumptions concern the modernization bias of the governance concept as currently used in the social sciences, which requires some conceptual innovation. These innovations, however, might even shed new light on the transformation of modern statehood. Thus, exposing the governance concept to areas of limited statehood yields new insights with regard to governance under conditions of consolidated statehood.

These issues do not only have academic and theoretical implications, but also far-reaching political and practical consequences. First, the international community is oriented almost completely toward the ideal of developed and democratic Western statehood in its state-building efforts and its democratization and development strategies. If, however, areas of limited statehood are here to stay for the time being and become the rule rather than the exception, this strategic orientation of the international community becomes problematic for practical as well as normative reasons. If governance in areas of limited statehood requires the systematic inclusion of nonstate actors, a reliance on nonhierarchical modes of steering, and the continuous involvement of the international community, we need to figure out the scope conditions for the success and failure of these "new" modes of governance. What alternative modes of governance can we think of that provide functional equivalents of modern democratic and developed statehood without constantly assuming the Western model as the underlying cultural script?

Second, we need to think anew about the international democratization, development, and state-building strategies, if only to counter the widespread suspicion that "good governance" is nothing else than Western neocolonialism in disguise. As this book demonstrates, state-building efforts that simply try to reproduce the modernization package of the Western developed and liberal nation-state in areas of limited statehood are bound to fail. Rather, the international community should help to improve the capacity of states to enforce and implement decisions and to see to it that the preconditions of governance are enabled in areas of limited statehood.[8] This implies a "light footprint," but also requires more innovation with regard to strengthening functional equivalents to consolidated statehood (Draude 2008; Börzel 2010; chapter by Brozus in this volume).

Last but not least, this book argues that multilevel governance, including shared sovereignty, is the reality of governance in areas of limited statehood. Thus, the global North is deeply entangled with the global South, and vice versa. As a result, we need be aware not only of the conceptual, empirical, and political pitfalls when governance travels to areas of limited statehood, but also of the consequences for the global North when governance travels back. This book can only serve as a starting point for such an exploration.

NOTES

1. I thank Tanja Börzel and two anonymous reviewers for very useful comments on the draft. I also thank Lars Brozus, Anke Draude, and Ursula Lehmkuhl for numerous discussions on the topic of this chapter.

2. This section builds upon Risse 2005; Risse 2008; Risse and Lehmkuhl 2007.

3. Weber's notion of legitimacy with regard to the control over the means of violence should not be confused with an empirically derived notion of a legitimate order that is considered just and fair. Rather, "legitimate monopoly over the means of violence" concerns the claim that the order is legitimate.

4. Data from "Detaillierte_Werte_BTI2010.xls," www.bertelsmann-transformation -index.de/bti/ranking/.

5. Here, I follow the usual definition of collective goods as characterized by non-exclusive access and/or nonrivalry in consumption. At least one of these conditions has to be present for a good to qualify as collective or common (see Héritier 2002).

6. Note that the effectiveness and problem-solving capacity of governance is not part of the definition. Institutionalized intentionality toward regulating social issues and providing collective goods is all that is needed.

7. While South Africa as an emerging economy certainly does not qualify as a failing state, it represents a good example of limited statehood in a particular policy area—environmental protection in this case.

8. Note that strengthening state capacity is not the same as establishing the state monopoly over the means of violence. If, for example, international actors provide sustainable security in areas of limited statehood, a fully consolidated state is not required to enable governance and the provision of collective goods.

REFERENCES

Beisheim, Marianne, Andrea Liese, and Cornelia Ulbert. 2008. "Transnationale öf-
fentlich-private Partnerschaften—Bestimmungsfaktoren für die Effektivität ihrer
Governance-Leistungen." In *Governance in einer sich wandelnden Welt*, edited by
Gunnar Folke Schuppert and Michael Zürn, 452–74. PVS–Politische Vierteljahresschrift, Sonderheft 41. Wiesbaden: VS Verlag für Sozialwissenschaften.

Beisheim, Marianne, and Gunnar Folke Schuppert, eds. 2007. *Staatszerfall und Governance*. Baden-Baden: Nomos.

Bendel, Petra, Aurel Croissant, and Friedbert W. Rüb, eds. 2002. *Hybride Regime. Zur
Konzeption und Empirie demokratischer Grauzonen*. Opladen: Leske and Budrich.

Benz, Arthur. 2001. *Der moderne Staat. Grundlagen der politologischen Analyse*. Munich
and Vienna: Oldenbourg.

———. 2004a. *Governance—Regieren in komplexen Regelsystemen*. Wiesbaden: VS Verlag für Sozialwissenschaften.

———. 2004b. "Multilevel Governance—Governance in Mehrebenensystemen." In *Governance—Regieren in komplexen Regelsystemen*, edited by Arthur Benz, 125–46. Wiesbaden: VS Verlag für Sozialwissenschaften.

Böckenförde, Ernst Wilhelm. 1976. "Die Bedeutung der Unterscheidung von Staat und Gesellschaft im demokratischen Sozialstaat der Gegenwart." In *Staat, Gesellschaft, Freiheit*, edited by Ernst Wilhelm Böckenförde, 395–431. Frankfurt/Main: Suhrkamp.

Börzel, Tanja A. 2007. "Regieren ohne den Schatten der Hierarchie: Ein modernisierungstheoretischer Fehlschluss?" In *Regieren ohne Staat? Governance in Räumen begrenzter Staatlichkeit*, edited by Thomas Risse and Ursula Lehmkuhl, 41–46. Baden-Baden: Nomos.

———. 2008. "Der 'Schatten der Hierarchie'—ein Governance-Paradox?" In *Governance in einer sich wandelnden Welt*, ed. Gunnar Folke Schuppert and Michael Zürn, 118–31. PVS–Politische Vierteljahresschrift, Sonderheft 41. Wiesbaden: VS Verlag für Sozialwissenschaften.

———. 2009. "New Modes of Governance and Accession: The Paradox of Double Weakness." In *Coping with Accession to the European Union: New Modes of Environmental Governance*, edited by Tanja A. Börzel, 7–31. Basingstoke: Palgrave Macmillan.

———. 2010. "Governance Without Government—False Promises or Flawed Premises?" Freie Universität Berlin: SFB 700, SFB Governance Working Paper Series, Berlin.

Börzel, Tanja A., Adrienne Héritier, and Anna Kristin Müller-Debus. 2007. "Der Regulierungsbeitrag von Großunternehmen im Kampf gegen HIV/AIDS in Südafrika." In *Regieren ohne Staat? Governance in Räumen begrenzter Staatlichkeit*, edited by Thomas Risse and Ursula Lehmkuhl, 272–91. Baden-Baden: Nomos.

Börzel, Tanja A., and Thomas Risse. 2005. "Public Private Partnerships: Effective and Legitimate Tools of International Governance?" In *Complex Sovereignty: Reconstituting Political Authority in the Twenty-first Century*, edited by Edgar Grande and Louis W. Pauly, 195–216. Toronto: University of Toronto Press.

Chojnacki, Sven, and Zeljko Branovic. 2007. "Räume strategischer (Un-) Sicherheit: Ein Markt für nicht-staatliche Gewaltakteure und Gelegenheiten für Formen von Sicherheits-Governance." In *Regieren ohne Staat? Governance in Räumen begrenzter Staatlichkeit*, edited by Thomas Risse and Ursula Lehmkuhl, 181–204. Baden-Baden: Nomos.

Conrad, Sebastian, and Shalini Randeria, eds. 2002. *Jenseits des Eurozentrismus. Postkoloniale Perspektiven in den Geschichts- und Kulturwissenschaften*. Frankfurt/Main: Campus.

Cutler, Claire A., Virginia Haufler, and Tony Porter, eds. 1999. *Private Authority and International Affairs*. Albany: State University of New York Press.

Czempiel, Ernst-Otto, and James Rosenau, eds. 1992. *Governance Without Government: Order and Change in World Politics*. Cambridge: Cambridge University Press.

De la Rosa, Sybille, Ulrike Höppner, and Matthias Kötter, eds. 2008. *Transdisziplinäre Governanceforschung. Gemeinsam hinter den Staat blicken*. Baden-Baden: Nomos.

Draude, Anke. 2007. "Wer regiert wie? Für eine äquivalenzfunktionalistische Beobachtung von Governance in Räumen begrenzter Staatlichkeit." SFB 700 Governance in Räumen begrenzter Staatlichkeit, FU Berlin, SFB Governance Working Paper Series, Berlin.

——. 2008. "Wer regiert wie? Eurozentrismus in der Governanceforschung und der Versuch einer methodischen Grenzüberschreitung." In *Transdisziplinäre Governanceforschung. Gemeinsam hinter den Staat blicken*, edited by Sybille De La Rosa and Matthias Kötter, 100–118. Baden-Baden: Nomos.

Erdmann, Gero. 2002. "Neopatrimoniale Herrschaft—oder: Warum es in Afrika so viele Hybridregime gibt." In *Hybride Regime. Zur Konzeption und Empirie demokratischer Grauzonen*, edited by Petra Bendel, Aurel Croissant, and Friedbert W. Rüb, 323–42. Opladen: Leske & Budrich.

Erdmann, Gero, and Ulf Engel. 2007. "Neopatrimonialism Reconsidered: Critical Review and Elaboration of an Elusive Concept." *Commonwealth and Comparative Politics* 45, no. 1:95–119.

Fearon, James D., and David D. Laitin. 2004. "Neotrusteeship and the Problem of Weak States." *International Security* 28, no. 4:5–43.

Fuhr, Harald, Markus Lederer, and Miriam Schröder. 2007. "Klimaschutz und Entwicklungspolitik: Der Beitrag privater Unternehmen." In *Regieren ohne Staat? Governance in Räumen begrenzter Staatlichkeit*, edited by Thomas Risse and Ursula Lehmkuhl, 292–308. Baden-Baden: Nomos.

Göhler, Gerhard, Ulrike Höppner, and Sybille De La Rosa, eds. 2009. *Weiche Steuerung. Studien zur Steuerung durch diskursive Praktiken, Argumente und Symbole*. Baden-Baden: Nomos.

Goldstein, Judith L., Miles Kahler, Robert O. Keohane, and Anne-Marie Slaughter, eds. 2000. "Legalization and World Politics." Special issue of *International Organization*. Cambridge, Mass.: MIT Press.

Grande, Edgar, and Louis W. Pauly, eds. 2005. *Complex Sovereignty. Reconstituting Political Authority in the Twenty-first Century*. Toronto: Toronto University Press.

Hall, Rodney Bruce, and Thomas J. Biersteker, eds. 2002. *The Emergence of Private Authority in Global Governance*. Cambridge: Cambridge University Press.

Héritier, Adrienne, ed. 2002. *Common Goods: Reinventing European and International Governance*. Lanham, Md.: Rowman & Littlefield.

——. 2003. "New Modes of Governance in Europe: Increasing Political Capacity and Policy Effectiveness?" In *The State of the European Union*, vol. 6, *Law, Politics, and Society*, edited by Tanja A. Börzel and Rachel A. Cichowski, 105–26. Oxford: Oxford University Press.

Hooghe, Liesbet, and Gary Marks. 2001. *Multi-level Governance and European Integration*. Lanham, Md.: Rowman & Littlefield.

——. 2003. "Unraveling the Central State, but How? Types of Multi-level Governance." *American Political Science Review* 97, no. 2:233–43.

Hurrelmann, Achim, Stephan Leibfried, Kerstin Martens, and Mayer Peter, eds. 2007. *Transforming the Golden-Age Nation State*. Basingstoke: Palgrave Macmillan.

Keane, John. 1988. "Despotism and Democracy. The Origins of the Distinction Between Civil Society and the State, 1750–1850." In *Civil Society and the State*, edited by John Keane, 35–72. London: Verso.

Keohane, Robert O. 2007. "Governance and Legitimacy." Keynote Speech Held at the Opening Conference of the Research Center (SFB) 700, (DFG Research Center [SFB] 700, SFB-Governance Lecture Series, February 23), Berlin.

Koehler, Jan, and Christoph Zürcher. 2004. "Der Staat und sein Schatten. Zur Institutionalisierung hybrider Staatlichkeit im Südkaukasus." *WeltTrends* 12, no. 45:84–96.

Kohler-Koch, Beate. 1998. "Einleitung. Effizienz und Demokratie. Probleme des Regierens in entgrenzten Räumen." In *Regieren in entgrenzten Räumen*, ed. Beate Kohler-Koch, 11–25. PVS–Sonderheft 29. Opladen: Westdeutscher Verlag.

Kohler-Koch, Beate, and Rainer Eising, eds. 1999. *The Transformation of Governance in the European Union*. London: Routledge.

Kooiman, Jan, ed. 1993. *Modern Governance: New Government-Society Interactions*. London: Sage.

Krasner, Stephen D. 1999. *Sovereignty: Organized Hypocrisy*. Princeton, N.J.: Princeton University Press.

——. 2004. "Sharing Sovereignty: New Institutions for Collapsed and Failed States." *International Security* 29, no. 2:85–120.

Ladwig, Bernd. 2007. "Gebotene Fremdbestimmung? Normative Überlegungen zum Umgang mit zerfallen(d)er Staatlichkeit." In *Regieren ohne Staat? Governance in Räumen begrenzter Staatlichkeit*, ed. Thomas Risse and Ursula Lehmkuhl, 354–73. Baden-Baden: Nomos.

Ladwig, Bernd, Tamara Jugov, and Cord Schmelzle. 2007. "Governance, Normativität und begrenzte Staatlichkeit." SFB 700 "Governance in Räumen begrenzter Staatlichkeit," Frei Universität Berlin, SFB-Governance Working Paper Series. Berlin.

Lake, David. 2009. *Hierarchy in International Relations*. Ithaca, N.Y.: Cornell University Press.

Leibfried, Stephan, and Michael Zürn, eds. 2005. *Transformations of the State?* Cambridge: Cambridge University Press.

Magen, Amichai, Thomas Risse, and Michael McFaul, eds. 2009. *Promoting Democracy and the Rule of Law: American and European Strategies*. Basingstoke: Palgrave-Macmillan.

Mayntz, Renate. 2004. "Governance im modernen Staat." In *Governance—Regieren in komplexen Regelsystemen*, ed. Benz, Arthur, 65–76. Wiesbaden: VS Verlag für Sozialwissenschaften.

——. 2008. "Von der Steuerungstheorie zu Global Governance." In *Governance in einer sich wandelnden Welt*, ed. Gunnar Folke Schuppert and Michael Zürn, 43–60. PVS–Politische Vierteljahresschrift, Sonderheft 41. Wiesbaden: VS Verlag für Sozialwissenschaften.

Menkhaus, Ken. 2006/2007. "Governance Without Government in Somalia: Spoilers, State Building, and the Politics of Coping." *International Security* 31, no. 3:74–106.

Meyer, John M. 1987. "The World Polity and the Authority of the Nation State." In *International Structure: Constituting State, Society, and the Individual*, edited by George M. Thomas, John W. Meyer, Francisco O. Ramirez, and John Boli, 41–70. London: Sage.

Müller-Debus, Anna, Christian Thauer, and Tanja A. Börzel. 2009. "Governing HIV/AIDS in South Africa: The Role of Firms." SFB 700 Working Paper 20, Berlin. SFB 700, Freie Universität Berlin.

O'Brien, Robert, Anne Marie Goetz, Jan Aart Scholte, and Marc Williams. 2000. *Contesting Global Governance: Multilateral Economic Institutions and Global Social Movements*. Cambridge: Cambridge University Press.

Prakash, Aseem. 2000. *Greening the Firm: The Politics of Corporate Environmentalism*. Cambridge: Cambridge University Press.

Prakash, Aseem, and Matthew Potoski. 2006. "Racing to the Bottom? Trade, Environmental Governance, and ISO 14001." *American Journal of Political Science* 50, no. 2:350–64.

Reinhard, Wolfgang. 2007. *Geschichte des modernen Staates*. Munich: C. H. Beck.

Rhodes, R. A. W. 1997. *Understanding Governance: Policy Networks, Governance, Reflexivity, and Accountability*. Buckingham and Philadelphia: Open University Press.

Risse, Thomas. 2005. "Governance in Räumen begrenzter Staatlichkeit. 'Failed States' werden zum zentralen Problem der internationalen Politik." *Internationale Politik* 60, no. 9:6–12.

——. 2008. "Regieren in Räumen begrenzter Staatlichkeit: Zur 'Reisefähigkeit' des Governance-Konzepts." In *Governance in einer sich wandelnden Welt*, edited by Gunnar Folke Schuppert and Michael Zürn, 149–70. PVS–Politische Vierteljahresschrift, Sonderheft 41, Wiesbaden: VS Verlag für Sozialwissenschaften.

Risse, Thomas, and Ursula Lehmkuhl, eds. 2007. *Regieren ohne Staat? Governance in Räumen begrenzter Staatlichkeit*. Baden-Baden: Nomos.

Rotberg, Robert I., ed. 2003. *State Failure and State Weakness in a Time of Terror*. Washington, D.C.: Brookings Institution Press.

——, ed. 2004. *When States Fail: Causes and Consequences*. Princeton, N.J.: Princeton University Press.

Schäferhoff, Marco. In preparation. "Transnational Health Partnerships in Areas of Limited Statehood—How Much State Is Enough?" Ph.D. diss. Fachbereich Politik- und Sozialwissenschaften. Berlin: Freie Universität Berlin.

Schäferhoff, Marco, Sabine Campe, and Christopher Kaan. 2009. "Transnational Partnerships in International Relations: Making Sense of Concepts, Research Frameworks, and Results." *International Studies Review* 11, no. 3:451–74.

Scharpf, Fritz. 1993. "Positive und negative Koordination in Verhandlungssystemen." In *Policy-Analyse*, edited by Adrienne Héritier, 57–83. Politische Vierteljahresschrift, Sonderheft 24. Opladen: Westdeutscher Verlag.

Schneckener, Ulrich, ed. 2004. *States at Risk: Fragile Staaten als Sicherheits- und Entwicklungsproblem*. Berlin: Stiftung Wissenschaft und Politik.

Schuppert, Gunnar Folke, ed. 2005. *Governance-Forschung. Vergewisserung über Stand und Entwicklungslinien*. Baden-Baden: Nomos.

——. 2007. "Was ist und wozu Governance?" *Die Verwaltung* 40, no. 4:465–514.

——. 2009. *Staat als Prozess. Eine staatstheoretische Skizze in sieben Aufzügen*. Frankfurt: Campus.

Schuppert, Gunnar Folke, and Michael Zürn, eds. 2008. *Governance in einer sich wandelnden Welt*. PVS–Politische Vierteljahresschrift, Sonderheft 41. Wiesbaden: VS Verlag für Sozialwissenschaften.

Weber, Max. 1921/1980. *Wirtschaft und Gesellschaft*. Tubingen: J. C. B. Mohr.

Williamson, Oliver E. 1975. *Markets and Hierachies: Analysis and Anti-Trust*. New York: The Free Press.

Zangl, Bernhard. 2008. "Judicalization Matters! A Comparison of Dispute Settlement under GATT and the WTO." *International Studies Quarterly* 52, no. 4:825–54.

Zangl, Bernhard, and Michael Zürn, eds. 2004: *Verrechtlichung—Baustein für Global Governance?* Bonn: Dietz.

Zürcher, Christoph. 2007. "When Governance Meets Troubled States." In *Staatszerfall und Governance*, edited by Marianne Beisheim and Gunnar Folke Schuppert, 11–28. Baden-Baden: Nomos.

Zürn, Michael. 1998. *Regieren jenseits des Nationalstaates. Globalisierung und Denationalisierung als Chance*. Frankfurt-am-Main: Suhrkamp.

——. 2005. "Global Governance." In *Governance-Forschung. Vergewisserung über Stand und Entwicklungslinien*, edited by Gunnar Folke Schuppert, 121–46. Baden-Baden: Nomos.

I

Insights from Law and History

2

Governance and Colonial Rule

Sebastian Conrad and Marion Stange

I N RECENT YEARS, GOVERNANCE HAS EVOLVED INTO a key concept in political science. The term is used to refer to processes and structures of regulation and rule that are either not at all, or at least not primarily and exclusively, based on hierarchically organized government action, but instead involve nonhierarchical modes of action by private, semiprivate, and public actors. According to the broad definition of the concept, governance is understood as the "collective regularization of societal matters" (Mayntz 2004, 66), thus comprising all agents contributing through their collective actions to the creation of public goods. These actors can be official government institutions as well as private persons or associations.

Originally applied to modern nation states of Western provenance in order to conceptually grasp the increasing adoption of classic state functions by private actors, the concept of governance has also proved to be useful in understanding modes of political organization and regulation in areas of limited statehood—that is, in areas in which core elements of modern statehood like effective territorial control or the state's monopoly on the use of physical force are absent. However, such limitations of central authority do not only exist in many countries on today's world map but can also be observed when looking at forms of political organization in historical perspective. Especially when studying modes of governing "before the state"— that is, in premodern and early modern societies, and, most conspicuously, when dealing with colonial rule—historians discern a plethora of governing practices that can only very inadequately be described by categories derived from the concept of modern statehood. Because the colonizing powers' central authority was debilitated by a diverse set of external and internal factors in virtually all colonies—whether in early modern times or during the age of high imperialism—the colonial state can be understood as a prototypical area of limited statehood. As a result of its weakness, it was highly dependent on the involvement and cooperation of nonstate actors, in particular among the colonized, to establish and maintain effective rule in the colonized territories.

By offering a wide perspective on governing modes that are not limited to hierarchical rule exerted by official agents but also comprise alternative forms of governing, the governance concept can thus be of use in the study of colonial rule. Governance provides a systematic approach to the question of the "how" and the "who" of political organization in historical perspective. Focusing on both the processes and the agents of governing, the concept allows for a comprehensive study of political rule in the colonial context. Governance can thus be fruitfully linked to recent developments in historiography. This literature stresses, first, the processual and negotiative character of early modern political rule. A good example for this trend is Greene's work *Negotiated Authorities* in which he argues that power was not a fixed constant in colonial American politics but instead had to be continuously negotiated and renegotiated between the rulers and the ruled (Asch and Freist 2005; Daniels and Kennedy 2002; Greene 1994; Hindle 2000; Meumann and Pröve 2004). Second, governance also ties into the rich historiography on formal versus informal empire, which essentially discusses the problematic of delegation of authority to nonstate actors (Dimier 2004; Doyle 1986; Louis 1976).

It is important to note, however, that since the governance paradigm has originally been developed against the background of the Western nation-state, notions of modern centralized statehood are necessarily inherent in it. An indiscriminate transfer of the governance concept to colonial contexts thus carries the risk of reiterating the mistakes made by earlier generations of historians who uncritically applied modern notions of statehood to historical contexts. A strict classification of governance actors along the lines of "public" and "private," for example, might be useful in the context of governance in today's Western societies but proves to be inadequate in the study of colonial rule because of the often hybrid nature of agents involved in colonial governance. Likewise, because colonies in many cases lacked clear territorial confines and often comprised a wide range of different ethnic groups with their own respective legal systems, it is not always possible to unequivocally determine the governance collective, that is, the group of people who were addressed by governance. Since these are conceptual problems arising not only in the colonial context but also when looking at many of today's fragile or failing states, the historical perspective can help to sharpen the concept of governance in areas of limited statehood.

This chapter therefore has a threefold aim. First, it purports to contribute to a historicization of the concept of governance. By shedding light on the variations in colonial political organization and on the diversity of actors, historical research thus serves as a corrective, demonstrating that the "new forms of governing" postulated by political scientists who study the changing character of statehood in OECD countries are not so new after all. The governance approach allows for a perspective on colonial governing that illustrates the historical contingency of the Western model of centralized statehood. As a result, the widespread notion of consolidated statehood as the necessary culmination of an evolutionary process that all polities pass through is challenged, resulting in a fresh perspective on alternative forms of governing in today's areas of limited statehood.

Second, we would like to argue that a critical reflection of the governance concept's applicability to historical contexts can provide important new insights both for historical research and political science. By linking the governance approach to the study of political organization and rule in colonies as prototypical areas of limited statehood, this chapter seeks to illuminate the potential benefits as well as the limitations of the concept when used in historical research. After a discussion of the specific conditions of rule in the colonial state, the chapter thus deals with the problems that historians incur when applying the governance concept to the colonial context. Bringing to light the underlying notions of modern statehood still inherent in the concept, the chapter's third section focuses on the binary differentiation between "public" or "state" actors on the one hand and "private" or "nonstate" actors on the other. This is a distinction that is at the center of many current governance debates but which proves to be inadequate for the colonial context, where the role of actors involved in political organization was often of a hybrid nature. By thus challenging tacit assumptions inherent in the concept, historians can contribute to a further adaptation of the governance concept so as to increase its applicability not only to historical contexts but also to modern-day areas of limited statehood.

Third, we argue that present-day predicaments and peculiarities of rule, in particular in areas of limited statehood, may be intimately linked with complex historical genealogies. This perspective enables us to shed light on the specific preconditions and historical origins of governing practices and conflicts that can be observed in present-day postcolonial societies. In many cases, legal traditions, political structures, and societal cleavages can only be understood when taking into consideration these countries' colonial pasts. Although this historical dimension is of particular importance when looking at today's areas of limited statehood in former colonies in Africa, Asia, or Latin America, it can also tell us a great deal about the roots of governing practices, ethnic divides, and legal systems in a country like the United States where colonial rule ended more than two centuries ago.

The Colonial State as an Area of Limited Statehood

The colonial states were set up on the belief that the model of the European state system could simply be applied to the colonies. But the practice on the ground turned out to be very different from the theory. The colonial state was not simply an extension of the western European model, but, as Jürgen Osterhammel suggests, "a political form in itself" (1995, 62). More importantly, even during its heyday in the age of high imperialism (1880–1914), the colonial state was essentially a weak state. It was therefore dependent on forms of governance in which power was delegated to local actors and native potentates. The acknowledgement of the instability and uncertainty of colonial rule is very much the result of recent scholarship. It runs counter to the traditional view of virtually unlimited state power in colonial settings. And it also runs counter to the fact that viewed in long-term perspective, colonial rule did indeed initiate a radical transformation in the nature of the state. It led to the creation of territorial states under international law that aspired to a state monopoly on power and to fixed external borders. Frequently, this took place in regions where boundaries had previously been imprecise and constantly changing, and where there had been a wide variety of different types of political order with very different degrees of centralization.

Especially in Africa, colonization introduced a completely new principle of political organization (Herbst 2000).

But recent scholarship, with its focus on the everyday dynamics of colonial rule, has relativized this macro perspective. Indeed, it has demonstrated that in many respects, colonial control was limited and that the colonial state was not able to exercise a monopoly of power. To be sure, any generalization needs to take into account the great variety of colonial experience. The laws and regulations that were applied differed greatly from one colony to the next. The structures of colonial power varied according to regional differences and different types of colony, and they followed different chronologies. They were also affected by local geography and by the dynamics of local societies. The level of control desired by the colonial state also depended on the objectives being pursued for each colony—in trading colonies like Hong Kong or Togo, the state's presence was limited to a small number of administrators, while in settlement and plantation colonies the presence of settlers and the demands for labor by landowners led to the state taking more control over local territories. Last but not least, colonial governing practices and structures and the power of the colonial state varied according to the time period in which colonization took place. While late nineteenth- and early twentieth-century colonies were ruled against the background of modern statehood in the colonizing countries, this was not the case with regard to premodern and early modern European colonies, for example in North America. Here, the limitations of centralized power were not only determined by the distance between colonizing power and colony and by the long lines of communication this distance entailed, but also by the absence of consolidated statehood in Europe where sovereign nation states basing their authority on an institutionalized form of abstract power were not yet existent (Lehmkuhl 2007).

In spite of this great diversity, it is possible to discern some general patterns of the specific weakness of colonial power. The following account examines the difference between the modern state, defined by Max Weber in terms of territoriality, monopoly on the use of physical force and bureaucracy, and the colonial state. While the argument is a general one, we will use examples from German colonialism, mainly in Africa, to illustrate our points. We will focus on two dimensions of colonial rule. First, the colonial state was generally weak in terms of the extent and depth of its control. This was partly related to its lack of legitimacy and ideological hegemony, the second issue we will examine.

The characteristic feature of the colonial state was that it only reached into local societies to a limited extent. There was a vast difference between the colonial powers' aspiration to total control of the colonies and social practice; the presence of the state was often very limited. In theory, colonial states were territorial states, which aspired to achieve a monopoly of power over the entire territory they claimed as theirs. Even if Germany's suggestion that effective control over an area would determine colonial rights was defeated in favor of Great Britain's insistence that the responsibility of the occupying power should be limited (at the Congo Conference in Berlin in 1884 and 1885), the monopoly of power remained the official ambition of the colonial bureaucracies (Förster 1988).

However, these visions remained largely unfulfilled; theory and social reality did not coincide. For the most part, the European colonial states did not exert full control over their territories. The colonial states were weak states, even though the office of governor was usually equipped with a wide range of competences. These included both executive and legislative powers, and, because governors could issue ordinances, they could add regulations to the legal system almost at will. The governor was the head of the colonial administration and commander-in-chief of the colonial military (Gann and Duignan 1978). In the German case, the Foreign Office, and, from 1907, the Reich Colonial Office, had very little control over the governors' actions—not least because the letters that were the main form of communication between Berlin and the colonies took two months to arrive. In addition, this concentration of powers in the office of the governor made continuity in colonial policies less likely. Each governor stayed in his post for only a few years; every change of governor could result in a change in focus or even a complete change of policy (Gann 1987; Pesek 2005).

Below the governor, the local administrative units were led by the district officers (*Bezirksamtmänner*) and station heads. They were the most important instances of colonial power and, like the British district commissioners and the French *commandants de cercle*, they had a range of competencies over which the governor, in his turn, had little control. They were the real creators of empire. Their local powers were such that in Togo, for example, one *Bezirksamtmann* dismissed every single one of the 544 chiefs in his district over the course of his twenty-year rule, appointing more favored candidates in their stead. Like their superior, the *Bezirksamtmänner* attempted an aristocratic style of power enforcement and insisted on their autonomy from the seat of government; they justified this with their superior knowledge of the situation on the ground. For this reason, we can describe the situation outside the main colonial cities as a form of subimperialism over which the governor had little actual control (Steinmetz 2007).

Because of this, the bureaucracies within the colonies were extremely heterogeneous. This was reinforced by the fact that a large number of other instances were involved at a local level, for example the members of expeditions sent out by antislavery committees and missionaries. They were independent of the colonial administration and did not feel bound to the latter's wishes. In fact, the colonial administration needed the cooperation of these individuals; given the costs involved, a large number of regions had no colonial presence at all. As Kwame Anthony Appiah has underlined, "the experience of the vast majority of [the] citizens of Europe's African colonies was one of an essentially shallow penetration by the colonizer" (Appiah 1992).

Here, too, we must differentiate. The administration's ability to control its territory generally increased over time; in the German colonies, this was the case especially after the Colonial Office was set up in 1907. It also varied from one colony to the next; a greater degree of control was possible in Kiaochow than, for example, in northern Cameroon. In towns and coastal regions, colonial rule was more thoroughly institutionalized than in the hinterlands. Dar es Salaam was completely transformed, becoming a modern colonial metropole. But outside these colonial centers, the creation of a full system of colonial rule remained incomplete. In 1900, 415 German officers and colonial administrators in East Africa were (supposedly) in charge of between eight and ten million African and immigrant inhabitants. At this level, the administrative presence was even slightly higher than in the British colonies, but some sixty times lower than in Japanese-occupied Korea. Over large areas of the colonies, then, real implementation of the supposed colonial monopoly on the use of force was impossible. Colonial administrators undertook travel outside the area of real control at their own risk. If an officer went on leave or was absent for any other reason, administrative activities often ceased for a considerable period. The few administrative stations within the country were "islands of power" (Pesek 2005) that struggled to maintain a semblance of authority.

In 1903, for example, there were only thirty German stations and military posts in German East Africa, and in many cases they were almost helpless to direct events in their surrounding regions. In most cases, the infrastructure available meant power could only really be exerted at isolated points. After the Reich Colonial Office was set up in 1907 and Rechenberg installed as

governor (in 1906), and with the changing focus on rational, "scientific" colonial policy, this began to change. Life in the colonial stations became strictly
regulated, and the separation between officers and troops, and Germans and
Africans, was implemented much more forcefully. Police regulations were
imposed on local societies, natives were obliged to greet every German they
encountered, and a curfew was introduced. All inhabitants were required to
register their address in order to make administration easier; they were also
banned from changing their names. In practice, however, these policies were
almost impossible to enforce. The African population was able to make use
of their superior knowledge of the local situation for their own purposes.
Mobility, in particular, continued to be used strategically by the rural population and the administration found this very difficult to control. In addition,
the stations in the colonial hinterlands were often dependent on the cooperation of local traders and power holders.

The second aspect of the weakness of the colonial state was related to
its lack of "grass-roots" legitimacy—the colonized did not believe that the
colonial rule was legitimate. Colonial regimes always attempted to create
the impression that their interventions were done for the benefit of those
ruled. Their main instrument in this regard was the promise put forward
by the "cultural mission"; the colonizers firmly believed that the state's organizational achievements would meet with the approval of the colonized
populations.

The *mission civilisatrice* promised to gradually modernize the colonized
societies and to improve individual standards of living. It was closely linked
to a worldview that thought in terms of development and of progress. It
was founded on a strong belief in the superiority of Western civilization and
the backwardness of African societies and a conviction that the achievements
of the colonial state would be such that those colonized would willingly go
along with colonial rule. Roads, railways, buildings, the teaching of reading
and writing, medical care, the creation of a Western system of education,
military superiority and a (compulsory) work ethic enforced by a regime of
physical punishment—all these were, in part or in full, the result of political
or economic interests, but it was also hoped that they would help to demonstrate to the native population the organizational powers of the colonial
state. In practice, however, these interventions, though propounded in terms
of the cultural mission, often triggered resistance and as such actually helped
to undermine colonial rule (Barth and Osterhammel 2005; Conklin 1997).

Another limit to the on-the-ground legitimacy of the colonial state was the fact that colonial rule always meant foreign rule. Even where the cultural and technological transformations met with the approval of the population, this deficit could never be completely overcome. Anticolonial national movements always picked up on this issue, even when they themselves were fundamentally interested in pursuing modernizing policies of the type that the colonial government had previously been engaged in. In structural terms, colonial rule was a form of "dominance without hegemony," as Ranajit Guha has described the rule of the British Empire in India. Following Antonio Gramsci, Guha uses *hegemony* to mean the broad acceptance of a particular cultural or ideological belief in a society not through force (i.e., dominance) but through the "agreement" of its members. In contrast, the colonial state had little chance of relying on shared beliefs and had to make use of force on a regular basis (Guha 1998).

This applied even when colonial government attempted to embrace local traditions. The British Empire in India was a model in this respect: the East India Company adopted the institutions of the defunct Mughal Empire in order to profit from the latter's prestigious status. Similarly, German colonies made use of indigenous customs and habits, typically in the context of institutions of indirect rule. This strategy was most successful in Samoa, but German officials in Africa also (increasingly) attempted to reconstruct local traditions and to ensure that German rule would make reference to them. The recovery and codification of what was called "native law," developed by legal experts such as Rudolf Asmis in Togo, was the most important element of these attempts to share in local structures of legitimacy (Knoll 2001; Steinmetz 2007).

Nevertheless, full rights of participation in modern societies remained inaccessible to the colonized population. This was one fundamental difference between colonial societies and European nation-states. Describing British-occupied Bengal, Partha Chatterjee has spoken of a "bi-furcated public sphere." Under the conditions of colonial rule, it was impossible for an independent civil society to emerge. Instead, the colonial state claimed and controlled large areas of the public sphere, not least by limiting education, freedom of expression and opportunities for codetermination (Chatterjee 1995). Similarly, the German colonies did not envisage any form of popular democratic representation.

This fundamental weakness of the colonial state—due to its limited resources and means of governmental control as well as its lack of legitimacy—

gave rise to the quintessential colonial form of governance: intermediarity, the delegation of power to local and regional power holders and elites. The new power holders had no option but to enter into alliances with locals, who themselves were pursuing their own goals. The strategy of divide and rule was, of course, not unique to Germany. This form of indirect rule was a common practice in the British colonial states, the famous example being Nigeria under Lord Lugard. The objective was to achieve careful modernization while maintaining traditional structures. The other end of the colonial spectrum—at least in theory, because in practice these differences tended to become blurred—was represented by France and Portugal, who aimed to achieve complete control over their colonies, with little scope for local agency. German policies were located somewhere in the middle. During the early phase of German colonialism, power was based on close cooperation with chiefs like Samuel Maharero in southwest Africa (although he was later to lead the armed resistance to German rule). Later, the Germans tended to involve selected local individuals in the colonial administration. Examples were the *Akida*, used as local administrators in the coastal regions of East Africa, or the *Luluai*, their counterparts in New Guinea. This was not indirect rule as such, because the power of the colonized was not derived from their own power resources; rather, they were taking on a role within the colonial administration (Dimier 2004).

Indirect rule, then, was devised as a form of governance by colonial powers to cope with the task of ruling over territories and populations largely outside governmental control. They used the prestige and authority of local potentates, so-called chiefs, to strengthen colonial rule by delegating limited powers. This strategy enabled colonial governments to rule over vast territories and large populations with only small armed forces and limited administrative personnel.

State Actors and Private Actors: Revisiting the Concept of Governance

A close look at the mechanisms of rule in colonial states has important implications for the general debate on governance in areas of limited statehood. Not least, it contributes to a historicization of the notion of governance. The incorporation of "private" actors into governmental strategies of rule is by no means a novel phenomenon. Given the precarious instability of imperial rule, governance was fundamental to colonial states from the very beginning. The colonial state, it is important to remember, was not just one among many examples of states that depend upon the incorporation of nonprivate actors and institutions. Instead, colonialism was the fundamental geopolitical and cultural condition that structured the global spread of the modern state. Analysis of governance patterns in colonial states thus helps to contextualize the concept of the modern state and its many historical manifestations (Dirlik 2007; Reinhard 1999).

Moreover, the case of the colonial state enables us to critically examine an aspect that lies at the heart of many current governance debates: the dichotomy of public and private. The dynamics of rule in colonial states render the binary category of public and private actors highly ambivalent and problematic, not least on normative grounds. The boundaries between public and private were blurred both among the colonizers and between the colonial bureaucracy and indigenous potentates. Moreover, in the colonial situation different governance collectives interacted and overlapped. This made it difficult to define the constituency for which governance services were provided. There are three components to this argument, which we will examine in greater detail here.

First, the differentiation of the colonizer population into state actors versus private actors remained largely theoretical. Most visibly in the early periods of colonial rule, but also later on, distinctions between state-funded administrative personnel and a wide range of nonstate actors were marginal. This was particularly obvious in the case of British India, where political power was deliberately delegated to the private East India Company. In the case of imperial Germany, the government invested colonial activists like Carl Peters with the right to annex territory for Germany. In the early 1880s, private entrepreneurs and companies also exercised quasi-state powers. To the extent to which the German colonial empire consolidated, these competences in foreign policy were monopolized by the colonial government. But in many other policy fields, private initiative remained crucial. This was true in particular for the education system that was largely built by mission societies and without state funds (Krause 2007).

While these forms of delegating power and authority seem to fit the definition of governance from the point of view of the colonized, the differences between state institutions, missions, plantation owners, traders, members of scientific explorations, and so on were marginal. This was not only the case in the early years in which, in Cameroon for example, the adjudication of criminal law was explicitly defined as the task of all Europeans (Schaper 2010). Even after colonial bureaucracies had been firmly installed, the categorical difference between state and private actors was not part of everyday colonial practice. From the perspective of the colonized population, the power of a plantation owner and even the head of a mission station did not fundamentally diverge from the authority of state administration.

Instead, what was crucial was the boundary of race. Colonial societies relied on the "rule of colonial difference," as Partha Chatterjee has called it in the case of British South Asia. By this he means the ideological and practical importance of the idea that there was a fundamental dichotomy between the colonial masters and the (supposedly inferior) colonized population. This concept was central even where the government and administration believed that their colonial subjects would at some point in the future be capable of becoming citizens with equal rights to those of citizens at home (Chatterjee 1993).

To be sure, the notion of race was not monolithic, and many competing strands of racial thinking coexisted. Moreover, in everyday practice the notion of racial difference could not be taken for granted but was, as Ann Stoler has convincingly argued, constantly rearticulated and negotiated (Stoler 1989; Stoler 2002). These qualifications notwithstanding, the segregating work of the color line was the fundamental reality of colonial rule. It was immediately apparent in the separation of living spheres in colonial cities, in the duality of the legal structure, and in the prohibitions to intermarriage and miscegenation. The prerogative of "race" implied that access to power and authority did not depend primarily on social difference, class, or indeed the characterization as public or private, but rather on notions of difference that reinforced the basic opposition of colonizers and colonized (Mühlhahn 2000; Wildenthal 2001; Zimmerer 2001).

Second, the definition of indigenous elites as private actors is highly problematic. Informal rule implied the delegation of authority to local potentates (frequently the so-called chiefs). This followed a classical governance pattern of employing indigenous actors and recruiting their networks and social prestige to make up for the weakness of the colonial state. From the perspective of the colonial government, these arrangements did indeed involve private actors who were temporarily invested with state competences. But for the historian, it is a normative assumption to declare the colonial administration a "state," and the local communities mere "private" institutions. Indeed, the local "chiefs" were selected by the colonial bureaucracy precisely because they were not mere "private" persons but rather fulfilled official functions in the local societies they represented. What was more, in many parts of the inaccessible hinterlands the colonial government did not even have the power to enforce their own orders, and the concept of indirect rule was clearly but a fiction. In northern Cameroon, for example, German rule should really be described as coexisting with local rule. The Islamic Fulbe rulers were formally subjugated through a series of military expeditions but the Germans had little real economic or political control. In fact, the Fulbe aristocracy themselves made use of the colonial power and were able, with the military support of the Germans, to expand their own area of domination (Hausen 1970; Wirz 1972).

What this means, then, is that the rhetoric of public versus private runs the danger of reifying colonialist categories and thus of naturalizing colonial rule. The colonial state was no more "public" than the multiple political entities it purported to govern. Instead, the complex mechanisms of colonial rule are better described as competing and overlapping forms of authority—involving both the colonial government and indigenous rulers. Depending on the context, the local rulers did not derive their authority from being invested by a colonial bureaucracy. Their rights to rule were equally based on the power structures of the local population and they aimed at representing a "state" that could claim higher legitimacy than the colonial state.

Third, the colonial setting renders the question of who constitutes the governance collective a highly complex one. Who were the individuals and groups addressed by governmental and private interventions? The boundaries of groups that benefited from governmental measures and were targeted as their beneficiaries were fluid and changing, and they are analytically hard to pin down for the historian. Within a given colony, highly diverse groups profited from the regulations and provisions of the state administration and its "private" partners. And as different social groups competed for rights and access to power, the addressees of institutional arrangements varied fundamentally.

Of course, governance always implies forms of bargaining between different groups and a trade-off between competing claims is therefore nothing peculiar. But the conditions under colonial rule were specific. For example, certainty of justice and the reliability and transparency of the law were values that the colonial government championed and used to legitimate its presence. But whose certainty of justice was it, and indeed, whose justice? From the perspective of the colonized population, the mechanism of legal

procedure worked primarily towards the reenforcement of colonial rule—
even if in concrete cases it may have served their individual or group interests.

To be sure, in this case it is important to stress that a straightforward
dichotomy of rulers and ruled is misleading, mainly for two reasons. On the
one hand, recent scholarship has complicated the strict dichotomy between
colonizers and colonized as posited in colonial discourse. A spate of theoretical and empirical work has explored and exposed the brittle boundaries
of whiteness, gender identities, and rulers and ruled in everyday colonial
practice. Instead of taking a racially based "rule of difference" for granted,
historians have looked increasingly at the shifting, negotiable "politics of difference" (Arnold 1983; Buettner 2000; Cooper 2005; Fischer-Tiné and Gehrmann 2009; Levine 2004; McClintock 1995). On the other hand, the differentiation between the colonial masters and the colonized, a differentiation
that was increasingly expressed in terms of "race," stood in opposition to the
concept of "elevation" preached by the proponents of the cultural mission
that was one of the main ideologies driving the colonial project. The civilizing mission aimed to promote comprehensive social "development": to facilitate technical progress, end despotic rule, create a social order that was based
on emancipation (for women for example) and participation, and introduce
"modern" cultural dispositions. But "elevation" and "development" were always conditional, as parity with the colonizers was constantly deferred. The
school system is a good example of the tension between assimilation and
difference, between "elevation" and the maintenance of fundamental differences that characterized the colonial project as a whole. Western education
was supposed to make its recipients familiar with the principles of European-
Christian civilization, but at the same time, teaching was limited to a very
basic level. To be clear, it did provide resources that colonized inhabitants
could access. It allowed the children of slaves and other dependent groups
(who were often the first to attend at mission schools) access to education
and, thus, the prospect of improving their social position. Many members
of the national elites who would later lead their countries to independence
also attended the mission schools. Emancipation was indeed a goal, but there
was never any intent for the students to become equal citizens. The schools
were established to create perfect "natives," not black Europeans (Barth and
Osterhammel 2005; Conklin 1997; Fischer-Tiné and Mann 2004).

All these complexities and contestations notwithstanding, the fundamental issue of legitimacy remains crucial to any evaluation of governance under
colonial conditions. Domination by a foreign power delegitimized, albeit to

different degrees, the interventions under colonial rule. While the state bureaucracy and its different "private" partners—such as mission societies and indigenous potentates—supplied the newly founded schools, the creation of Westernized medical services, the ongoing efforts to "educate the natives to work," and the introduction of Western legal standards, these services and programs were always tied to the interests of the European planters, settlers, merchants, and administrators. The forms of in- and exclusion based on the notion of race produced a binary discursive structure that made it difficult to embrace the "benefits" of governance provisions without recognizing the inherent connection to foreign domination.

Path Dependency?

Studying the processes, structures, and actors of colonial governing not only provides us with an understanding of what governance "before the state" could look like, it also helps us comprehend the origins of specific governing practices, legal traditions, or conflicts that can be observed, even today, in countries and regions that look back on a colonial past. The modes of governing established under colonial rule were not always completely abolished after a colony gained independence, but instead frequently had profound reverberations in the country's subsequent development. In many cases, the governance practices and structures that had evolved during the colonial era determined the shape and character of a country's legal and political system, the role of specific actors within the realm of political organization and rule, or the nature of societal cleavages.

The longevity of political structures and practices rooted in colonial times strongly suggests that there is a path dependency inherent in colonial governance. In order to understand present-day governance in formerly colonized countries it is therefore indispensable to take into account their colonial pasts. This is not only true for those African, Asian, or Latin American countries that are viewed as areas of limited statehood today, but also for stable democracies like Canada or the United States. Even in the United States where British and French colonial rule ended more than two hundred years ago, the legacies of the country's colonial past continue to influence the character of the political and legal system. In this context, the use of the governance concept proves to be of value, since it allows for a perspective on colonial rule that not only focuses on the colonies' official political structure, but also takes into view informal modes of governing and the role of nonofficial and semiofficial actors in processes of political organization—characteristics of colonial rule that were often much more persistent than the formal structures established by the colonizing powers.

In the following paragraphs, the long-term consequences of colonial governance are illustrated on the basis of two case studies. While the first example deals with the political heritage of early modern settler colonies in North America, the second one looks at the legacies of colonial rule in Africa during the era of high imperialism. Although the long-acting effects of colonial rule that can be observed in these two cases differ quite substantially from each other, the continuities of governing practices that emerged in colonial times are clearly visible in both contexts.

Various features of the United States' political and legal system on the local, regional, and national level can be traced back to the country's colonial past. A conspicuous example of the colonial heritage inherent in United States politics is the extraordinary strength of the individual states within the federal system of government. When the thirteen original British colonies in mainland North America declared their independence from Great Britain in 1776, it was a matter of course for many former colonists that the newly created states should be the principal centers of power and that a centralized federal government should be vested with as little discretionary power as possible—a position that found expression in the Tenth Amendment of the U.S. Constitution, ratified in 1791 (Wood 1998). The reason behind this was not only the fear that central authorities would abuse power at the states' expense—the exact same constellation that had induced the colonists' resistance against British rule in the first place—but also because long-standing political structures and traditions had evolved in each colony independently over the course of several decades. During most of the colonial era, the commercial, political, and social relations that each colony maintained with Great Britain were much stronger than those existing between the North American colonies themselves. Due to this lack of intercolonial exchange and cooperation and the relative freedom that Britain left her colonies with regard to the handling of internal affairs, it was thus possible for each colony to develop its own governing practices and structures. Even more diversity was added to this picture when former French and Spanish colonies like Louisiana or Florida became part of the United States. These differences in the political development had important consequences for the colonies' subsequent position and self-conception as states in the newly-founded country's constitutional make-up as well as for the shape and character of regional and local governance. The issue of the states' autonomy and political power in relation to the federal government has been a contentious topic throughout United States history and remains so even today. The most vivid historical example is the heated discussion of "states' rights" during the antebellum period and its culmination in the American Civil War (Drake and Nelson 1999). But the debate concerning the influence of state versus federal government continues to affect current governance in the United States, as could be observed, for example, in the immediate aftermath of Hurricane Katrina in New Orleans in 2005. While the local level of government ceased functioning because of damages caused by the catastrophe, state and federal authorities were split over the question of who was ultimately responsible for the coordination of emergency relief. This confusion of responsibilities resulted in delays in extending effective assistance and evacuating the city and contributed substantially to the high death toll in the city during the days following the storm. This led to a renewed discussion of the advantages and disadvantages of the federal system (Griffin 2007).

But the persistence of colonial legacies in the United States' political and juridical system does not only become visible with regard to the status and influence of the individual states in the country's federalist system. Colonial traditions are of similar importance with regard to governing practices and structures on the regional and local levels of political organization. Many of the differences in the individual states' formal political structures existing today can be traced back to their colonial pasts. Even the original thirteen British colonies' local governing practices and structures, though all based on British models, varied considerably. Massachusetts, for example, featured a relatively decentralized political system based on townships as units of local political organization, while power in centrally organized South Carolina was concentrated in the colony's capital Charleston, with only the Anglican church parishes serving as local governing units. Together with the different socioeconomic conditions prevalent in the two colonies—with South Carolina being dominated by an extremely wealthy slave-holding planter and merchant elite that was concentrated in the colony's coastal area, whereas the Massachusetts population consisted mostly of small-scale farmers, merchants, and craftsmen who were scattered throughout the province—these structural features led to entirely distinct governance patterns (Middleton 2002). Even today, town meetings in which the registered voters of each town transact town business by majority vote are an important part of local governing in Massachusetts and other New England states, while such practices of direct democracy are absent in other parts of the United States, such as South Carolina (Berman and Murphy 2003).

The long-term consequences of colonial governing practices for present-day local governance can also be observed in the state of Louisiana. Placed under French control during most of the eighteenth century—with a thirty-year intermezzo of Spanish rule during the latter half of the eighteenth century—Louisiana's development took a completely different direction from that of the British colonies in mainland North America. Legacies of French and Spanish colonial rule are particularly persistent with regard to the role and influence of certain groups within the sociopolitical sphere on the local level. During the latter half of the eighteenth century, a three-caste society evolved in Louisiana. It consisted of free whites, mostly enslaved blacks (like other North American colonies), as well as a third, intermediary group of people called *gens de couleur libres*. These "free people of color" (later also referred to as Creoles of Color) were either the offspring of mixed-race relationships, usually between white males and free black females, or emancipated African slaves. The status of blacks and the interaction between blacks and whites in Louisiana was regulated by the *Code Noir* which had been enacted by the French crown in 1724 and was later adopted by the Spanish authorities. According to this law, manumissions were much easier and therefore more frequent in Louisiana than in areas under British or, after the founding of the United States, under American rule. While the ordinance prohibited marriage between whites and blacks in general, mixed-race unions between whites and free blacks without marriage were tolerated, resulting in a relatively large number of mixed-race children. Although freed slaves also existed in the British colonies, the status of the free people of color in French and Spanish Louisiana was unique in colonial North America because they enjoyed, with very few exceptions, the same rights and privileges as the white Louisiana settlers. Like colonists of European origin, they could own property and freely choose their professions. Many of them worked as artisans, traders, or merchants and a few even owned slaves and operated plantations. During colonial rule, the free people of color thus emerged as an important and self-confident socioeconomic group within colonial society that had to be reckoned with by the ruling authorities in political and social matters (Möllers 2008, 48–52).

By the time of the Louisiana Purchase, the free people of color made up almost one-fifth of New Orleans' overall population, their number having further increased during the 1790s due to the influx of free blacks from the Caribbean during and after the Haitian Revolution. Their position had become so strong that the newly established American government saw no other alternative than to continue the French and Spanish authorities' policy toward them. Even though resentments among whites against the state's free black population considerably increased during the 1840s and 1850s, the free people of color managed to maintain their high economic status throughout the late antebellum period. They did so in part by forming tight-knit social networks. Living in the same neighborhoods, attending church together, providing for a joint education of their children, and promoting marriages of their children only with other Creoles of Color of a similar economic standing, they successfully secured their intermediary position between whites and the mass of enslaved blacks until the end of the Civil War. With the emancipation of all slaves, they lost their special legal status and were forthwith, at least officially, on the same level as the freed slaves (Schweninger 1989). But because of their former status and their superior education, they managed to exert a disproportionate amount of political influence during the Reconstruction (1863–77). All of the black delegates sent to the 1868 state constitutional convention from the states' prairie regions, for example, were Creoles of Color. Although the dividing lines between Creoles of Color and the rest of Louisiana's black population became increasingly blurred, the former free people of color maintained their cultural identity throughout the following decades. Even when eventually joining forces with the mass of the Louisiana blacks in the course of the civil rights movement, they were still disproportionately influential due to their former privileged status and their self-conception as a distinctive group. Once again the Creoles of Color assumed a leadership role within Louisiana's black community. During the past decades, most of the black officeholders in the prairie counties have been Creoles of Color. And their influence also continued in New Orleans politics. With the election of Ernest Morial in 1977, a Creole of Color became the city's first nonwhite mayor (Brasseaux et al. 1996, 104–26; Hirsch 1992).

A second example concerns the long-term effects of colonial rule during high imperialism. An analysis of colonial structures of governance suggests that current conflicts and difficulties in areas of limited statehood cannot be explained without reference to their colonial past. Quite to the contrary, it is possible to speak of path dependencies that connect colonial structures of rule to postcolonial predicaments. A good example is the taxonomy with which the colonial bureaucracies in many states in colonial Africa defined, for different "tribes," their specific customary law according to which they were to be ruled. This kind of intervention contributed to the construction, and fixation, of "tribes" and ethnic groups based on legal (but not cultural) separation. The colonial state thus acquired aspects of a federation of different ethnically defined entities that were subjected, as local states, to overarching colonial rule.

Frequently, this specific colonial order based on the legal reification of "tribes" had long-lasting consequences. The 1994 mass killings of Tutsis in Rwanda, conventionally rendered as a paradigmatic example of the dangers of limited statehood, is a case in point. Of course, the genocide was the product of a complex set of factors that cannot be reduced to issues of historical continuity (Malkki 1995; Straus 2006; Uvin 2001). But among the long-term origins of the conflict was the strict differentiation of Hutu and Tutsi under German (and then Belgian) colonial rule. The administrative segregation of ethnic groups that in everyday practice were not at all separate was a concern of the colonial state that relied on a *divide et impera* strategy to safeguard its rule. The establishment of different legal spheres, reinforced by partial political autonomy, was organized by colonial administrators who both employed and produced the relevant anthropological and legal knowledge of the time (see, for example, the "Instructions for ethnographic observations and collections in German East Africa," written by Felix von Luschan, director of the Anthropological Museum in Berlin, specifically for colonial bureaucrats) (Honke 1990; Servaes 1990). Colonial rule was thus intimately tied to colonial knowledge, and the structures it created lived on to shape life in the region well into postcolonial times (Mamdani 1996b; Newbury 1998; Schmuhl 2000).

Mahmood Mamdani has convincingly demonstrated that this was a general pattern. The access to rights and power remained conditioned on indigenous status. "If we look at the definition of citizenship in most African states, we will realize that the colonial state lives on. . . . In privileging the indigenous over the non-indigenous we turned the colonial world upside down, but we did not change it" (Mamdani 2001, 658). As a colonial legacy to postcolonial times, a culture of entitlement developed in which ethnic categories were not only employed to define cultural identity, but also to legitimize social and political claims. When in the context of mobility and labor migration spawned by capitalist development an increasing number of people came to live on the territory of a "foreign" ethnic group, they always carried their minority rights with them. This transferability of competing legal orders exacerbated social problems and political conflicts and at the same time posed limitations on the ability of the state to intervene and control. The problematic of limited statehood in contemporary Africa, in other words, can be traced in part to this colonial legacy. Mahmood Mamdani therefore goes as far as to say that the institutionalization and politicization of the status of "indigenous" was the most influential and long-lasting effect of colonial rule (Mamdani 1996a).

Conclusions

The use of the governance concept in the study of colonial rule presents the historian with both opportunities and problems. On the one hand, the notion of governance proves to be highly useful for systematically inquiring into the mechanism of colonial rule. In particular, it allows identifying path dependencies of colonial governing practices and structures, as we have argued in the fourth section of the article. Providing a broad perspective on modes of political organization existent in colonial contexts, the governance approach allows for a view on colonial governing that not only focuses on the official systems of rule established by the colonizing powers, but also on the informal (and at times cooperative) forms of governing that evolved during colonial times and in many cases proved to be more persistent in the long run than the formal institutional structures. As the case study on the legacies of colonial rule in Africa demonstrates, the long-term consequences of colonial governance are still keenly felt in many of the formerly colonized regions of Africa, resulting in postcolonial predicaments that have stymied the development of stable polities on the continent until today. In the United States, although quite different from the African case and much less dramatic and negative in their effects, colonial legacies are also still visible in the country's political system, as the example of states' rights and of the peculiarities of local governing practices and structures illustrate.

In contrast, the critical discussion of the concept's transferability to the colonial context in the third part of this chapter has vividly demonstrated the limitations of a classic understanding of governance when applied to colonial contexts. The diversity of actors involved in colonial governing processes and the often hybrid nature of their roles in colonial rule cannot be adequately described using the binary categories of "public" and "private" that are of central importance in many of the current debates on governance. Likewise, due to ethnic divides, the varying influence of specific social groups, and the colonies' blurred territorial boundaries, a clearly defined and coherent governance collective as the object of governing did not exist in the colonial context, rendering the task of clearly distinguishing between the rulers and the ruled more complex.

The conceptual weaknesses of the governance concept when applied to the colonial past may also be of relevance for the study of governing practices and structures in modern-day areas of limited statehood. A first step to accommodate this criticism would be to understand governance as "institutionalized modes of social coordinative action geared towards the production and implementation of binding rules or towards the allocation of collective goods," and thus to strip the concept of any underlying notions of modern statehood formerly inherent in it. In contrast to conventional definitions that implicitly assume the existence of a consolidated society with specific expectations regarding the regularization of certain issues, this modified understanding of governance need not contain such presumptions. Speaking more neutrally of "binding rules" and "collective goods," it instead merely implies that a group of individuals addressed by certain rules is aware that compliance with these rules is expected of it (if compliance is actually achieved it is irrelevant in this context), and that in contrast to private goods, collective goods have to be openly accessible, not exclusive, and nonrival with regard to their consumption (Sonderforschungsbereich 700 2009, 4).

Apart from these minimal requirements, the actual definition of what a collective good is in a given society or community remains a question of social and political negotiation within the society itself. Moreover, an understanding of governance suited for the study of colonial rule needs to rethink the strict dichotomy of "public" and "private" spheres of society typical for classical approaches to governance and statehood as it was applied to modern Western nation states. Acknowledging the fact that the lines between these two categories are often blurred in areas of limited statehood, it seems appropriate instead to merely differentiate between "official" and "nonofficial" agents—even though this very dichotomy may have differed, in historical practice, depending on the perspectives of the social actors.

To keep the definition of governance open thus seems imperative when applying it to historical contexts—and also to many present-day constellations outside the purview of the Western nation-state. Used in this way, it may serve as a heuristic instrument that enables us to take a broad look at modes of governing and at the actors involved therein in a historical perspective. In particular, it helps focus our attention equally on the structures and processes of governing, and on the institutions of rule as well as the informal modes of governing.

REFERENCES

Appiah, Kwame Anthony. 1992. *In My Father's House: Africa in the Philosophy of Culture*. New York: Oxford University Press.

Arnold, David. 1983. "White Colonization and Labour in Nineteenth-Century India." *Journal of Commonwealth History* 11:133–58.

Asch, Ronald G., and Dagmar Freist, eds. 2005. *Staatsbildung als kultureller Prozess. Strukturwandel und Legitimation von Herrschaft in der Frühen Neuzeit*. Cologne: Böhlau.

Barth, Boris, and Jürgen Osterhammel, eds. 2005. *Zivilisierungsmissionen. Imperiale Weltverbesserung seit dem 18. Jahrhundert*. Konstanz: UVK.

Berman, Larry, and Bruce A. Murphy. 2003. *Approaching Democracy*. Upper Saddle River, N.J.: Prentice Hall.

Brasseaux, Carl A., Keith P. Fontenot, and Claude F. Oubre. 1996. *Creoles of Color in the Bayou Country*. Jackson: University Press of Mississippi.

Buettner, Elizabeth. 2000. "Problematic Spaces, Problematic Races: Defining Europeans in Late Colonial India." *Women's History Review* 9:277–99.

Chatterjee, Partha. 1993. *The Nation and Its Fragments: Colonial and Postcolonial Histories*. Princeton: Princeton University Press.

——. 1995. "The Disciplines in Colonial Bengal." In *Texts of Power: Emerging Disciplines in Colonial Bengal*, edited by Partha Chatterjee, 1–29. Minneapolis: University of Minnesota Press.

Conklin, Alice. 1997. *A Mission to Civilize: The Republican Idea of Empire in France and West Africa, 1895–1920*. Stanford: Stanford University Press.

Cooper, Frederick. 2005. *Colonialism in Question: Theory, Knowledge, History*. Berkeley: University of California Press.

Daniels, Christine, and Michael V. Kennedy, eds. 2002. *Negotiated Empires: Centers and Peripheries in the Americas, 1500–1820*. New York: Routledge.

Dimier, Véronique. 2004. *Le gouvernement des colonies, regards croisés france-britanniques*. Brussels: Édition de l'université de Bruxelles.

Dirlik, Arif. 2007. *Global Modernity*. Boulder, Colo.: Paradigm Press.

Doyle, Michael W. 1986. *Empires*. Ithaca, N.Y.: Cornell University Press.

Drake, Frederick D., and Nelson, Lynn R., eds. 1999. *States' Rights and American Federalism: A Documentary History*. Westport, Conn.: Greenwood Press.

Fischer-Tiné, Harald, and Susanne Gehrmann, eds. 2009. *Empires and Boundaries: Rethinking Race, Class, and Gender in Colonial Settings*. London: Routledge.

Fischer-Tiné, Harald, and Michael Mann, eds. 2004. *Colonialism as Civilizing Mission: Cultural Ideology in British India*. London: Anthem Press.

Förster, Stig, ed. 1988. *Bismarck, Europe, and Africa: The Berlin Africa Conference, 1884–1885, and the Onset of Partition*. Oxford: Oxford University Press.

Gann, Lewis H. 1987. "Marginal Colonialism: The German Case." In *Germans in the Tropics: Essays in German Colonial History*, edited by Arthur J. Knoll and Lewis H. Gann, 1–17. New York: Greenwood Press.

Gann, Lewis H., and Peter Duignan. 1978. *African Proconsuls: European Governors in Africa*. New York: Free Press.

Greene, Jack P. 1994. *Negotiated Authorities: Essays in Colonial Political and Constitutional History*. Charlottesville: University of Virginia Press.

Griffin, Stephen M. 2007. "Stop Federalism Before It Kills Again: Reflections on Hurricane Katrina." *St. John's Journal of Legal Commentary* 21, no. 2:527–40.

Guha, Ranajit. 1998. *Dominance Without Hegemony: History and Power in Colonial India*. Cambridge, Mass.: Harvard University Press.

Hausen, Karin. 1970. *Deutsche Kolonialherrschaft in Afrika: Wirtschaftsinteressen und Kolonialverwaltung in Kamerun vor 1914*. Zurich: Atlantis.

Herbst, Jeffrey. 2000. *States and Power in Africa: Comparative Lessons in Authority and Control*. Princeton: Princeton University Press.

Hindle, Steve. 2000. *The State and Social Change in Early Modern Britain, c. 1550–1640*. Basingstoke: Macmillan.

Hirsch, Arnold R. 1992. "Simply a Matter of Black and White: The Transformation of Race and Politics in Twentieth-Century New Orleans." In *Creole New Orleans: Race and Americanization*, edited by Arnold R. Hirsch and Joseph Logsdon, 262–319. Baton Rouge: Louisiana State University Press.

Honke, Gudrun. 1990. "Ins Innerste Afrika. Europäer und Ruander entdecken einander." In *Als die Weißen kamen: Ruanda und die Deutschen, 1885–1919*, edited by Gudrun Honke, 83–98. Wuppertal: Hammer.

Knoll, Arthur J. 2001. "An Indigenous Law Code for the Togolese: The Work of Dr. Rudolf Asmis." In *Kolonialisierung des Rechts: Zur kolonialen Rechts- und Verwaltungsforschung*, edited by Rüdiger Voigt and Peter Sack, 271–92. Baden-Baden: Nomos.

Krause, Ingo. 2007. *Koloniale Schuldlüge? Die Schulpolitik in den afrikanischen Kolonien Deutschlands und Britanniens im Vergleich*. Hamburg: Verlag J. Kovac.

Lehmkuhl, Ursula. 2007. "Regieren im kolonialen Amerika: 'Colonial Governance' und koloniale 'Gouvernementalité' in französischen und britischen Siedlungskolonien." In *Regieren ohne Staat? Governance in Räumen begrenzter Staatlichkeit*, edited by Thomas Risse and Ursula Lehmkuhl, 111–33. Baden-Baden: Nomos.

Levine, Philippa, ed. 2004. *Gender and Empire*. Oxford: Oxford University Press.

Louis, William R., ed. 1976. *Imperialism: The Robinson and Gallagher Controversy*. New York: New Viewpoints.

Malkki, Liisa. 1995. *Purity and Exile: Violence, Memory, and National Cosmology Among Hut Refugees in Tanzania*. Chicago: University of Chicago Press.

Mamdani, Mahmood. 1996a. *Citizen and Subject: Contemporary Africa and the Legacy of Late Colonialism*. Princeton, NJ: Princeton University Press.

——. 1996b. "From Conquest to Consent as the Basis of State Formation: Reflections on Rwanda." *New Left Review* 216:3–36.

——. 2001. "Beyond Settler and Native as Political Identities: Overcoming the Political Legacy of Colonialism." *Comparative Studies in Society and History* 43:651–64.

Mayntz, Renate. 2004. "Governance im modernen Staat." In *Governance—Regieren in komplexen Regelsystemen*, edited by Arthur Benz, 65–76. Wiesbaden: VS.

McClintock, Anne. 1995. *Imperial Leather: Race, Gender, and Sexuality in the Colonial Contest*. New York: Routledge.

Meumann, Markus, and Ralf Pröve, eds. 2004. *Herrschaft in der Frühen Neuzeit. Umrisse eines dynamisch-kommunikativen Prozesses*. Münster: LIT.

Middleton, Richard. 2002. *Colonial America: A History, 1565–1776*. Oxford: Blackwell.

Möllers, Nina. 2008. *Kreolische Identität: Eine amerikanische Rassengeschichte zwischen Schwarz und Weiß—Die Free People of Color in New Orleans*. Bielefeld: transcript.

Mühlhahn, Klaus. 2000. *Herrschaft und Widerstand in der 'Musterkolonie' Kiautschou: Interaktionen zwischen China und Deutschland, 1897–1914*. Munich: Oldenbourg.

Newbury, Catharine. 1998. "Ethnicity and the Politics of History in Rwanda." *Africa Today* 45:7–24.

Osterhammel, Jürgen. 1995. *Kolonialismus: Geschichte, Formen, Folgen*. Munich: C. H. Beck.

Pesek, Michael. 2005. *Koloniale Herrschaft in Deutsch-Ostafrika: Expeditionen, Militär und Verwaltung seit 1880*. Frankfurt: Campus.

Reinhard, Wolfgang, ed. 1999. *Verstaatlichung der Welt? Europäische Staatsmodelle und außereuropäische Machtprozesse*. Munich: Oldenbourg.

Schaper, Ulrike. 2010. "Koloniale Herrschaft des Rechts—Recht der kolonialen Herrschaft." Ph.D. diss., Freie Universität. Berlin.

Schmuhl, Hans-Walter. 2000. "Deutsche Kolonialherrschaft und Ethnogenese in Ruanda, 1897–1916." *Geschichte und Gesellschaft* 26:307–34.

Schweninger, Loren. 1989. "Antebellum Free Persons of Color in Postbellum Louisiana." *Louisiana History* 30, no. 4:345–65.

Servaes, Sylvia. 1990. "Die ethnographische Erforschung Ruandas." In *Als die Weißen kamen: Ruanda und die Deutschen, 1885–1919*, edited by Gudrun Honke, 99–111. Wuppertal: Hammer.

Sonderforschungsbereich 700, ed. 2009. *Grundbegriffe der Governance-Forschung*. Berlin.

Steinmetz, George. 2007. *The Devil's Handwriting: Precoloniality and the German Colonial State in Qingdao, Samoa, and Southwest Africa*. Chicago: University of Chicago Press.

Stoler, Ann Laura. 1989. "Rethinking Colonial Categories: European Communities and the Boundaries of Rule." *Comparative Studies in Society and History* 31:134–61.

——. 2002. *Carnal Knowledge and Imperial Power: Race and the Intimate in Colonial Rule*. Berkeley: University of California Press.

Straus, Scott. 2006. *The Order of Genocide: Race, Power, and War in Rwanda*. Ithaca, N.Y.: Cornell University Press.

Uvin, Peter. 2001. "Reading the Rwandan Genocide." *International Studies Review* 3:75–99.

Wildenthal, Lora. 2001. *German Women for Empire, 1884–1945.* Durham: Duke University Press.

Wirz, Albert. 1972. *Vom Sklavenhandel zum kolonialen Handel: Wirtschaftsräume und Wirtschaftsformen in Kamerun vor 1914.* Zurich: Atlantis.

Wood, Gordon S. 1998. *The Creation of the American Republic, 1776–1787.* Chapel Hill: University of North Carolina Press.

Zimmerer, Jürgen. 2001. *Deutsche Herrschaft über Afrikaner: Staatlicher Machtanspruch und Wirklichkeit im kolonialen Namibia.* Münster: LIT.

3

Law Without a State?

A "New Interplay" Between State and Nonstate Actors in Governance by Rule Making

GUNNAR FOLKE SCHUPPERT

T HE AIM OF THIS CHAPTER IS TO CONTRIBUTE TO the understanding of "Governance in Areas of Limited Statehood" by discussing these issues in the broader context of new developments in the area of rule making. What can be witnessed here—the decoupling of state and law, the emergence of new modes of governance by rule making in the process of transnationalization—are developments that are of immediate importance for understanding areas of limited statehood. Furthermore, it would improve—at least in the long run—the research on governance in areas of limited statehood if this research would stay in close touch with the broader discussion about changes in governance.

The State and the Territoriality of the Law

The process of the emergence of the modern state—and consensus exists on this point among representatives of the science of history (Schilling 1999)— can be described as a process of the achievement of three monopolies that are characteristic of the modern state.[1] These are the monopolies on legitimate violence, taxes, and legislation. Ever since the enforcement of these three key state monopolies, law is mainly state law (Schuppert 2003). It is this close link between law and state that Peter Badura (1971) hints at in the following sentences: "Law is a state legal order whose validity depends on the fulfilment of certain formal criteria which are usually defined in the constitution. . . . The state holds the prerogative of lawmaking within a certain territory. . . . The idea and reality of the modern sovereign state constitute the historical and ideological basis of this statist concept of law."[2]

The modern state emerged based upon territorial sovereignty (Brunner 1965). State authority therefore is both territorially based and limited (Badura 2006, para. 1). In order to paraphrase once again this inextricable link between the state and the law, which is expressed in the concepts of statehood and the territoriality of the law, I will draw upon the following influential formulations: Michael Mann's (1994) characterization of political power as territorially centralized regulatory power, and *Territory—Authority—Rights*, the significant title of Saskia Sassen's (2006) widely quoted book, which invokes a triad that pinpoints the essence and functional logic of the modern state.

If, therefore, law is state law and territorially limited law, the question arises as to what "happens" with the law in the face of evident and increasing processes of *Entstaatlichung*[3] and the deterritorialization of political rule. Extensive evidence of this is presented in the literature on the change in statehood (see Leibfried and Zürn 2005; Schuppert 2008). This question is particularly relevant to areas of limited statehood that are by definition characterized by the weak role of state and government agencies, and where *governments* are governance actors among others. Here, the concept of state law lacks much of its plausibility. Instead, one finds a plurality of complementary—and also competing—forms of regulations and norm settings that are only partially state law. If the law falls by the wayside as a result of these processes of *Entstaatlichung*, then the following questions must be asked. Is national law losing its significance? Will it succeed in assimilating these developments and responding to them through *Entstaatlichung* and deterritorialization?

It is not possible to answer these questions comprehensively within the scope of this chapter. Thus, I shall limit myself to three fragmentary aspects that demonstrate something about legal or quasi-legal governance services in areas of limited statehood. I will first look at certain manifestations of nonstate self-regulation so as to establish the conditions under which such self-regulation actually functions. Only through understanding the functional logic and effectiveness of such nonstate self-regulation can one draw reasonable conclusions regarding the "opportunities and risks" associated with the *Entstaatlichung* of law. Second, I will examine in greater detail the meaning of the reference to the emergence of a transnational law and whether this could constitute a credible example of a deterritorialized and denationalized form of law. Third, I will look at sets of regulations that clearly do not constitute classical state law, but—as has been specified in the literature (Hommelhoff and Schwab 2001)—have been enacted by private standards bodies that replace the state, and that, although not legally binding, display a high level of de facto governance. Having completed this broad survey of the world of nonstate law, I will then be in a position to draw some initial relevant conclusions about areas of limited statehood and, perhaps also, to formulate some preliminary hypotheses.

Manifestations of "Nonstate Rule Making"

Nonstate Rule Making in Microsocieties, or "Governance by Reputation"

The intention in this section is to address the discussion that has been under way among U.S. legal scholars for the past ten years under the heading of "private ordering" (for more detail, see Richman 2004). This discussion is concerned with the functional conditions of private regulatory systems in microsocieties. The ways in which such private regulatory systems emerge and—the ultimate acid test—how they are implemented have been described in a series of detailed case studies. The classical examples in this literature on private ordering (cf. the summary presentation in Nils Ipsen 2008) concern the sets of rules that replace state law among Jewish diamond dealers in New York (Richman 2006), the American cotton trade at the Memphis Cotton Exchange (Bernstein 2001), and conflict resolution among farmers in Shasta County (Ellickson 1991). The focus of these studies, the results of which shall be reported in brief, is not, therefore, global or transnational, but local and—it may be said—profession-specific. They may not prove particularly helpful in the study of areas of limited statehood.

A particularly instructive example concerns the Jewish diamond dealers in New York who belong to the New York Diamond Dealers Club and base their business transactions on self-defined rules. The club monitors compliance with these rules through the provision of regular information about the business behavior of its members. As a result the club plays a role in the decisions made about the members' reputations and, in the case of a permanent loss of reputation, ultimately issues the threat of expulsion. Barak D. Richman refers aptly to the "reputation-based enforcement" (2004, 2328) of the self-defined rules, a formulation that prompts us to refer more generally to a case of the application of "governance by reputation." To simplify and summarize the results of the case studies, a mode of governance of this nature presupposes two things. First, a functioning exchange of information about the business behavior of certain people (usually traders), and second, the existence of a social group or social network, within which the reputation of the members is important. I shall refer to such social groups using a term I have chosen myself, *reputation communities*.

With regard to the exchange of information, Nils Ipsen (2008, 38–39) points out that the "dissemination of information and publication of the individual reputations must first be guaranteed." Distinguishing groups of different sizes, Ipsen assumes that "in very small groups, such as the neighbouring ranchers in Shasta County, this can take place informally." Larger groups, in contrast, shall require special institutions that offer this service. Ipsen presents the example of the New York Diamond Dealers Club, within which most of the global trade in diamonds takes place: "[The DDC] not only offers a secure trading hall but also acts as a chamber of commerce. Based on this, the DDC defines the rules governing diamond trading and provides a mandatory private arbitration system."

But the DDC not only provides the infrastructure for the trading. It furthermore enables and guarantees the exchange of information on the reputation of the individual dealers with various means so as to ensure compliance with the rulings of its own arbitration body. For this purpose, photographs of visitors and new traders are displayed on the walls of the common trading hall with information about their reputations and their personal references. These are complemented by photos of those who have failed to pay their debts, a practice that reminds Ipsen of "the infamous 'wanted' posters in the Wild West." In Ipsen's opinion, this system facilitates easy access to information about the reputation of a potential trading partner for all dealers.

As a second example, Ipsen (2008, 39) describes the American cotton market that usually takes place at the Memphis Cotton Exchange. A system very similar to DDC has been established here: historically, the members of the MCE located their offices on one street in Memphis where a shared market center enabled the rapid exchange of information.

The existence of such a social network, which I refer to as a reputation community, can involve a professional group with specific professional-ethical standards or, as in the case of the Jewish diamond traders, a religious group. The community of Jewish diamond traders in New York clearly exercises "reputation-based rule enforcement" as specified here, not just vis-à-vis the actual diamond traders but also vis-à-vis the diamond cutters who live with the omnipresent temptation to steal the diamonds they work on.

According to Ipsen (2008, 41–42), the situation among the diamond cutters is different. Due to their low level of income and due to the informality of the business arrangements that makes it easy to embezzle or steal the diamonds, the incentive to violate the agreements is extremely high. Besides, these ultraorthodox Jews want neither to remain in the business permanently nor to pass it on to their descendants, but would much rather follow the ideal of the life-long study of the Torah. The breach of the rules, however, is out of the question as Ipsen points out: as ultraorthodox Jews they also have particularly strong ties with their religious community and flight would involve the abandonment of this community. Moreover, the community attaches great importance to the appropriate behavior of its members in public. Offences are sanctioned through a kind of court of arbitration headed by a rabbi. In the case of the diamond trade, this connection runs so deep that the arbitration courts can be invoked directly by diamond traders. Those who break their word are threatened with the withdrawal of religious honors, temporary exclusion from community festivities, and, in extreme cases, expulsion from the community.

Thus, Ipsen (2008, 42) concludes that the enforcement of the rules is achieved through the connection with the religious community. The breach of the rules has such far-reaching consequences for the individual believers that it is unlikely to occur even with the significant incentive. Based on this support from a social network, the private regulatory system is superior to the state legal system and, in Richman's view (2004), constitutes a decisive competitive advantage and hence the main reason for the high proportion of Jews among the diamond traders.

As can be generalized on the basis of the findings of the private-ordering literature, in a functioning nonstate regulatory system, the system and the network are mutually dependent: "While the social network ensures compliance with the regulatory system, the existence of such a system ensures that conflicts can be resolved without necessitating the intervention of a third party (the state), which may only be able to resolve these conflicts inadequately and thus could jeopardize the existence of the social network" (Ipsen 2008, 43). If this is correct, the question that requires clarification is how such sets of private rules arise, which of course do not just simply appear but require a fertile ground that promotes the emergence of rules. Nils Ipsen refers here to a publication by Amitai Aviram (2003) that deals with this question and establishes convincingly that private regulatory systems do not arise "spontaneously" out of nothing, but build on an existing institutional infrastructure consisting of social or religious networks. Aviram cites as examples the Pax Dei movement and the German Hanse or Hanseatic League.

In order to explain the functioning of such social and religious networks, Aviram (2003, 20) distinguishes two different stages of the evolutionary process that results in a private legal system: "First, a network creating a centralized bonding mechanism would form (most likely, not as an end of its own, but as a side effect of some other function the network serves)." And second, "the network would undertake regulating behavior, using its enforcement ability." Social networks, Aviram points out, facilitate centralized bonding and for this purpose use reputation bonds. Such reputation bonds would be ineffective when individuals expect the network to fail. Many social networks, however, would continue to exist over long periods of time. As an example, he refers to "one's neighbors" who "will continue to affect one's social life indefinitely." Besides, he assumes that social networks may spontaneously form, while regulating networks tend to fail if they form spontaneously.

Aviram describes the reputation and punishment mechanism of the social network as follows: "By gossiping about each other within the social network, and by reacting to the gossip according to common norms, the social network can align most members' responses to any member's deviant behavior. When members of the same social circle are also part of another network that attempts to regulate behavior, they will care for their reputations, for while the regulating network cannot in itself harm them, the negative reputation they build will carry on to the social network, and there the centralized bonding mechanism will punish them." However, in Aviram's opinion there is no need for two separate networks, one to regulate and the other to punish deviance. In fact, "if there is demand for certain regulation and networks are the efficient providers, existing networks that enable centralized bonding—such as social networks, religious groups, etc.—will evolve to provide the required regulation."

Aviram's thesis is that such social and religious networks initially only fulfill functions with low implementation costs, but with the strengthening of the implementation mechanisms the aspect of cost becomes less important. Thus, according to his conclusion, when a need for regulation arises the existing networks continue to develop so as to provide this necessary regulation. The precondition for the emergence of a private regulatory system of this kind is always the existence of a network-like demonstrable homogenous group—a close-knit community comprised of members united by similar convictions and values.

From the findings on the microsocieties examined, one learns that, as a rule, the emergence of nonstate regulatory systems necessitates the existence of social and religious networks that, based on this institutional infrastructure, are in a position to steer the membership of their members quite effectively through the governance mode of "reputation-based rule enforcement." In this view, it is more than tempting to apply these insights to areas of limited statehood.

Nonstate Transnational Regulatory Systems

INTERNATIONAL SPORTS LAW AS A LARGELY INDEPENDENT REGULATORY SYSTEM

I shall now change the focus and turn to the wider transnational arena, in which, according to many authors, a new kind of law is emerging in the form of transnational law (e.g., Callies 2004; Hanschmann 2006). As a form of private legislative process beyond the nation-state, this law fills the gaps in regulation that arise because state law is either lagging behind societal developments, a phenomenon known as legal lag, or is unable to keep up with transnational regulatory requirements, a phenomenon known as regulatory gap (Ware 2006). The most popular examples of such self-formulated rules, the rise of which is mainly due to the overcoming of national bottlenecks in rule making (Röthel 2007), are the *lex mercatoria* (i.e., the Law Merchant, an agreement between merchants on certain trade practices and transaction rules), the *lex electronica*, which refers to the regulation of the Internet, and the *lex sportiva*, the self-defined rules of international sports. As this chapter is not intended to be legal-theoretical in nature (see Schuppert 2009), I would like to leave the question as to whether it is possible to refer here to a transnational law as a type of independent law unanswered at this point (for a skeptical view, see Ipsen 2008). Instead I will focus my attention on the question of which of these three sets of rules actually functions well as a result of formulating clear rules that are largely observed by their target groups and are also robustly implemented in the case of noncompliance.

When stated in these terms, the answer is obvious: it is *lex sportiva* — the transnational sports law — that stands on the winners' platform. According to Nils Ipsen (2008, 121–22), the main reason is the quality of sports law as a law of associations that focuses on the rules and regulations of the sporting associations. Principally, each association is autonomous and can enact its own set of regulations. However, together the sporting associations form a hierarchically structured pyramid whose functioning corresponds in full to the Weberian ideal of a hierarchical organization.

In order to outline the hierarchically structured pyramid, Ipsen relates to the level of integration of association regulations by examining the institutional organization of international (Olympic) sports. The International Olympic Committee (IOC) stands at the apex of the pyramid and holds the exclusive rights to the Olympic Games (Rule 7, Olympic Charter) — a right that was never seriously challenged. As a result, the IOC holds a monopoly at the highest level of competitive sports.

Furthermore, Ipsen points out that within the Olympic movement the one-association principle applies. This means that there can only be one top international association for each kind of sport, and only one National Olympic Committee for each nation (Rule 29, Olympic Charter). This principle also applies at lower levels; the top international association also recognizes only one national association. This gives rise to a hierarchical pyramid within competitive sport with the IOC at its apex, the national sports associations below it, followed by any existing regional sports associations, the local sports associations, and at the bottom the individual athletes.

Finally, the pyramid structure allows us to apply the same rules for one kind of sport — which are defined by the top associations — at an international level to achieve the essential comparability of performance. According to Rule 23 of the Olympic Charter, any sporting association that contravenes or fails to recognize the Olympic principles or the World Anti-Doping Agency's World Anti-Doping Code runs the risk of exclusion from the Olympic Games. Thus, the relevant competition rules have universal applicability.

A particular feature of the area of the *lex sportiva*, which makes a crucial contribution to its qualification as an independent regulatory system, is the existence of a superior court of sport in the form of the Court of Arbitration for Sport, which is based in Lausanne. This is an actual court of arbitration for sports-related disputes and has now been recognized by all Olympic and non-Olympic associations. Even so, the court's decisions only have jurisdiction within the limits set by the state courts, which "in exchange" refrain from intervening in the core area. This relationship between the state courts and the sporting associations is referred to in some cases in the literature as a "constitutional equilibrium" (Beloff, Kerr, and Demetriou 1999), in others as a relationship of "concordance" (Hess 2006) and, in any case, as a relationship "which constitutes the basis and precondition for the development of a (partly) independent law of sport" (Ipsen 2008, 147).

THE RELATIONSHIP BETWEEN THE STATE AND TRANSNATIONAL REGULATORY SYSTEMS

If one wishes to determine in greater detail the relationship between state and transnational regulatory systems discussed in the literature, three roles of the state come into consideration (Ipsen 2008, 204 ff):

- The state as model
- The state as beneficiary
- The state as guarantor

The reference to the state as model is suggested by the observation that the state or state law provides a model for the private regulatory systems in two respects. First, they base their material content on existing state regulations—either voluntarily or as a result of pressure from the state—and second, the procedures for the creation of norms or arbitration procedures are often based on state processes. This observation is also applicable to the area of international standard-setting, which will be examined later.

Referring to the state as beneficiary is justified by the idea that in the transnational arena, in particular, the state is forced to experience the limitations of its own national regulatory options and must, therefore, explore other regulatory options. In the absence of a global state or other international regulatory bodies, one such option is the respect of private self-regulation and hence the use of the lawmaking competency of societal subsystems for the compensation of its own excessive regulatory demands.

The second variant—the role of the state as beneficiary—is even more interesting, as it involves the use of the private regulatory systems as a substitute for state law. Ipsen (2008, 207–208) accounts for this structure with the pace of society's continuing development: lawmaking is unable to keep up with this pace and regulatory lags arise wherever new societal or technical developments cannot immediately be covered by law. These lags can be filled by private regulatory systems, albeit in many cases only temporarily. In the two cases of sports and the Internet, participants initially had to regulate their relationships themselves. At the outset, leisure-related sports activity did not seem to require any state intervention and the success of the Internet could not be foreseen. Private regulatory systems have to initially take the place of state regulatory systems since public law making cannot and could never attempt to regulate all relevant issues in a field in advance.

However, if these regulatory areas assume increasing public and political relevance, the state must ask itself whether and to what extent independent regulatory intervention is necessary. Thus, it is unsurprising that attempts to impose state regulation in the area of the Internet are increasing and that an increasing exertion of influence by the state can also be observed in the area of sports, mainly because of the out-of-control doping problem.

The third role of the state vis-à-vis transnational regulatory systems is that of the guarantor. It guarantees to citizens that their essential rights will also be recognized in such transnational regulatory systems. The image of the state as guarantor requires it to be ready to use its legal system as a kind of safety net (on this point, cf. Kirchhof 1987, 522ff.). Technically, the state fulfils these expectations through the "ordre public" caveat, which ensures in the case of both national and international rulings that they may not be recognized or implemented if the outcome would contravene the public order. According to a definition of the German Federal Court of Justice (Bundesgerichtshof, BGHZ 27:249, 254) such a contravention of the "ordre public" arises if an arbitration ruling "ignores a core area of norms of mandatory law which affect the bases of state and economic life (in a free society) and were enacted on the basis of certain state, social or economic policy objectives."

This completes my exploration of the state's trinity of roles in relation to private transnational regulatory systems.

Rule Making That Replaces the State: The World of Standards and Standard Setters

To conclude my overview, I would like to take a brief look at the world of standards, a world that is increasingly gaining significance (Brunsson and Jacobsson 2000). Because standards close a regulatory gap left open by the nation-states, either voluntarily through the "outsourcing" of legislation (Röthel 2007) or involuntarily due to a lack of transnational regulatory competence, standard setting is progressing to become a central type of regulation beyond the nation-state. This aspect will not be examined in greater detail here; what I will focus on instead is the question as to whether requirements of this kind of nonstate standard setting are made and how these requirements are specified. In this way, I can, perhaps, obtain an initial indication as to the character of a meta-law of nonstate lawmaking, which will also assist with exploration of areas of limited statehood.

Standards are not limited to the formulation of technical or scientific insights, and in particular those that define limit values or specify in another way what is authorized or reasonable. But standards also express political compromises and processes of public understanding. The similarity of standardization and lawmaking was pointed out by Harm Schepel (2005, 6). In his opinion, standards are rarely derived "from the customs and practices of social life or deduced from the immutable laws of nature. Standards are products of discussion, negotiation, deliberation and compromise between engineers, manufacturers, academic experts, professionals, trade unionists, representatives of consumer organisations and public officials meeting in boards, committees, task forces and working groups in associations and other organisations." Standards interlock different social perspectives as they "bring to the table economic, political, moral and technical arguments and ultimately arrive at a solution that will to some extent hurt some groups and in some degree benefit others—consumers or producers, importers or domestic manufacturers." Summing up, Schepel calls standardization a "microcosm of social practices, political preferences, economic calculation, scientific necessity, and professional judgement" that "looks a lot like lawmaking."

As rule making through standardization is similar to lawmaking, similar normative requirements—"standardization standards"—apply. This claim is brought forward by Harm Schepel (2005, 6) when he points out that "standardisation procedures have developed into a remarkably consistent set of truly global principles of 'internal administrative law.'" He identifies five aspects that the standardization procedures—"partly influenced by legal instruments, partly by the ethics of the engineering and other professions and structured by an extensive process of global reciprocal normative borrowing between the public and private spheres at various levels"—provide for at a minimum:

> 1. Elaboration of draft standards in technical committees with a balance of represented interests (manufacturers, consumers, social partners, public authorities); 2. A requirement of consensus on the committee before the draft goes to; 3. A round of public notice and comment, with the obligation on the committee to take received comments into account, 4. A ratification vote, again with the requirement of consensus rather than mere majority, among the constituency of the standards body, and 5. The obligation to review standards periodically.

Thus, what is mainly involved here are requirements relating to the organization and process of standardization, which can be summarized under the heading of "structural requirements" of standardization. How these struc-

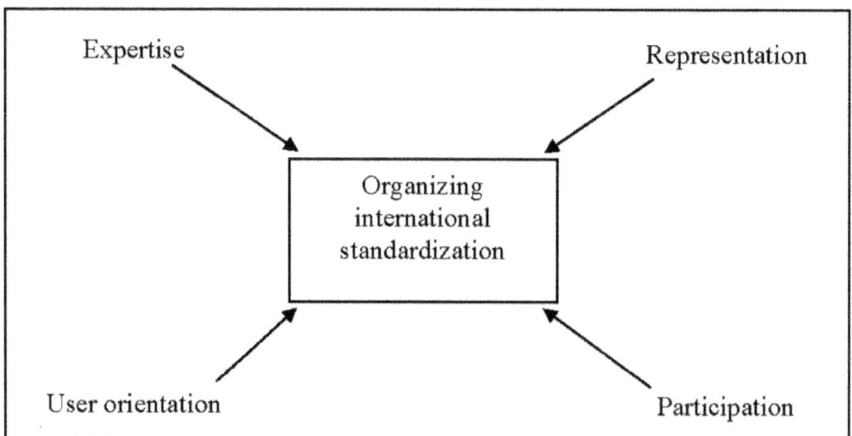

FIGURE 3.1. Four principles of organization for an international standardization body. *Source*: Tamm Hallström 2000, 93.

tural requirements can be developed in detail and postulated normatively will be discussed in the next section.

In her article entitled "Organizing the Process of Standardization," Kristina Tamm Hallström (2000) presented four organizational principles, which are represented graphically in figure 3.1. This brief look at the world of standards should suffice, and in my view, the time has come to draw some interim conclusions.

Interim Conclusions

If one reviews the outcome of the reflections presented thus far, the following insights would appear to be noteworthy:

1. Private regulatory systems are particularly likely to emerge, be enforced, and implemented if they are based on an existing institutional infrastructure, in particular in the form of a social or religious network. The more close-knit the network and the more homogenous the social group in question, the more the enforcement and implementation of the rules can be guaranteed through the governance mode of "governance by reputation."

2. Private regulatory systems are particularly effective when the supporting infrastructure is associative in nature. The more monopolistic and hierarchical this associative structure is, the more likely the self-defined association law is to be enforced among the individual members of local associations. Private association law clearly reaches its limits in cases in which the protection of the basic rights of its members is at stake and against which they can appeal to the state courts, or in cases in which the regulatory problem assumes such a high level of societal relevance that it calls for a solution that goes beyond the association.

3. Private regulatory systems with a high level of de facto binding force raise legitimation problems from the perspective of the individual, as a nonstate self-regulation can also mean heteronomy and, in view of its enforcement claim, requires justification. The examination of standards and other self-regulatory rule systems reveals that certain criteria are required to qualify a regulatory system of de facto binding force as worthy of compliance. The following may be considered as such criteria:

• First, a certain level of authority of the rule-setting institution, be this authority based on knowledge or expertise (as in the case of standards) or—in the Weberian sense—on tradition, charisma, or religious authority.

- Second, certain requirements of the composition and procedures of the standard-setting bodies to guarantee maximum possible representativeness and responsiveness of the standard setting.

Which of these criteria assumes the prominent position differs according to the type of regulatory system in question and the nature of the political culture that prevails in a social and political community.

4. Private regulatory systems do not in essence stand in opposition to state rule making, but can substitute it to varying degrees, complement it, or be based on it so as to prove worthwhile regulatory options. Moreover, the relationship between the enforcement of state and nonstate law is always precarious and in need of clarification based on the field of action in question.

This last observation prompts us to reflect on the relation between state and nonstate lawmaking more systematically and in greater detail in the next section.

A "New Interplay" Between State and Nonstate Actors in Governance by Rule Making

The more intensively one engages the manifestations and functional conditions of nonstate regulatory systems, the more obvious it becomes that one is not dealing with either the dichotomous opposition of state and nonstate lawmaking—and not with a categorical "either/or"—or with manifold variants of rule making between the state and society (Augsberg 2003). To demonstrate this finding, which is ultimately difficult to question, I shall limit myself to four key headings, explained briefly here.

Rule Making in the Shadow of the Law

What is meant by this key heading can perhaps best be explained using the example of the German Corporate Governance Code (Deutscher Corporate Governance Kodex, CGK). This nonstate and nonlegally binding code of conduct was formulated by a commission established by the federal government, publicized in the *German Federal Gazette* and referred to in section 161 of the German Stock Corporation Act (Aktiengesetz) to the extent that companies quoted on the stock exchange are subject to a duty to disclose whether they wish comply with the code or not ("comply or explain"). As summarized by Johannes Köndgen (2006, 496), "if one attempts to make sense out of all that, the status of the CGK can best be described using a variation of a formula familiar in the German sociology of law for 30 years: the code is 'rule-making in the shadow of the law.' It is state-initiated private law-making, subject, however, to the state's right of revocation at any time."

Regulated Self-Regulation

The second key heading is also very familiar and discussed in German literature in particular as a governance concept of the "ensuring state" (*Gewährleistungsstaat*) (Die Verwaltung 2001). A plausible example to consider would be the case of collective bargaining, in which private rule production actually takes place—facilitated and channeled through state agenda setting. A summarizing commentary in a contribution by Gerd Bender (2006, 361) makes the following point: "The most spectacular of these evolutionary achievements, which are embodied by self-regulation in the economic system and crucially concern the 'cooperative state,' is the initially much vaunted and now almost notorious collective bargaining. . . . It is this mechanism of rule production by private collective entities through state procedural law, which is so central to the German variant of capitalism," that made a "strong contribution to the history of regulation in Germany."

Having presented these two evident and largely familiar examples, I would now like to formulate some more general conclusions under the next two headings.

Embedded Self-Regulation

My thesis, to the effect that it makes little sense to consider self-regulation and state lawmaking as dichotomous opposites, finds valuable support in the ideas of Thomas Conzelmann and Dieter Wolf. They (2007, 175) suggest that one should understand the relationship between private self-regulation and state lawmaking as a relationship based on the functional division of labor between public and private actors. In their opinion, the idea of the opposition of public and private sector regulation is misleading. Rather, private-sector self-regulation can only function as a form of governance *embedded* in a public regulatory structure if it is to contribute to governance compatible with the common good. In return it can underlie, complement, and unburden public regulation and compensate for the inherent deficits and limitations of pure interstate governance.

However, if the relationship involved is one based on the functional division of labor, it is necessary to determine the relevant share—or as one would, perhaps, express it in criminal law, determine the relevant "contribution to the act"—of the state or private actor. Conzelmann and Wolf (2007, 175) distinguish five different dimensions of the role of the state in the concept of "embedded self-regulation." It

> (1) provides the constitutional framework for private self-regulation and ensures the functioning of the markets and of a critical public; (2) plays a part in the design of the regulatory environment of private self-regulation and (co-) legitimates the standards represented there; (3) maintains the possibility of a binding public regulation as a fall-back option so as to, first, link the self-regulation initiatives back to common-good criteria and, second, to further develop minimum standards of socially and ecologically responsible action; (4) supports monitoring systems for private self-regulation; and (5) avoids negative external effects through the linking and coordination of different sectoral self-regulation initiatives.

Hybrid Regulation

The fourth and final heading that one should explore is that of hybrid regulation. This term can be used to describe a coordination structure (Schuppert 2007) that consists of both private and state regulatory elements and can therefore be located between the extremes of pure state sanction-based regulatory elements (public ordering) and the completion of a transaction entirely on the basis of private agreement and self-implementation.

In a recent publication, Klaus Heine (2008, 3) examines this mode of governance of hybrid regulation in greater detail from an economic perspective. He distinguishes four generic modes of regulation that he derives from two components: a substantive component, which specifies the cases for which and ways in which the regulation should take effect, and an implementation component, which ensures compliance with the regulation through the recourse of a sanctioning mechanism. If the two components are privately determined Heine calls this "private ordering," whereas if the two components are determined by the state, he calls this "public ordering." Based on this, "hybrid regulation" is involved if one of the two components arises through "private ordering" and the other through "public ordering." Thus, four generic modes of regulation arise for problem resolution, which can entail specific advantages and disadvantages, depending on the situated context.

Heine's examples of prototypes of hybrid regulation are hardly surprising: first, the German Corporate Governance Code and, second, the International Accounting Standards, which are formulated by the private-law-based International Accounting Standards Board and then transformed into European Community Law through a committee procedure (Kirchner and Schmidt 2006). Heine (2008, 12) identifies the first important advantage guaranteed by hybrid regulation as the fact that specific regulatory knowledge that is required "is availed of." He assumes that an initial possible advantage of private regulation exists in its relation to the quality of the regulation. High-quality regulation exists from the perspective of regulation seekers if the regulation is tailored to their needs or aims to achieve a fair balancing of interests between the parties affected by the regulation. In order to illustrate private regulation, Heine gives the example of the International Accounting Standards Board. As it concentrates entirely on the design of an issue in need of regulation, the regulator can accumulate substantial expertise in this area. Heine points out that the learning processes that lead to the production of the high-quality regulation design are not as broadly based as those involved in the case of a state regulator, which must regulate a large number of different issues. But they are developed in depth in relation to a single regulatory object.

A second advantage of private regulations from a reputation-seeker's point of view is their greater credibility and higher reputation as compared with state regulations (Heine 2008, 13). Credibility, in his understanding, means that the addressee of the regulation can rely on the fact that the future application of a regulation will take place as expected by them at the time of the selection of the regulation. Credibility in this sense, however, does not necessarily refer to the stability of the regulation, as it can also consist of the belief that a regulation design will be developed on a continuous basis and

TABLE 3.1 Generic Modes of Regulation

Implementation	State	Private
State	state regulation	hybrid regulation
Private	hybrid regulation	private regulation

adapted to changing situations. In Heine's opinion, if a regulation is repeatedly credible in this way, the regulation gains reputation. Regulation seekers prefer approved regulations because conclusions can be drawn regarding future regulatory practices from the application of the regulation observed in the past. As a result, the costs and benefits of a regulation are identifiable on a comparatively reliable basis.

Interim Conclusions

All four headings outline a consistent finding: the area of "rule making" is increasingly less concerned with exclusively private or state lawmaking and there is greater dovetailing and overlapping of the public, private, and tertiary sectors (Schuppert 2000). As a result, the interaction between state and nonstate actors in the production of rules needs to be examined more closely, and questions need to be asked about the contextual conditions, which, first, give rise to the careers of such hybrid forms of regulation and, second, determine the shares of the different actors in this process of functional division of labor.

Lessons to Learn: Rule Making and Rule Enforcement in Areas of Limited Statehood

In closing, I would like to draw some conclusions for governance in areas of limited statehood that provide an outline for a future research program. First, it has clearly emerged that law is not necessarily state law. A large variety of nonstate rule making clearly exists that can be approached in a wide variety of contexts, from the informal customs of Jewish diamond traders in New York to the hierarchically organized international sports law, a variety to be found in areas of functioning statehood. Thus, there is all the more cause to watch for manifestations of nonstate rule setting in which the territorial nation-state is absent as monopolistic legislator—that is, in the transnational arena or areas of limited statehood. In both of these areas, other types of rules and standard setters play the role of the state and thus fill the regulatory gap. This role is fulfilled in the transnational arena by what is known as transnational law. To name the main ones, the corresponding systems of law in areas of limited statehood, which need to be studied in greater detail, include customary law, local law, traditional law, and religion-based law. This medley of systems should be analyzed and systematized.

Second, if one reviews the aforementioned candidates for a form of rule making that replaces or complements state lawmaking, it is of crucial importance not to think in terms of the state-private or public-private pairs of opposites and not to be taken in by this misleading dichotomy. As was seen in the study of the problems of governance in sub-Saharan Africa, the differentiation between state and private and public and private areas in areas of limited statehood is either nonexistent or merely rudimentary. Moreover, a central problem in areas of limited statehood appears to consist of the fact that effective territorial sovereignty only extends to part of the state territory—e.g., Kabulistan, archipelago states—and thus what is mainly being dealt with here is manifestations of local governance (Risse and Lehmkuhl 2007). If this is the case, and moreover, the key local governance actors are religious or ethnic authorities, it becomes questionable as to whether one can refer here to "governance by the state" or to a boundary line between state and private that, in reality, is almost impossible to locate.

Third, if one reviews the examples addressed in this chapter, it becomes clear that the main research questions for areas of limited statehood involve identifying the institutional infrastructure, in particular in the form of social and religious networks that can be considered as regulatory and reputation communities. Which collectives produce regulatory systems? What qualities do they have? How is their enforcement ensured? In my view, these questions are key ones and cannot be adequately answered in the absence of expertise in the areas of the science of religion and the social anthropology of law.

Finally, it should be clarified how these nonstate regulatory systems behave vis-à-vis the outcomes of state lawmaking. The question that arises here is whether one can refer to a functional division of labor between state and nonstate standard production or instead to the coexistence or overlap of different regulatory systems, as in the case of colonial statehood, or the coexistence of state and local, ethnic and religious sets of rules. It will also be impossible to answer these questions in the absence of a detailed knowledge of the relevant governance area and its historical and cultural context. Thus, a theory of the role of the law in areas of limited statehood can only be one that is empirically well founded.

NOTES

1. I would like to express my sincere gratitude to Matthias Kötter for his persistent willingness to engage in discussion, his valuable comments, and his constructive insistence on the adoption of a clear position.

2. Quotations from German texts have all been translated by the author.

3. The German term *Entstaatlichung* refers to processes of denationalization, Europeanization, globalization, privatization, the demise of the state, and so on.

REFERENCES

Augsberg, Steffen. 2003. *Rechtsetzung zwischen Staat und Gesellschaft. Möglichkeiten differenzierter Steuerung des Kapitalmarktes*. Berlin: Duncker & Humblot.

Aviram, Amitai. 2003. "The Paradox of Spontaneous Formation of Private Legal Systems." Law and Economics Working Paper No. 192, Olin Program, University of Chicago Law School, www.law.uchicago.edu/files/files/192.aa_.spontaneous.pdf.

Badura, Peter. 1971. "Recht, Theorie des Rechts, Rechtsphilosophie." In *Recht*, edited by Peter Badura, Erwin Deutsch, and Claus Roxin, 118–37. Frankfurt: Fischer.

——. 2006. "Der räumliche Geltungsbereich der Grundrechte." In *Handbuch der Grundrechte*, vol. 2, edited by Detlef Merten and Hans-Jürgen Papier, §47, 1059–78. Heidelberg: C.F. Müller.

Beloff, Michael, Tim Kerr, and Marie Demetriou. 1999. *Sports Law*. Oxford: Hart.

Bender, Gerd. 2006. "Regulierte Selbstregulierung, Der Fall Tarifautonomie." In *Selbstorganisation. Ein Denksystem für Natur und Gesellschaft*, edited by Miloš Vec, Marc-Thorsten Hütt, and Alexandra M. Freund, 355–71. Cologne, Weimar, and Vienna: Böhlau-Verlag.

Bernstein, Lisa. 2001. "Private Commercial Law in the Cotton Industry: Creating Cooperation Through Rules, Norms, and Institutions." *Michigan Law Review* 99:1724–90.

Brunner, Otto. 1965. *Land und Herrschaft*. 5th ed. Darmstadt: Wissenschaftliche Buchgesellschaft.

Brunsson, Nils, and Bengt Jacobsson, eds. 2000. *A World of Standards*. Oxford: Oxford University Press.

Callies, Gralf-Peter. 2004. "Transnationales Verbrauchervertragsrecht." *Rabels Zeitschrift* 68:244–87.

Conzelmann, Thomas, and Klaus-Dieter Wolf. 2007. "Doing Good While Doing Well? Potenzial und Grenzen grenzüberschreitender politischer Steuerung durch privatwirtschaftliche Selbstregulierung." In *Macht und Ohmmacht internationaler Organisationen*, edited by Andreas Hasenclever, Klaus Dieter Wolf, Michael Zürn, 145–75. Frankfurt: Campus.

Die Verwaltung. Beiheft 4/2001. "Regulierte Selbstregulierung als Steuerungskonzept des Gewährleistungsstaates." *Ergebnisse des Symposiums aus Anlass des 60. Geburtstages von Wolfgang Hoffmann-Riem*, Berlin: Duncker & Humblot.

Ellickson, Robert C. 1991. *Order without Law: How Neighbors Settle Disputes.* Cambridge, Mass.: Harvard University Press.

Hanschmann, Felix. 2006. "Theorie transnationaler Rechtsprozesse." In *Neue Theorien des Rechts*, edited by Sonja Buckel, Ralph Christensen, and Andreas Fischer-Lescano, 347–69. Stuttgart: Lucius & Lucius.

Heine, Klaus. 2008. "Hybride Regulierung—Zum Einfluß politischer Institutionen auf private Regelsetzung." In *Ökonomische Analyse politischer Institutionen, Schriften des Vereins für Sozialpolitik*, edited by U. Vollmer, 113–20. Berlin: Duncker & Humblot.

Hess, Burkhard. 2006. "Vom Konflikt zur Konkordanz—das Europäische Gemeinschaftsrecht und der Sport, dargestellt am Beispiel der Freizügigkeit der Sportler." In *Prisma des Sportrechts*, edited by Klaus Vieweg, 1–31. Berlin: Duncker & Humblot.

Hommelhoff, Peter, and Martin Schwab. 2001. "Staatsersetzende Privatgremien im Unternehmensrecht." In *Festschrift für Heinrich Wilhelm Kruse*, edited by Walter Denseck and Roman Seer, 693–718. Cologne: Verlag Otto Schmidt.

Ipsen, Nils. 2008. *Private Normenordnungen als Transnationales Recht?* Berlin: Duncker & Humblot.

Kirchhof, Ferdinand. 1987. *Private Rechtsetzung.* Berlin: Duncker & Humblot.

Kirchner, C., and M. Schmidt. 2006. "Hybride Regelsetzung im Recht der Unternehmensrechnungslegung—Fehlentwicklungen im Europäischen Gemeinschaftsrecht." *Betriebswirtschaftliche Forschung und Praxis* 58:387–407.

Köndgen, Johannes. 2006. "Privatisierung des Rechts. Private Governance zwischen Deregulierung und Rekonstitutionalisierung." *Archiv für die civilistische Praxis (AcP)* 206:477–525.

Leibfried, Stephan, and Michael Zürn, eds. 2005. *Transformations of the State?* Cambridge: Cambridge University Press.

Mann, Michael. 1994. *Geschichte der Macht*, vols. 1 and 2. Frankfurt: Campus.

Richman, Barak D. 2004. "Firms, Courts, and Reputation Mechanisms: Towards a Positive Theory of Private Ordering." *Columbia Law Review* 104:2328–68.

——. 2006. "How Community Institutions Create Economic Advantage: Jewish Diamond Merchants in New York." *Law and Social Inquiry* 31:383–420.

Risse, Thomas, and Ursula Lehmkuhl. 2007. *Regieren ohne Staat? Governance in Räumen begrenzter Staatlichkeit.* Baden-Baden: Nomos.

Röthel, Anne. 2007. "Lex mercatoria, lex sportiva, lex technica—Private Rechtsetzung jenseits des Nationalstaates?" *Juristenzeitung* 62:755–63.

Sassen, Saskia. 2006. *Territory—Authority—Rights: From Medieval to Global Assemblages.* Princeton: Princeton University Press.

Schepel, Harms. 2005. *The Constitution of Private Governance: Product Standards in the Regulation of Integrating Markets.* Oxford: Irish Academic Press.

Schilling, Heinz. 1999. *Die neue Zeit. Vom Christenheitseuropa zum Europa der Staaten, 1250 bis 1750*. Berlin: Siedler Verlag.

Schuppert, Gunnar Folke. 2000. *Verwaltungswissenschaft. Verwaltung, Verwaltungsrecht, Verwaltungslehre*. Baden-Baden: Nomos.

——. 2003. *Staatswissenschaft*. Baden-Baden: Nomos.

——. 2007. "Was ist und wozu Governance?" *Die Verwaltung* 40:463–511.

——. 2008. "Was ist und wie misst man Wandel von Staatlichkeit?" *Der Staat* 47, no. 3:325–58.

——. 2009. *Governance by Rule-Making. Von der Gesetzgebungslehre zur Regelungswissenschaft*. Baden-Baden: Nomos.

Tamm Hallström, Kristina. 2000. "Organizing the Process of Standardization." In *A World of Standards*, edited by Nils Brunsson, Bengt Jacobson, et al., 85–100. Oxford: Oxford University Press.

Ware, Glenn T. 2006. "Filling the Regulatory Gap: The Emerging-Transnational Regulator." *Global Governance* 12:135–39.

II

Governing Areas of Limited Statehood

The Role of Nonstate Actors

4

New Modes of Security

The Violent Making and Unmaking of Governance

in War-Torn Areas of Limited Statehood

SVEN CHOJNACKI AND ZELJKO BRANOVIC

W AR-TORN AREAS OF LIMITED STATEHOOD SUCH
as Afghanistan, Somalia, or the eastern parts of the Democratic
Republic of Congo pose a special challenge for the linkage of
security and governance. Theoretically, the question arises as to what extent
security can be established in such zones of violent conflict. Conventional
wisdom holds that the answer is clearly negative: a complex mixture of
residual state control and emerging nonstate armed groups are in fact tending
to promote strategic insecurity. Processes of political disintegration and the
lack of security guarantees frequently provide the rationale for local militias
or rebel groups to pursue permanent strategies of violence, enrich themselves
economically, and profit from insecurity. But what if the answer is positive
and security appears even in the social and political processes of substate
violence? Under such conditions, which forms of security governance can
emerge?

In contrast to the conventional wisdom, we assume, first, that security
can in fact be provided without the state or even its rudimentary structures,
and, second, that the governance approach can in turn be usefully applied to
analyze security dynamics in areas of limited statehood. Thereby, we define
security in a narrow sense as the absence of threats to a defined social group

or, more precisely, as a situation in which means applied with the intention of maintaining protection against a defined group succeed in reducing the risk level with respect to existential threats. Thus, even under the conditions of violent conflict, there are times and spaces in which nonstate armed actors arrive at collectively binding decisions and are interested in a minimum of security. In this context, however, it is theoretically necessary to take into account a twofold transformation in the provision of security: first, an increasing fragmentation of participants in the respective security markets;[1] and second, the ever greater complexity of security that varies between being a public and a private good.

Under conditions of political disintegration and violent conflicts, two types of security-defined areas theoretically emerge: first, areas of *strategic insecurity,* characterized by a specific shortage of armed protection, a fragmentation of the spectrum of rapacious armed groups, and a lack of collectively binding regulations; second, areas of *strategic security*, in which security is provided to various degrees of scope and inclusiveness, and by various actors. Security can be provided both intentionally by armed actors (security governance as the institutionalization of territorial control of violence), and through the patterns of self-defense by victimized groups (self-protective security).[2] In our view, the governance concept can be usefully applied precisely to these processes of partially institutionalized macronetworks of strategic security. This idea is not completely new, but rather builds upon initial approaches to interpret the violent activity of nongovernmental armed actors in areas of limited statehood as "new" forms of governance (cf. Duffield 2001; Keen 2000; Reno 2000; Jackson 2003).[3] Nonetheless, from a governance perspective, a number of questions arise: When and under which conditions do armed groups provide security as a governance service, and when do they rather resort to strategies of violence that tend to heighten insecurity? Which forms and qualities does security take on and in which way do the addressees of governance actually receive these services? Last but not least, in which way do continuous violent conflicts lead to the formation of security markets and which market logic does the trade in protection commodities follow? To approach answers to these questions, we have on the one hand developed ideas on the structure and dynamics of security markets in areas of limited statehood that follow economic approaches. On the other hand, we have used the concept of opportunity structures in order to encompass the changing material and geographical conditions of control over the use of force.

In terms of configurations of limited statehood, we focus on the territorial and temporal loss of both, the monopoly of the use of force and the ability to make and enforce collectively binding decisions (cf. Risse, chapter 1, this volume). The lack of state authority in such areas leaves space and time for nonstate armed actors to recalibrate their interaction with the civilian population and invest in the provision of security. Contrary to the conventional differentiation between *strong*, *weak*, *failed* and *collapsed* states (Rotberg 2003, 2004) that uses the state as central unit of analysis, "limited statehood" is thus a configurational conception reflecting spatial variations of security and allowing for the analysis of specific security dynamics within *or* across territorial boundaries.

The chapter starts with explaining three unique modes of security in areas of limited statehood. We then connect these modes theoretically with the logic of security markets and the opportunity structures that come along with them. The chapter closes with an assessment concerning the usefulness of linking security with governance. The underlying assumptions are that the formation and the paths of security governance are closely linked, first, to the logics of security markets that emerge from a lack of monopolization of the legitimate use of force, and, second, to material opportunities that change over time. Specific economic or geographical opportunity structures do not constitute simply an explanatory factor for the outbreak or the dynamics of violent conflict, they also provide information about the conditions under which providers of security determine the functions of the use of force.[4]

New Modes of Security in Areas of Limited Statehood

As we will argue in the subsequent sections, the probability of the provision of security is tied both to the market of violence and the material and geographical structures of opportunity that influence the strategies of the use of force. However, in order to measure the quality of security, one has to consider the logic of consumption first. Who actually consumes the security as a commodity and what range does that consumption assume? If security is defined narrowly as the absence of physical force and an increasing reliability of protection, then violent groups such as rebel organizations or warlords systems can produce internal and external security in a defined territory, just as states can.[5] Territoriality and the extent of consumption of specific protection measures are thus not only closely interconnected, but also constitute the core elements for the identification of areas of strategic security or insecurity.

However, territorial control and the ability to reduce external threats do not in and of themselves constitute indicators for the quality of security, since that control of the use of force can also be used for indiscriminate violence and the systematic massacre of the population in the territory. As long as rebels or local militias provide security only sporadically and in a territorially undefined context, security remains a rival commodity that can be excluded from consumption (cf. Brauer 1999, 6–7). Stated differently: by the strategic maintenance of insecurity and the simultaneous existence of various forms of security within an area, not only is the effectiveness and stability of the security system called into question, but security also does not attain the quality of a public good. Nevertheless, there are ways out of insecurity and the "protection screw" (Mehlum, Moene, and Torvik 2002, 448), which permit security as a good to once again move more markedly from the private toward the public realm on a quality axis.

Ideally, in war-torn areas of limited statehood, two basic forms of security without or beside the state can be ascertained: (1) security by coercion and a certain degree of institutionalization and reliability; and (2) self-organized forms of protection against internal or external threats (self-protective security). A third conceivable alternative form of security production is the delegation of protection functions to commercial suppliers.[6] All three variants are brought together systematically in table 4.1.

If we define security governance as the intentional provision of the collective good security for a defined group of protection recipients, the first type is best qualified to be considered security governance in the narrower sense. This involves the specific strategies of militarily potent actors who invest in the establishment of monopolies on the use of force, and advance processes of governance formation—that is, the establishment of institutionalized political and economic systems of rule. First of all, dominant and sanction approved armed actors use their abilities to control territory and social relations (i.e., the civilian population) to build up internal and external protection systems; second, they no longer finance themselves by means of organized looting, but rather through institutionalized taxation systems. Prototypes are rebel groups as the Fuerzas armadas revolucionarias de Colombia (FARC) or the Sudan People's Liberation Army (SPLA) in southern Sudan. But even local warlord factions in Afghanistan or in Somalia have invested in the build

TABLE 4.1 Forms and Qualities of Security

Type	Form	Quality
Coercive security	• Protection provider: monopolist • Mechanism: institutionalized system of taxation and order • Range: territorial control • Means: military protection of the external borders, internal control (e.g., police functions)	Security equals public good (no selectivity within the territory)
Self-protective security	• Protection provider: recruitment among "own people" • Mechanism: reactive to violent context, pooling of resources • Range: territorially limited to a defined group (i.e., selective and excludable) • Means: patrols, fortification systems, hiring of local militias	Security equals pool and club commodity (group members clearly identifiable)
Commercialized security	• Protection provider: commercial security companies • Mechanism: competition and prices, delegation by state and private groups • Range: persons, property • Means: diverse range of services	Security equals private commodity (however, there is an implementation of security governance)

up of political and social regulatory structures, which produce both a certain degree of mutual expectations and collectively binding decisions for a defined group. Thus, the assumption of governance formation applies to different degrees of institutionalization and to a large number of forms of nonstate armed organizations. In successful cases, security in such situations increasingly takes the form of a public good.

If security is ranked in a hierarchy of public goods as the central precondition for a functioning political order (cf. Rotberg 2003; Konrad and Skaperdas 2005), which is necessary to obtain positive beneficial effects in other realms, it follows that the rudimentary institutionalization can be restricted to the establishment of a system of protection and taxation. This implies, first, formal and informal institutions that organize the monetary transaction between the provider and the recipients of protection, and also an organizational framework that guarantees territorial integrity toward third parties. From a neoinstitutional perspective, this process gives rise to security expectations, both on the part of the civilian population and of the dominant armed actors. The civilian population can assume, on the bases of information as to the military capacities of the protection provider, a certain degree of effectiveness, that is, the protection provider in fact appears as a reliable security monopolist in the eyes of the population (cf. Weinstein 2006, 169–70). Moreover, it is assumed that the productivity of the civilian population will increase because of the perceived territorial security, since more time and resources can be invested in production than in self-protective means. In turn, the armed organization achieves reliability regarding a regular income that it obtains through the institutionalized taxation system. Thus armed groups secure not only their own organizational structures, but also take into account future investment decisions that can therefore take on the quality of a public good—if the investments are made in sustainable economic means of production. In sum, one could posit the hypothesis that the success or stability of such nonstate control systems depends on the quality of formal and informal decision-making rules related to the system of protection and taxation, the credibility of deterrence of internal and external military challengers, and the reliability of agreements between the military leadership and the civilian population. Over time, however, even violent actors have to engage themselves in processes of legitimation. Theoretically, it can be assumed that coercive political orders tend to establish an endogenous or exogenous frame of stabilization over time. Related to the former, an expansion of public related services into other sectors (e.g., finance, health, education) characterizes the development of quasi-state structures (e.g., Somaliland) that require a minimum of output-legitimacy (cf. Bakonyi and Stuvøy 2005). In case of exogenous stabilization one has to consider the benefits that come along with statehood (e.g., licensing, credits, development aid). It is not surprising that coercive modes of security governance may possibly change into statehood (as happened in Liberia with Charles Taylor) and make use of externally guaranteed sovereignty.[7]

Self-protective security, by contrast, is usually a reaction to continual attacks by looting violent groups. Under these conditions, individuals or civilian groups affected by insecurity can decide to counter the restrictions of the violent environment with investments in their own security through protective capacities. Such forms of the provision of security are usually restricted to the units involved (peasants, villages) and are inclusive. Self-protection is promoted primarily and intentionally with no other end such as territorial expansion or gaining state control. The military capacities of these units vary with the type of strategic alliance. While alliances between village units and self-defense groups usually promise only a lesser degree of security, collaboration with governments or strong rebel groups may promise greater levels of security, at least temporarily. The frame of reference for the recipients is the protected area and the particular benefit. From the perspective of economics, security here takes the form of a *pool good* in which resources and capacities are merely mobilized for the purpose of providing security to the groups involved in the coordination. Situations of self-protective security might therefore better be considered as temporary, transitional phenomena. By assuming that the civilian population ultimately has four action options — to become the victim, to flee, to engage themselves in nonproductive armament, or to associate with stronger armed groups (cf. Skaperdas and Konrad 2004) — the probability increases that in the long run, forms of self-protective security will merge into governmental or nongovernmental orders of violence.

Commercialized security, that is, the delegation of security services to the private sector, is a special case of security production. As a rule, only very specific security functions, as the protection of persons or buildings, are provided as a private commodity for special security risks (e.g., counterinsurgency measures, participation in special military operations). From the point of view of governance consumers, security here is enormously selective, since only those who can pay for security services receive the benefits of protection. Examples are multinational corporations (securing access to resources), humanitarian organizations (protecting the humanitarian space from looting), or international organizations (e.g., protection of persons or buildings, mine-clearing). The activities of commercial security companies are clearly defined functionally (protection of an oil field or of governmental buildings) and directed toward a narrowly defined group of beneficiaries (members of a company or the public employees of a transitional administration). Certainly, the delimitation toward the public-security structures is often fuzzy. For example, commercial security companies engaged to protect buildings may certainly produce positive externalities for the immediate neighborhood and extend the range of the protection services they provide. The protection of administrative facilities and the construction of security structures in Iraq and Afghanistan, including the training of police, can also certainly benefit all potential consumers of security, and thus become an integral component of governance strategies. This implies theoretically that commercialized protection services can produce different forms and qualities of security. Additionally, the potential security outcome is dependent on the functional context: in cases of the use for the protection of persons or buildings, it ultimately involves a private good. However, commercial protection services assigned for societal and institutional reconstruction can also serve to implement security governance on behalf of third parties. In this context, private security-service providers proceed on the basis of existing regulatory structures. Regardless of this, the logic of action of the "new mercenary" remains oriented toward defending against perceived threats and security risks in the interests of his employer—and not to act in his own interests to prevent the dangers of wartime or postwar orders.

At the end of the day, the processes of security governance discussed here indicate that security can be provided by various institutional forms. As an alternative to the state, institutionalized orders of violence arise, which intentionally provide protection from internal and external threat. The resulting protection commodities can be labeled as security governance commodities or as paths of governance formation at least. Insecurity, however, remains a dominant feature if the monopolist on the use of force depends on repressive strategies, if insufficient revenues are obtained by taxation, or if military challengers endanger a weakly institutionalized system of rule. But even if these partial orders of violence are frequently unstable, it should be clear that the minimum prerequisite for the classification as governance consists primarily in the quality of security as a collective good as well as the implications of consumption and territoriality.

To explain why and under which conditions violent actors engage in security governance, in the next section we make use of the concept of security markets by assuming that the market structures and economic logics in the security domain encompass the terms under which violent actors shape their preferences, select strategies for action, and make decisions.

Security Markets

Security, and in the narrower sense, protection, are not ordinary market commodities and differ in many ways from other consumer goods.[8] As Skaperdas (2001) and Skaperdas and Konrad (2004) have plausibly demonstrated, the competition in the provision of protection differs from classic economic concepts regarding the factors of production, pricing mechanisms, and the resulting quality of the market product. Private protection providers do not compete via price mechanisms; rather, they use violent means to gain control of territory and revenues resulting from protection services. Moreover, it is necessary to take into account that ownership of goods and services is not exchanged voluntarily, but is rather acquired by force (Elwert 1999, 87). Unlike ordinary commodity markets, greater competition in the protection-providers' segment therefore does not lead to more but rather less gain in benefits for all (Skaperdas 2001, 174). At the same time, competition between nonstate armed actors with no regulating central authority means that security dilemmas and arms races arise that favor an increase in violence. Without any effective protection of their lives or property rights, large segments of the population are prevented from engaging in economically productive activities and are forced to invest in their own protection instead (Bates, Greif, and Singh 2002, 613). This necessity to invest in the means of violence reduces economic productivity and efficiency (Skaperdas, 2001, 187).[9] Under conditions of overt violence, resources cannot be effectively distributed. Survival in areas of limited statehood and the possibilities of profiting from the provision of protection services thus depend on one's relative ability to exercise violent control of resources and social relations. Violence therefore becomes a necessary—albeit not a sufficient—condition for the ability to participate as a competitive actor in the security market. In this context, the growth of self-defense groups in Afghanistan that protect themselves against attacks by the Taliban or by units of the Northern Alliance has to be considered just as much as that of security-market participants and well-organized and militarily powerful rebel groups.

The spectrum of market participants can be extended still further. In sub-Saharan Africa, this category includes not only rebel groups and local militias, but also criminal cartels, traditional fighters like the *Kamajors* in Sierra Leone, and ad hoc groupings like the Area Boys in Lagos (Nigeria) who collect protection money on transportation routes and at weekly markets (see Bakonyi, Hensell, and Siegelberg 2006). Another critical group of actors who is contributing to the increased complexity of security markets and conflict structures in war and settings of postconflict peace building is that of Private Military Companies (PMCs). Militarily highly specialized PMCs not only offer a variety of services on today's security markets but also operate according to free-enterprise calculations. Such internationally operating companies as Blackwater or DynCorp are the visible expression of a system of the politically sanctioned delegation of selected security functions to commercial enterprises by states or private groups (cf. e.g. Avant 2005; Leander 2003; Musah 2002; Singer 2003). However, the involvement of this group of actors affects the military power relationship and local conflict dynamics, as well as the calculations of state and nonstate actors to outsource certain forms of the military activity to private specialists. These security dynamics turn out to have particularly serious consequences in Colombia and Iraq. External interventionists who support internal armed groups become themselves competitors for resources and aggravate both the available informational asymmetries and the intensity of conflicts.[10]

From the perspective of conflict theory, the problem underlying the increase of armed actors is that reliable information about competitive groups as well as mutually binding security guarantees become increasingly insecure (Walter 1997; Cunningham 2006). However, the greater the number of potentially violent state and nonstate parties to a conflict is and the more intense the competition becomes, the more significant are informational asymmetries and commitment problems. Such dynamics not only affect the conflict behavior of armed actors, but also heighten the vulnerability of societal groups (i.e., the civilian population) who cannot provide for their own security by private means.

In terms of economic theory, the market structures in the security realm can be described as an unusual form of monopolistic competition: each group establishes its own, spatially delimited monopoly of protection, in which it must provide credible proof of its ability to provide security (Skaperdas 2001, 187).[11] The prices that can be demanded for protection services are thus contingent on the number of armed actors, the degree of spatial separation between competitors, material opportunity structures, and alternative options for action for the affected population (e.g., flight or the construction of self-defense units). More specifically, it can be expected that greater competition among armed actors will lead to greater investment in combat and resources and at the same time increase information deficits and the difficulties in achieving credible commitments (Skaperdas 2002, 435).

Moreover, economic models assume that decision makers—be they armed actors or potential entrepreneurs of governance—will consider the relative benefits of two forms of economic activity: investments in the production of civilian goods and services or the investments in conflict perpetuating means.[12] In other words, violent actors can choose between the institutionalization of a political order that guarantees ownership rights and organizes the interaction between providers and recipients of protection via a tax system, or a violence-mediated state of conflict, in which the civilian population is used as spoils, or as an extractable resource, to finance the capability of these actors for violent activity. But even under the conditions of armed contest between two or more violent groups, time-limited forms of cooperation are not impossible. A prime example is the formation of a time-limited alliance in Sierra Leone during the mid-1990s between the government, commercial security companies (Gurkha Security Guards Limited, Executive Outcomes, and Sandline International), and the self-defense groups of the Kamajor militias to fight the rebels of the Revolutionary United Front (RUF) (Abdullah and Muana 1998, 185).

Fundamentally, these considerations mean that armed groups can strategically choose between the provision of security and the maintenance of insecurity. However, the more promising military and economic profits become, and the more uncertain a future under conditions of peace appears (Fearon 2004), the higher the value of insecurity strategies should become. In view of the structural characteristics of insecurity, Stergios Skaperdas (2002, 444) assumes a reverted shadow of the future, particularly in areas of warlord competition. The prospect of the elimination of competitors and of resulting greater profits increases the value of violent conflict strategies, compared to negotiated settlements. For the civilian population this has fatal consequences. First, the demand for protection services rises with the increasing degree of insecurity; however, the free choice of protection providers is greatly limited. Second, the risk increases that actors in the conflict will turn to strategies of indiscriminate violence (Kalyvas 2006; Weinstein 2006; Olsen 2007; Wood 2008) and promote diffuse insecurity. Both empirical evidence and formal models have provided evidence that arbitrary violence and destruction of property are more probable in zones of strategic insecurity because of an asymmetric distribution of information and multiple material insecurities (Skaperdas 2001, 188; Kalyvas 2006; Weinstein 2006). However, the ability to cause either security or insecurity (or both) becomes a political and economic resource, and hence an alternative source of power. As a result, the price for protection services increases with the military capabilities of potent armed actors (Mehlum, Moene, and Torvik 2002). Theoretically, the production of (in-)security is thus immediately tied to the logic of violence and resource extraction.

To sum up, in the context of an increasing tendency toward fragmentation of the actors' spectrum, as well as the associated implications for the forms of security, the concept of the security market describes the structure and composition of the supply and demand side in the provision of protection commodities and its temporal and spatial coincidence in areas where the provision is not monopolized. Similar to corporations on regular markets, violent groups calculate their profit margin of investments in the supply of security— that is, whether to invest in the production of a secure environment (areas of strategic security) or to perpetuate the violent appropriation of resources.

"Opportunity Makes Thieves"

The structure and dynamics of security markets, like the question of the quality of security, cannot be adequately understood without considering the changing opportunity structures in areas of limited statehood. If there is any truth to the popular saying "opportunity makes thieves," it should be considered that the absence or breakdown of states creates extraordinary opportunities for entrepreneurs of violence to either enrich themselves by looting, extortion, or resource exploitation, or else to offer protection against looting by violent groups.

Theoretically, structures of opportunity encompass the conditions under which actors formulate preferences, make decisions, and act (Siverson and Starr 1991; Most and Starr 1980; Collier and Hoeffler 1998). In the research into the causes of war, they have often been used as explanatory factors for the probability of the outbreak of both internal and international warfare.

However, both the twin concepts of opportunity and willingness developed by Benjamin Most and Harvey Starr (Starr 1978; Most and Starr 1980) and the opportunity model of the World Bank group around Paul Collier (Collier and Hoeffler 1998, 2004)[13] are oriented toward the relatively static boundary conditions of methodological nationalism (including borders, number of the neighboring states, or primary-goods exports). Beyond that, the approach developed by the World Bank group relates the motivation of armed actors primarily to greed and the relative share of the export of primary goods to the overall volume of export (cf. the critique by Cramer 2002; Fearon 2005). Moreover, Collier and Hoeffler (1998) see structures of opportunity as preexisting factors in conflicts between rebel group and governments that primarily reflect the conditions that increase the risk of the outbreak of civil wars involving two conflicting parties. But precisely under the conditions of failing states, opportunity structures and the configuration of actors may shift, both in time and space. Resources may be completely exploited, the emergence of splinter factions, and the intervention of external actors may change the balance of power between conflicting parties, or one of these parties may over time establish a dominant position within a defined territory. The term *opportunity structures* is therefore used herein as a broad category that encompasses all material and territorial options actors find under conditions of time and space, and thus refers both to incentive structures favoring the perpetuation of violence and to those factors promoting the establishment of orders of violence. Dominant armed actors can then decide how and to what end they wish to apply force: unilaterally against the population, offensive against competing violent groups, or defensively as reliable protection provider for the civilian population against internal and external threats. Economic and geographic structures of opportunity, which we will discuss in greater detail in the following section, are thus theoretically especially informative in this context.

Economic Opportunities

The lack or breakdown of security guarantees offered by the institutions of the sovereign state favor both conflicts over access to resources and targeted looting strategies. Basically, material structures of opportunity refer to all available resources that can be extracted and thus used to guarantee one's own capability to exert force. Areas of strategic insecurity are therefore most likely to arise in resource-rich areas: the greater the wealth of resources, the higher the probability that new entrepreneurs of violence will appear on the security market and compete with one another. Consequently, the incentive structure to continuously apply military force and to produce insecurity will be greater. The insight that the type of resource itself affects the risks of the occurrence and perpetuation of organized violence is even more fundamental. Empirical studies reveal that the effect of diamonds and oil is highly significant, while agricultural goods, by contrast, are hardly significant at all (Fearon 2005; Lujala, Gleditsch, and Gilmore 2005; Ross 2004). The extraction practice of guaranteeing one's own freedom of action by mining mineral resources leads to a different logic of security and different constraints than does the looting of the civilian population. While the extraction of natural resources primarily poses logistical challenges, such as the securing of extraction and storage sites and transportation routes, the taxation of humanitarian aid and the looting of the civilian population by predatory gangs, rebel groups, or regular soldiers tends to be carried out in a more ad hoc and often uncoordinated manner. To put it in more general terms, the forms of the financing of violence can vary in time and space, even within single conflict zones, and in each case generate specific strategies of violence and insecurity.

Resources not only create the risk of the emergence of violent conflicts and provide opportunities for enrichment, they are also a critical quantum both for the survival of the civilian population and of various types of armed organizations. While the civilian population in resource-rich zones is subjected to the specific risks of indiscriminate violence (Weinstein 2006), the recruitment of new fighters is more difficult in resource-poor regions if they cannot be economically compensated. However, a substitute strategy is available for the leadership of armed groups under certain conditions: if rebel groups, warlords, or local militias are unable to distribute profits or maintain material motivation, they can rely on social relationships and provide credible promises of future payments (Weinstein 2005, 599).

Particularly specialized entrepreneurs of violence make profits by looting *and* protection services, thus jacking up the "protection screw" (Mehlum, Moene, and Torvik 2002). Looting has a dual function here: first, it enables better mobilization of resources to permit the financing of combat; second, it permits expenditures for the pay for combatants to be reduced (Azam 2006). In the long run however, the looting of the civilian population also raises two problems: on the one hand, the number of competitive armed groups can rise over time, and hence, too, the number of violent incidents; on the other, this situation permits no phases of regeneration for the population, during which they might produce new resources to loot. Both problems imply a marginal utility of looting over time.

These issues are closely related to organizational dynamics—that is, to the degree of organization of the armed organization. If military capacities expand, the expenditures for the maintenance of a military organization—payment for the combatants and maintenance of military equipment—increase at the same time. In other words, an increased degree of organization implies higher maintenance expenses and hence an increased demand for resources. The marginal utility of looting can therefore occur in a dual manner: first, via overlooting, by which noncoordinated looting and the potential increase of armed groups in effect result in overplundering and the loss of potential profits; and second, the profit no longer covers the regular expenditures of maintenance. According to economic theory, the positive beneficial effects for the civilian population increase with a minimum of security, since it can invest in production instead of protection services. A well-established armed organization can therefore certainly seize a dominant position in the course of the conflict and then take the opportunity of sharing in the profits of increasing productivity by taxation of protection in a defined territory—and thus institutionalize the initial rudiments of an order of violence.

In areas with only weakly organized armed organizations by contrast, the civilian population can theoretically be considered as a freely accessible resource, and is thus constantly endangered by overlooting (see Kurrild-Klitgaard and Svendsen 2003, 257).[14] In situations of competition between armed groups, these conditions in fact intensify. Under conditions of incomplete information armed groups most likely come to no mutual agreement as to where and to what degree looting is to be undertaken, so that the probability of overlooting increases. Altogether, it is to be assumed that areas of limited statehood are often exposed to the risk of overlooting. A sustainable practice of extraction that allows for regeneration phases for the population can theoretically hardly be expected in situations in which armed groups are highly fractured into splinter factions and in which there is a high demand for resources and specific organizational structures.

Geographic Opportunities

In addition to the material structures of opportunity, geography is intuitively a critical momentum for the explanation of the dynamics of violence and also for the development of security markets. Appropriately, research on international war began as early as the 1970s to conceptualize such geographical conditions as direct neighborhood and spatial distance as explanatory factors for the occurrence and diffusion of armed conflicts and wars (e.g., Diehl 1991; Starr 1991). Somewhat belatedly, recent civil war research has discovered the "geography of war." Current studies show that topographical variables, like forests and mountains, not only affect the manner in which internal violent conflicts are carried out but also are important in determining the prospect of winning a battle or the war (cf. Gates 2002; Buhaug and Gates 2002; Buhaug and Rød 2006). At the same time, geography also limits the number of potential violent actors and provides information for an understanding of organizational logics of violent groups. Both formal models and empirical evidence indicate that greater distance between contending groups affects the probability that competitive violent groups will emerge (Gates 2002, 127).

Particularly linked to geographic opportunity structures is the concentration of resources affecting the possibilities of carrying out certain forms of violent control and making profits from the resource extraction. First, one has to bear in mind that natural resources differ considerably in their concentration and location (Le Billon 2001, Ross 2004). Second, centralized resources such as petroleum and easily accessible mines are considerably easier to monitor than geographically widely dispersed resources, such as opium plantations, alluvial diamonds, or tropical forests. Third, a critical aspect is the proximity to the headquarter of a rebel group or the capital of the state. It has been demonstrated empirically that natural resources that are located near the capital of a country can be monitored more easily by the existing government than more remote extraction sites (Le Billon 2001). The reverse is just as true: the further a potential extraction site is away from the state center, the easier it is for nonstate armed groups to appropriate and the more probable will it be that violent conflicts, and hence areas of strategic insecurity, arise. Rebel organizations that operate in resource-rich regions will, in the course of the conflict, in turn be confronted with a "principal-agent problem" (Ross 1973): if their combatants operate in remote areas, they will be difficult to coordinate and monitor internally. To respond to this dilemma, there are two contrary strategies: either, a high degree of military and social control, such as guerilla movements prefer, or more decentralized organizational forms, as in the case of the phenomenon of warlord systems (Bakonyi, Hensell, and Siegelberg 2006). But even without access to valuable resources, the distance from the capital or from state security guarantees may accelerate a decision to accumulate the means of exerting force and to emerge as a local security provider.

One weakness of previous approaches has been that the analyses have remained state-centered and oriented solely toward conflicts between governments and rebel groups. However, in areas of limited statehood, one can assume neither the presence of a state with a fully functioning regular army nor a dyadic conflict structure (state versus rebel group). Instead, these areas are characterized by the fact that the state's control of the use of force is severely limited or has broken down and several entrepreneurs of violence compete as providers of security or perpetrators of insecurity. An immediate result of these developments is the vulnerability vis-à-vis outside threats (see, for example, the external interventions in Somalia and Democratic Republic of Congo).

Geography has yet another dimension. It not only creates certain structures of opportunity for political action or certain risks for the escalation of violent conflicts, but also has an inherent significance and an identity-building function for the development of security-related governance structures or even statehood (Knight 1994; Murphy 1996). Referring to Sack (1986), we understand territoriality here as a spatial principle of the organization of social interaction and control. On the one hand, territoriality refers to the structural problem of shared boundaries and neighborhood; on the other hand, it also has a clear political-organizational spatial frame of reference and involves a linkage of space and time with control and power.[15] Territorial control thus is an indispensable precondition for the specific and independent extraction of natural resources and the implementation of control by military force. At the same time, this has implications for our understanding of governance: security is more closely tied to the conditions of territoriality than other consumable durables. Even "new" forms of orders of violence, such as the warlord systems in Liberia, the Democratic Republic of the Congo, or Somalia during the 1990s, draw upon the norm of territoriality.

Conclusions

Linking security with governance stimulates an interest in the handling of violent conflicts and threats, in scrutinizing the modes of protection, the provision of security services, their linkage at different levels of analyses, and, thereby, in the formation of alternative security structures. Since areas of limited statehood can be characterized both by zones of permanent insecurity and by the institutionalization of protection and taxation systems (areas of strategic security), structures of political and social order emerge only in the second variant that are interesting from a governance perspective—and which should ultimately be examined in terms of efficiency, effectiveness, and also aspects of stability and legitimacy.

Security as a governance commodity is directly connected to the ability to perform control over violent means and to provide protection goods. Therefore, it must be taken into account that the provision of security has an explicitly territorial component and is tied to the logic of the use of force and of resource extraction. Changing geographical and economic structures of opportunity contribute to the fact that even nonstate armed groups may prefer the provision of security to the use of violence against the population, particularly if considerations of efficiency predominate. In this context, the making of governance should be expected as a preferred strategy of exerting control over a defined territory and population under certain material conditions (i.e., within economic valuable territories) in order to overcome or balance the risks of survival and negative economic effects (overplundering) in zones of permanent violence. The formation of security structures may fail or turn into the unmaking of governance if armed groups abstain to provide both a minimum of internal security and deterrence from external threats, resources are limited or become scarce, and support within the armed group or population decreases. While Somaliland (1991–) and Puntland (1998–) clearly represent alternative formations of security governance beyond the state, partially institutionalized macronetworks of strategic security like "Taylor-Land" in Liberia (1991–96), "Nkunda-Land" (2004–) in the Eastern Congo or the Islamic Courts in Somalia (1999–2006) stand for the conflictual making of security structures within war-torn areas of limited statehood *and* for the failure or transitional character of such orders of violence.

The potential paths of governance formation discussed here suggest, first, that the provision of security as a governance service can be provided by a variety of nonstate groups without the state; second, that it may be organized on the basis of a variety of regulatory structures and processes (different organizational forms and degrees of institutionalization); and third, that it varies in its effective range (territoriality and consumption). Moreover, recourse to considerations of conflict theory (opportunity structures) and formal economics (markets of security or protection) in governance research is more than worth it. As it has been shown, the quality of security has to be linked to the functional logic of the markets of security in areas of limited statehood. At the same time, economic or geographical opportunity structures shed light on the conditions under which entrepreneurs of security governance choose between strategic actions (production of goods and services versus investments in conflict perpetuating means).

Conceptually, our configurational logic of (in)security in areas of limited statehood shows similarities to other considerations concerning the coexistence of alternative institutionalized orders such as "de facto states" (Pegg 1998), "states-within-states" (Kingston and Spears 2004), or "unrecognized quasi-states" (Kolstø 2006). More specifically, our approach indicates conscious points of reference to the concept of "markets of violence" (Elwert 1999),[16] which has been systematized recently along a continuum of the institutionalization of power. Jutta Bakonyi and Kirsti Stuvøy (2005; 2006) distinguish between two ideal types of nonstate orders of violence: warlord configurations, which constitute an only weakly institutionalized type of order, are not territorially consolidated, and hardly have any organizational apparatus; and quasi-states, which are best characterized as highly institutionalized orders of violence akin to basic functions of the state, but which may not enjoy formal recognition by the international community (such as Somaliland). Nonetheless, quasi-states have monopolized the provision of security within their territorial areas of influence and control parts of a territory, together with its economic resources (cf. Bakonyi and Stuvøy 2006, 41–42). Both variants ultimately indicate the coexistence of alternative structures of security arrangements in areas of limited statehood. But whereas Bakonyi and Stuvøy reflect security only as a byproduct of the institutionalization of power, the advantage of linking security with governance lies in focusing attention on the intentional provision of security for defined social groups and providing both microfoundations for the institutionalization of different qualities of security and for changes in the temporal and spatial dynamics of violence.

That does not mean that the state loses its significance entirely in such areas. It may very well remain the central framework of reference for nonstate armed actors and also fits well into the logic of structures of opportunity. The example of "Taylorland," which at times embraced over 90 percent of Liberian territory and developed a currency and even a banking system of its own, demonstrates that institutionalized security systems can break down again relatively rapidly if the constellations change. Despite the territorial and economic independence that Charles Taylor established within his system of rule, Taylor finally, in 1997, aimed for the presidency of all of Liberia—with the well-known result of the renewed escalation of violence in the war in Liberia and his arrest in March 2006. Aside from the ultimate fate of Taylor himself, it is clear that the state apparatus and the perspective of international recognition remain important resources, both internally (political legitimacy, advantages over political rivals) and externally (e.g., in the form of international financial aid or by access to international assistance). It can therefore be assumed that opportunity structures such as the form of a state and the norm of sovereignty will in the future continue to determine the options for action of (some) private armed groups.

Notes

1. The concept of the "security market" refers to the structure and composition of the spectrum of actors as well as the interaction of supply (provision) and demand of and for security.

2. Security governance thus incorporates the regulatory structures and processes by means of which security is provided intentionally as a collective good for a defined group of recipients. Hence, the present article operates with a minimal definition of governance, without addressing here the broad range of differing definitions. Our understanding of security governance also differs from Krahmann (2003), who applies the term to the emergence of complex security structures in Europe and North America.

3. The analytical distinction common in the debate over the privatization of security between *top-down* processes of the delegation of functions to private suppliers, and *bottom-up* processes of local self-organization of security appears adequate at the outset, in order to obtain an overview of the multifarious suppliers of security (cf. Mandel 2003; Bryden 2006). In contrast, its analytical utility is restricted: first, it establishes no immediate theoretical correlation between the shortage and the active provision of security; second, neither the forms and expressions nor the quality of security are differentiated.

4. The central goal functions of the use of force are in the short term one's own survival, the ability to finance one's capabilities to use force, and the seizure of control of an area. In the long term, they include the protection of the control against internal and external challengers.

5. We thus offer a middle-ground strategy between the classical definition of security as the absence of existential threats to a political unit (see, for a comprehensive

discussion, Baylis 2005) and widening the concept to include nonstate actors as entrepreneurs of security governance strengthened by state collapse and the dynamics of internal wars.

6. We concentrate here on security dynamics without or beside the state and will, therefore, not discuss other possible forms such as "governance with government." A good example for the latter is provided by Elisabeth Jean Wood (2008). By exploring different social processes of civil war she illustrates the emergence of "insurgent governance" in Sri Lanka by the Liberation Tigers of Tamil Eelam (LTTE). Since the early 1990s the LTTE has drawn on state administrations and has cooperated with government civil services, but at the same time has maintained core functions of protection and control over territory (Wood 2008, 551).

7. Empirically, this pattern often can be found in cases, in which former rebel groups or warlords take part in elections to run for office.

8. In this context, we will distinguish between security and means of protection. While security can be seen as an aggregate state characterized by the absence of physical violence toward a defined group over time, protection encompasses all measures necessary for the production of security. Protection is thus the active process of the provision of security and hence the major asset traded on security markets.

9. These considerations are based on the guns-and-butter model (cf. in greater detail Powell 1999, chap. 2), which compares investment in civilian means of production versus military capacities.

10. Particularly in areas of limited statehood some security companies take their pay in the form of exploitation licenses for the extraction of valuable resources and become protagonists in the war-economy systems. They not only profit from zones of insecurity but also contribute to their perpetuation (Musah and Fayemi 2000; Pech 2000).

11. Andreas Mehler (2003) argues that over time, homogeneous or heterogeneous oligopolies of violence emerge. Such considerations on the production of violence and security via market mechanisms, while innovative, nonetheless go only halfway. First, the concept is confined to violent actors directly involved; and second, it fails to adequately theorize the question of the consumption of security.

12. Hirshleifer (2000) as well as the excellent summary by Garfinkel and Skaperdas (2006).

13. Collier and Hoeffler argue that the outbreak of warfare can be explained less by the political motivation of the actors than by the opportunities for economic extraction and accumulation in crisis-torn areas, i.e., via "atypical circumstances that generate profitable opportunities" (2004, 564).

14. Nonetheless, such overlooting-related arguments like those developed by

Olson (1993) or Kurrild-Klitgaard and Svendsen (2003) have the problem that they merely attach the extraction logic of violent actors to the civilian population, but leave aside alternative structures of opportunity.

15. Sack (1986, 19) defines territoriality as "attempt by an individual or group to affect, influence, or control people, phenomena, and relationships, by delimiting and asserting control over a geographic area."

16. Elwert (1999, 86) defines "markets of violence" as "economic fields dominated by civil wars, warlords or robbery, in which a self-perpetuating system emerges which links non-violent commodity markets with the violent acquisition of goods." As highly profitable systems these markets may achieve stability for certain periods of time.

REFERENCES

Abdullah, Ibrahim, and Patrick Muana. 1998. "The Revolutionary Front of Sierra Leone: A Revolt of the Lumpenproletariat." In *African Guerrillas*, edited by Christopher Clapham, 172–95. Oxford: James Currey.

Avant, Deborah. 2005. *The Market for Force: The Consequences of Privatizing Security*. New York: Cambridge University Press.

Azam, Jean-Paul. 2006. "On Thugs and Heroes: Why Warlords Victimize Their Own Civilians." *Economics of Governance* 7:53–73.

Bakonyi, Jutta, Stephan Hensell, and Jens Siegelberg, eds. 2006. *Gewaltordnungen bewaffneter Gruppen. Ökonomie und Herrschaft nicht-staatlicher Akteure in den Kriegen der Gegenwart*. Baden-Baden: Nomos.

Bakonyi, Jutta, and Kirsti Stuvøy. 2005. "Violence and Social Order Beyond the State: Somalia and Angola." *Review of African Political Economy* 32, no. 104:359–82.

——. 2006. "Zwischen Warlordfigurationen und Quasi-Staat. Ansätze zu einer Typologie bewaffneter Gruppen." In *Gewaltordnungen bewaffneter Gruppen. Ökonomie und Herrschaft nicht-staatlicher Akteure in den Kriegen der Gegenwart*, edited by Jutta Bakonyi, Stephan Hensell, and Jens Siegelberg, 38–52. Baden-Baden: Nomos.

Bates, Robert, Avner Greif, and Smita Singh. 2002. "Organizing Violence." *Journal of Conflict Resolution* 46, no. 5:599–628.

Baylis, John. 2005. "International and Global Security in the Post–Cold War Era." In *The Globalization of World Politics*, 3rd ed., edited by John Baylis and Steve Smith, 297–323. Oxford: Oxford University Press.

Brauer, Jürgen. 1999. "An Economic Perspective on Mercenaries, Military Companies, and the Privatization of Force." *Cambridge Review of International Affairs* 13, no. 1:130–46.

Bryden, Alan. 2006. "Approaching the Privatisation of Security from a Security Governance Perspective." In *Private Actors and Security Governance*, edited by A. Bryden and M. Caparini, 3–19. Geneva: Geneva Centre for the Democratic Control of Armed Forces.

Buhaug, Halvard, and Scott Gates. 2002. "The Geography of War." *Journal of Peace Research* 39, no. 4:417–33.

Buhaug, Halvard, and Kjetil Rød. 2006. "Local Determinants of African Civil Wars, 1970–2001." *Political Geography* 25, no. 3:315–35.

Chojnacki, Sven. 2007. "(Un-)Sicherheit, Gewalt und Governance. Theoretische Herausforderungen für die Sicherheitsforschung." In *Staatszerfall und Governance*, edited by Marianne Beisheim and Gunnar Folke Schuppert, 236–63. Baden-Baden: Nomos.

Collier, Paul, and Anke Hoeffler. 1998. "On the Economic Cause of Civil War." *Oxford Economic Papers* 50, no. 4:563–73.

——. 2004. "Greed and Grievance in Civil War." *Oxford Economic Papers* 56, no. 4:563–95.

Cramer, Christopher. 2002. "Homo Economicus Goes to War: Methodological Individualism, Rational Choice, and the Political Economy of War." *World Development* 30, no. 11:1845–64.

Cunningham, David E. 2006. "Veto Players and Civil War Duration." *American Journal of Political Science* 50, no. 4:875–92.

Diehl, Paul F. 1991. "Geography and War: A Review and Assessment of the Empirical Literature." *International Interactions* 17, no. 1:11–27.

Duffield, Mark. 2001. *Global Governance and New Wars: The Merging of Development and Security*. London: Zed Books.

Elwert, Georg. 1999. "Markets of Violence." In *Dynamics of Violence: Processes of Escalation and De-Escalation in Violent Group Conflicts*, edited by Georg Elwert, Stephan Feuchtwang, and Dieter Neubert, 86–101. Berlin: Duncker & Humblot.

Fearon, James D. 2004. "Why Do Some Civil Wars Last So Much Longer Than Others?" *Journal of Peace Research* 41, no. 3:275–301.

——. 2005. "Primary Commodity Exports and Civil War." *Journal of Conflict Resolution* 49, no. 4:483–507.

Garfinkel, Michelle R., and Stergios Skaperdas. 2006. "Economics of Conflict: An Overview." In *Handbook of Defense Economics*, 2nd ed., edited by Todd Sandler and Keith Hartley, 649–709. Amsterdam: Elsevier.

Gates, Scott. 2002. "Recruitment and Allegiance: The Microfoundations of Rebellion." *Journal of Conflict Resolution* 46, no. 1:111–30.

Hirshleifer, Jack. 2000. "The Macrotechnology of Conflict." *Journal of Conflict Resolution* 44, no. 6:773–92.

Jackson, Paul. 2003. "Warlords as Alternative Forms of Governance." In *Small Wars and Insurgencies* 14, no. 2:131–50.

Kaldor, Mary. 1999. *New and Old Wars: Organized Violence in a Global Era*. Stanford: Stanford University Press.

——. 2005. "Warfare in Civil Wars." In *Rethinking the Nature of War*, edited by Isabelle Duyvesteyn and Jan Angstrom, 88–108. London: Franc Cass.

Kalyvas, Stathis N. 2006. *The Logic of Violence in Civil War*. Cambridge: Cambridge University Press.

Keen, David. 2000. "Incentives and Disincentives for Violence." In *Greed and Griev-ances: Economic Agendas in Civil Wars*, edited by Mats Berdal and David M. Malone, 19–41. Boulder, Colo.: Lynne Rienner Publishers.

Kingston, Paul, and Ian Spears, eds. 2004. *States Within States: Incipient Political Enti-ties in the Post–Cold War Era*. New York: Palgrave Macmillan.

Kitschelt, Herbert P. 1986. "Political Opportunity Structures and Political Protest: Anti-Nuclear Movements in Four Democracies." *British Journal of Political Science* 16, no. 1:57–85.

Knight, David B. 1994. "People Together, Yet Apart: Rethinking Territory, Sover-eignty, and Identities." In *Reordering the World: Geopolitical Perspectives on the Twenty-first Century*, edited by George J. Demko and William B. Wood, 71–86. Boulder, Colo.: Westview Press.

Kolstø, Pål. 2006. "The Sustainability and Future of Unrecognized Quasi-States." *Journal of Peace Research* 43, no. 6:723–40.

Konrad, Kai A., and Stergios Skaperdas. 2005. "The Market for Protection and the Origin of the State." CESIFO Working Paper No. 1578.

Krahmann, Elke. 2003. "Conceptualizing Security Governance." *Cooperation and Con-flict* 38, no. 1:5–26.

Kurrild-Klitgaard, Peter, and Gert Tinggaard Svendsen. 2003. "Rational Bandits: Plunder, Public Goods, and the Vikings." *Public Choice* 117, nos. 3/4:255–72.

Leander, Anna. 2003. "The Commodification of Violence, Private Military Compa-nies, and African States." IIS-Working Paper 11, Copenhagen.

Le Billon, Philippe. 2001. "The Political Ecology of War: Natural Resources and Armed Conflicts." *Political Geography* 20, no. 5:561–84.

Lujala, Päivi, Nils Petter Gleditsch, and Elisabeth Gilmore. 2005. "A Diamond Curse? Civil War and a Lootable Resource." *Journal of Conflict Resolution* 49, no. 4:538–62.

Mandel, Robert. 2003. *Armies Without States: The Privatization of Security*. Boulder, Colo.: Lynne Rienner Publishers.

Mehler, Andreas. 2003. "Legitime Gewaltoligopole. Eine Antwort auf strukturelle Instabilität in Westafrika." Working Paper No. 22, GIGA Focus Africa, Hamburg.

Mehlum, Halvor, Karl Ove Moene, and Ragnar Torvik. 2002. "Plunder & Protection Inc." *Journal of Peace Research* 39, no. 4:447–59.

Most, Benjamin A., and Harvey Starr. 1980. "Diffusion, Reinforcement, Geo-politics, and the Spread of War." *American Political Science Review* 74:932–46.

Murphy, Alexander B. 1996. "The Sovereign State System as a Political-Territorial Ideal: Historical and Contemporary Considerations." In *State Sovereignty as Social Construct*, edited by Thomas J. Biersteker and Cynthia Weber, 80–120. Cambridge: Cambridge University Press.

Musah, Abdel-Fatau. 2002. "Privatization of Security, Arms Proliferation, and the Process of State Collapse in Africa." *Development and Change* 33, no. 5:911–33.

Musah, Abdel-Fatau, and Kayode Fayemi. 2000. "Africa in Search of Security: Mercenaries and Conflicts, an Overview." In *Mercenaries: An African Security Di-lemma*, edited by Abdel-Fatau Musah and Kayode Fayemi, 13–42. London: Pluto Press.

Olsen, Kasper Thams. 2007. "Violence Against Civilians in Civil War: Understanding Atrocities by the Lord's Resistance Army in Northern Uganda." Conflict Research Group, Working Paper No. 8, Gent.

Olson, Mancur. 1993. "Dictatorship, Democracy, and Development." *American Political Science Review* 87, no. 3:567–76.

Pech, Khareen. 2000. "The Hand of War: Mercenaries in the Former Zaïre." In *Mercenaries: An African Security Dilemma*, edited by Abdel-Fatau Musah and Kayode Fayemi, 117–54. London: Pluto Press.

Pegg, Scott. 1998. *International Society and the De Facto State*. Aldershot: Ashgate.

Powell, Robert. 1999. *In the Shadow of Power: States and Strategies in International Politics*. Princeton: Princeton University Press.

Reno, William. 2000. "Shadow States and the Political Economy of Civil War." In *Greed and Grievances: Economic Agendas in Civil Wars*, edited by Mats Berdal and David M. Malone, 43–68. Boulder, Colo.: Lynne Rienner Publishers.

Risse, Thomas, and Ursula Lehmkuhl. 2006. "Governance in Areas of Limited Statehood—New Modes of Governance?" SFB-Governance Working Paper Series, No. 1.

Ross, Michael L. 2004. "What Do We Know About Natural Resources and Civil War?" *Journal of Peace Research* 41, no. 3:337–56.

Ross, Stephen A. 1973. "The Economic Theory of Agency: The Principal's Problem." *American Economic Review* 63, no. 2:134–39.

Rotberg, Robert I. 2003. "Failed States, Collapsed States, Weak States: Cause and Indicators." In *State Failure and State Weakness in a Time of Terror*, edited by Robert I. Rotberg, 1–25. Cambridge, Mass.: World Peace Foundation.

——, ed. 2004. *When States Fail: Causes and Consequences*. Princeton: Princeton University Press.

Sack, Robert David. 1986. *Human Territoriality: Its Theory and History*. Cambridge: Cambridge University Press.

Singer, Peter W. 2003. *Corporate Warriors: The Rise of the Privatized Military Industry*. Ithaca, N.Y.: Cornell University Press.

Siverson, Randolph M., and Harvey Starr. 1991. *The Diffusion of War: A Study of Opportunity and Willingness*. Ann Arbor: University of Michigan Press.

Skaperdas, Stergios. 2001. "The Political Economy of Organized Crime: Providing Protection When the State Does Not." *Economics of Governance* 2, no. 3:173–202.

——. 2002. "Warlord Competition." *Journal of Peace Research* 39, no. 4:435–66.

Skaperdas, Stergios, and Kai Konrad. 2004. "What Kind of Order out of Anarchy? Self-Protective Security, Autocracy, and Predatory Competition." Paper WP2004/2, Institute of Governmental Studies, University of California, Berkeley.

Starr, Harvey. 1978. "'Opportunity' and 'Willingness' as Ordering Concepts in the Study of War." *International Interactions* 4, no. 4:363–87.

——. 1991. "Joining Political and Geographic Perspectives, Geopolitics, and International Relations." *International Interactions* 17, no. 1:1–9.

Walter, Barbara F. 1997. "The Critical Barrier to Civil War Settlement." *International Organization* 51, no. 3:335–64.

Weinstein, Jeremy M. 2005. "Resources and the Information Problem in Rebel Recruitment." *Journal of Conflict Resolution* 49, no. 4:598–624.

——. 2006. *Inside Rebellion: The Politics of Insurgent Violence*. Cambridge: Cambridge University Press.

Wood, Elisabeth Jean. 2008. "The Social Processes of Civil War: The Wartime Transformation of Social Networks." *Annual Review of Political Science* 11:539–61.

5

Transnational Public-Private Partnerships

and the Provision of Collective Goods

in Developing Countries

ANDREA LIESE AND MARIANNE BEISHEIM

T RANSNATIONAL PUBLIC-PRIVATE PARTNERSHIPS (PPPs) are often described as an innovative form of governance, in which nonstate actors (e.g., nonprofit organizations, companies) together with state actors (e.g., international organizations, donor agencies) perform functions and provide services that previously rested firmly within the authority of sovereign states.[1] These actors jointly govern across multiple levels (transnational to local). In the OECD world, community-level PPPs often complement or supplement governmental regulation or services (Vaillancourt Rosenau 2000). In areas of limited statehood (see Risse, chapter 1 in this volume; and Risse and Lehmkuhl 2006, 66), however, the situation is quite different. Here, PPPs often have the goal of providing collective goods: They may provide rules or services that were simply absent before, or, alternatively, PPPs might substitute state activities in a situation of state failure (cf. Posner 2004, 239). For instance, a transnational PPP such as "Water and Sanitation for the Urban Poor" aims at providing access to water and sanitation for people in urban slums.

In this chapter, we seek to explain under which conditions transnational PPPs successfully provide collective goods in areas of limited statehood. In other words, why are some transnational PPPs highly effective while others are not? We use a range of theories on (the design of) international institutions and on compliance to develop hypotheses on PPP effectiveness that guide our empirical research. We draw our findings from our database of twenty-one PPPs in the areas of health, social, and environmental governance.[2]

The chapter is structured as follows: the following section defines PPPs and briefly describes their governance role in areas of limited statehood. We then introduce our concept of effectiveness and describe its operationalization. This part also gives an overview of the effectiveness of the twenty-one transnational PPPs in our database. In the next section we draw on the literature on compliance and the three most prominent mechanisms associated with institutions (coercion, management, legitimacy) to develop our conceptual framework. We identify five hypotheses and apply them to selected transnational PPPs in our research sample. Finally, we discuss the results.

Our focus on features of the institutional design of PPPs has provided valuable new insights for the analysis of PPP effectiveness. In particular, we find very strong support for the hypothesis that obligation, precision, and delegation matter (Abbott et al. 2000). Furthermore, we find support for the relevance of process management (Hemmati et al. 2002). A closer look reveals specific patterns with regard to three types of PPPs: service-providing, standard-setting, and knowledge-transfer partnerships. For example, while the degree of obligation, precision, and delegation significantly influences the effectiveness of service-providing partnerships, it matters less for PPPs engaging in knowledge transfer. And while we find less support for the relevance of a high level of inclusion of stakeholders in our overall sample, this factor seems to matter for standard-setting PPPs.

Transnational PPPs and Governance in Areas of Limited Statehood

What is a transnational public-private partnership? PPPs are "governance tools" (Börzel and Risse 2005) that are set up by public and private actors. They have been defined as "cooperative relationships between government, profit-making firms, and nonprofit private organizations to fulfill a policy function" (Linder and Vaillancourt Rosenau 2000, 5) and are composed of "people and organizations from some combination of public, business, and civil constituencies who engage in voluntary, mutually beneficial, innovative relationships to address common social aims through combining their resources and competencies" (Nelson and Zadek 2000). In a comprehensive discussion of literature on PPPs, Schäferhoff et al. (2009) propose an explicitly nonnormative definition of transnational PPPs as institutionalized transboundary interactions between public and private actors that aim at the provision of collective goods, a definition we ascribe to.

Since the beginning of the new century, and even more so in the aftermath of the Johannesburg Conference on Sustainable Development held in 2002, transnational public-private partnerships have not only become a hot topic in international politics, but also a much covered issue in the governance literature (for a comprehensive overview see Schäferhoff et al. 2009). PPPs are being promoted as a means to overcome the widespread lack of implementation of international policies and targets, specifically the Millennium Development Goals to which all of the PPPs in our sample refer to. All health, social, water, or energy PPPs that we look at are set up in the transnational realm but aim to execute governance also at the national or local level in areas of limited statehood. It would not be correct to view them as the result of shrewd state policies, mere delegation of implementation tasks and services, or even a form of privatization (about a characterization applicable to many community-level PPPs in the OECD world). Rather, in most cases, it is not governments that initiated or steer the PPPs. In areas of limited statehood, in particular, governments supervise PPPs only in a very limited fashion. Further, transnational PPPs always bring in their own rules and regulations, sometimes called "soft law" or "project law" (Randeria 2007) that may substitute or even compete with state law. Hence, we think it is correct to label their work as a separate form of governance.

Much of the literature on governance and private actors assumes that PPPs increase the effectiveness of both purely public and purely private governance, because they pool the resources of different actors, allow burden-sharing, and lead to win-win situations. In this vein, Reinicke et al. argue that PPPs narrow the "operational gap" that has opened up wherever policymakers have found themselves lacking the information, knowledge, and tools they need to respond to the complexity of governance in a globalizing world (Reinicke et al. 2000, xii, 57, 113). Their core assumption is that the private sector can bring in material resources and knowledge that public actors lack, while the public sector brings in legitimacy (cf. Börzel and Risse 2005, 209). Beyond this aspect of pooling resources, the inclusion of norm addressees—for example companies—in multisectoral partnerships is also regarded as a viable strategy to increase the likelihood of compliance with agreements and to further the implementation of norms (Mayntz 1983). Several critics, on the other hand, question the effectiveness of PPPs, especially concerning their value in improving governance in developing countries, and interpret them more as a neoliberal policy instrument to advance the special interests of private business (Richter 2003; Zammit 2003). More moderate critics point out typical risks and side effects of private sector involvement, such as a fragmentation of the U.N. system and a redesign of policies according to private interests instead of public needs (Bull et al. 2004; Martens 2007; Brühl 2007). Our research speaks to the debate just mentioned, in that it systematically explores the effectiveness of PPPs.

Measuring Effectiveness

When do PPPs attain their goals, and when are they effective? In order to determine and explain effectiveness, we first must define this concept. As Raustiala and Slaughter observe, "Effectiveness is a concept defined in varying ways: for example, as the degree to which a rule induces changes in behavior that further the rule's goals; improves the state of the underlying problem; or achieves its policy objective" (Raustiala and Slaughter 2002, 539). Drawing on Easton (1965) and Young (1994, 140ff.; 1999) and the compliance literature, we define effectiveness along three dimensions: output, outcome, and impact. In doing so, we consistently relate effectiveness to the goals set by the PPP itself.

"Output" signifies the immediate activities of a PPP, whether it is setting up institutional structures, convening meetings, setting rules, disseminating policy papers, or delivering medication, counseling, or treatment. These activities might cause changes in the behavior of the involved actors or have other effects during the further implementation of measures, that is, what we call "outcome." Outcome can be observed when members or target groups of a PPP alter their behavior, "either by doing things they would not otherwise have done or by terminating or redirecting prior patterns of behavior" (Young 1994, 145). Hence, a PPP as an institution is effective to "the extent that its operation impels actors to behave different than they would if the institution did not exist or if some other institutional arrangement were put in its place" (Young 1992, 161). However, we are not only talking about a narrow understanding of "compliance": for example, after a health PPP has delivered training for medical personnel (output), more cases of disease might be correctly managed at health facilities (outcome). Outcome is, moreover, not limited to behavioral effectiveness alone. Other indicators may include case detection rates or treatment success rates in cases of health PPP delivering medication and therapy. There is a direct and immediate link between this outcome of treatment and the potentially reduced prevalence, mortality, or morbidity rates—the "impact." Impact refers to the broader results of PPP activities, in particular to their contribution to problem solving. We furthermore have to discount for negative side effects. The impact of PPP activities is hard to measure because reliable data are rarely available and there are many attribution problems in a dense web of complex causal relations. Therefore, we chose to collect data on the solution of problems, such as mortality rates, and then evaluated whether this success may be attributed to PPP activities.

As stated earlier, we are mostly interested in the effectiveness of PPPs in relation to their goal attainment (Young 1994, 144). PPP goals may focus on the output, outcome, and/or impact dimensions. Some health PPPs, for example, either want first and foremost to hand out medication (output), alter behavior that causes the spread of infectious diseases (outcome), or eradicate an entire disease (impact). An HIV/AIDS initiative might be extremely successful in distributing condoms (output), but may nevertheless contribute little toward solving the problem of HIV/AIDS (impact) because of a lack of willingness or knowledge (outcome). For this very reason, most PPPs try to be active in all three dimensions. We can nonetheless identify a primary focus in their work.[3]

In order to rate the effectiveness of our sample of transnational PPPs, we use a three-point ordinal scale (see table 5.1), which is mostly based on qualitative indicators—the nature of a PPP's work is hard to compare or evaluate otherwise. Our data are based on evaluations, documents, and nearly 150 interviews with PPP members and experts. Our comparison of twenty-one transnational PPPs in the areas of environmental, health, and social policy reveals that the effectiveness of PPPs varies to a great extent. We can group them into three categories: (a) PPPs with high effectiveness, which achieve most of their goals and provide output, outcome, and impact; (b) PPPs with medium effectiveness, which have reached some goals but failed on other dimensions; and (c) PPPs with low effectiveness (sometimes near ineffectiveness), which

TABLE 5.1 Qualitative Indicators for Effectiveness

	Output	*Outcome*	*Impact*
High (3)	Provision or adoption of knowledge, standards, services as envisioned in the stated goals	Substantial change in behavior of targets, extensive application/ implementation of knowledge, standards, services	Substantial contribution to solution of problem
Medium (2)	Substantial policy papers and some provision of knowledge, standards, services, but failure to achieve all stated goals	Some change in behavior of targets, some application or implementation of knowledge, standards, services	Some contribution to solution of problem
Low (1)	Mere paperwork and meetings with no or few results	No or low change in behavior of targets, hardly any application/ implementation of knowledge, standards, services	No or low contribution to solution of problem

struggle to provide the desired output and fail with regard to most of their goals, and the outcome and impact dimension (for an overview see table 5.2). Within each dimension of effectiveness, we rank each PPP as compared to the others, thereby identifying the relative effectiveness of each. We will now present one case for each category to demonstrate how we applied our indicators in the coding process.

TABLE 5.2 Effectiveness of PPPs

	PPP	*Goal*	*Effectiveness*
1.	GAVI Alliance	Extend the reach and quality of immunization coverage	3
2.	Global Fund to Fight AIDS, Tuberculosis and Malaria (GF)	Attract, manage, and disburse resources to fight the three diseases	3
3.	Water and Sanitation for the Urban Poor (WSUP)	Provide access to water and sanitation in urban slums	2
4.	Global Alliance for the Elimination of Leprosy (GAEL)	Attain elimination of leprosy at a national level in all endemic countries	2
5.	International AIDS Vaccine Initiative (IAVI)	Accelerate the research and development of an HIV vaccine	2
6.	Common Code for the Coffee Community (4C)	Develop a voluntary code of conduct comprising basic social, environmental, and economic practices in mainstream coffee production, processing, and trading	2
7.	Social Accountability 8000 (SA 8000)	Establish an auditable certification standard based on international workplace norms	2
8.	Global Network on Energy for Sustainable Development (GNESD)	Carry out policy analysis on energy issues that can facilitate attaining the Millennium Development Goals	2
9.	Global Alliance for Improved Nutrition (GAIN)	Fight vitamin and mineral deficiencies in developing countries	2

TABLE 5.2 Effectiveness of PPPs *(continued)*

	PPP	Goal	Effectiveness
10.	World Commission on Dams (WCD)	Develop internationally accepted standards for the planning and construction of large dams	2
11.	United Nations Global Compact (GC)	Mainstream ten principles in business activities around the world and catalyze actions in support of broader U.N. goals	2
12.	Building Partnerships for Development in Water and Sanitation (BPD)	Promote the effective delivery of safe water and sanitation services to poor communities in developing countries	2
13.	Global Public Private Partnership for Handwashing with Soap (PPPHW)	Spread awareness about the importance of handwashing with soap to prevent diseases	2
14.	Renewable Energy and Energy Efficiency Partnership (REEEP)	Promote renewables and energy efficiency in developing countries	2
15.	Global Water Partnership (GWP)	Support countries in the sustainable management of their water resources	1
16.	Global Alliance for Workers and Communities (GAWC)	Improve workplace experience and future prospects of workers in developing countries	1
17.	Global Village Energy Partnership (GVEP)	Increase access to sustainable modern energy in rural areas in developing countries	1
18.	Roll Back Malaria Partnership (RBM)	Halve the global burden of malaria by 2010	1

TABLE 5.2 Effectiveness of PPPs *(continued)*

	PPP	*Goal*	*Effectiveness*
19.	International Alliance against Hunger (IAAH)	Increase the public awareness of hunger, mobilize public campaigns, and facilitate local and national initiatives against hunger	1
20.	World Committee on Tourism Ethics (WCTE)	Promote the Global Code on Ethics in Tourism and reconcile disputes about code compliance	1
21.	Children's Vaccine Initiative (CVI)	Develop new and improved vaccines	1

PPP WITH HIGH EFFECTIVENESS

Two partnerships in the area of transnational health, GAVI Alliance and the Global Fund, provide examples of highly effective PPPs (cf. Beisheim et al. forthcoming; Schäferhoff 2009; Ulbert 2008). While initially criticized for not being effective, the Global Fund to Fight AIDS, Tuberculosis and Malaria (GF), a PPP with the goal to attract, manage, and disburse resources to fight the three aforementioned diseases, is now also reaching an increasing number of people and regions with HIV/AIDS drugs and therapies, tuberculosis therapies, and insecticide-treated nets and malaria treatment. For example, concerning the GF's output until 2009, 2.5 million people living with HIV/AIDS in the developing world received antiretroviral treatment (ART), 6 million people received a therapy to treat tuberculosis, and 104 million insecticide-nets (ITN) were distributed to prevent malaria. Between 2007 and 2009, the GF's output was even more impressive.

The GF also tries to measure its impact on morbidity, mortality, and prevalence rates (Global Fund 2007). While the GF has not met all of its initial (and perhaps overly ambitious) targets, it has substantially improved its performance over the years and is becoming more and more effective. Furthermore, the GF is increasing its contribution to the strengthening of national health systems, and it has been successful in disbursing funds relatively quickly and

TABLE 5.3 Output Measurement for Global Fund

Output Indicators	2006	2007	2008	2009
HIV: People on ARV Treatment	770,000	1.4 million	2 million	2.5 million
TB: Cases Treated Under DOTS[a]	2 million	3.3 million	4.6 million	6 million
Malaria: ITNs Distributed	18 million	46 million	70 million	104 million
[a] Directly Observed Treatment, Short-course.				
Sources: Global Fund 2007, 2009, 2010.				

in spending only a small proportion (3 percent) of its budget on operational costs. Hence, we rate the Global Fund as highly effective.

PPP WITH MEDIUM EFFECTIVENESS

Several PPPs in the areas of social rights, health, and water and sanitation have been partially effective. The United Nations Global Compact (GC), probably the best-known transnational PPP, has the goal to mainstream ten principles in business activities around the world and to catalyze actions in support of broader U.N. goals, such as the Millennium Development Goals. To achieve these objectives, the GC facilitates policy dialogues, also within national or local networks, and partnership projects. And indeed, the GC produced an impressive output in that respect. Outcome and impact of its work are hard to measure and arguably rather low. An evaluation by McKinsey estimates, for example, that 90 percent of projects pertaining to Corporate Social Responsibility (CSR) would have taken place even without membership in the GC (McKinsey&Company 2003; Mohaupt et al. 2005, 9, as quoted in Kaan 2008b). Yet, especially for companies in developing countries, the GC has often led the sole initiative to make them familiar with the principle of corporate social responsibility. Consequently, we rank the GC's effectiveness as medium: the GC achieved most of its objectives concerning output. However, while most members comply with the GC's rule to produce an annual Communication on Progress, the impact of these activities in terms of mainstreaming the GC's ten principles in business activities around the world is barely visible.

PPP WITH LOW EFFECTIVENESS

The Global Code on Ethics in Tourism is a standard set by the World Tourism Organization's General Assembly in 1999. The World Committee on Tourism Ethics (WCTE), a public-private reconciliation body—composed of delegates from member states and representatives of labor and employer organizations—is responsible for the proliferation of the code, its evaluation and monitoring, and dispute settlement. While one output has been to translate the code into thirty-three languages, the output of proliferation has not been met. Furthermore, the outcome is low: the private sector hardly knows about the code or prefers other initiatives, such as the Global Compact. Furthermore, the committee has so far failed to fulfill its task of dispute settlement. During its five annual meetings, the committee "has not decided on any major issue of dispute" (Kaan 2007b, 2). Hence, WCTE has hardly achieved its goals and provided only low output, low outcome, and no impact. Compared to others in the sample, the effectiveness of the initiative is ranked as low.

How can we account for the different degrees of effectiveness? In the following section, we will turn to the institutional design of the PPP as our major explanatory variable.

Explaining the Effectiveness of PPPs— Our Conceptual Framework

Our comparison of the selected twenty-one PPPs reveals that they are, on the one hand, not as perfect as proponents of the concept would think, but, on the other hand, more effective than critics would assume. Overall, PPPs produce very different output, outcome, and impact and differ greatly with regard to attaining their goals.

In the following section, we introduce a conceptual framework that attempts to explain these varying degrees of effectiveness. We use assumptions and hypotheses from the legalization debate, the literature on organizational learning, and theories of compliance to identify a number of testable hypotheses. Overall, they all rely on three distinct mechanisms of social control: coercion, self-interest, or legitimacy (Hurd 1999). Neorealist theories and the legal enforcement school focus on sanctions and other forms of coercion, which are seen as the only mechanism to manipulate the cost-benefit calculations of actors. Instead, a neoliberal theory of international relations assumes that actors follow rules because it is in their interest to do so. In contrast, sociological or constructivist approaches regard the legitimacy of norms as a crucial determinant of actors' compliance. For our research, we draw on these assumptions to develop three sets of hypotheses on the relevance of PPP institutional setup for their effectiveness.

Degree of Institutionalization: Obligation, Precision, and Delegation

Following the literature on legalization, we assume that the success of a PPP is highly dependent on three features of its rules: namely their obligatory status, their relative precision, and the delegation of their interpretation and application to a third party. *Obligation* means that actors "are legally bound by a rule or commitment in the sense that their behavior there under is subject to scrutiny under the general rules, procedures, and discourse of international law" (Abbott et al. 2000, 401). *Precision* means "that rules and commitments unambiguously define the conduct they require, authorize, or proscribe" (Ibid., 412). By defining "clearly and unambiguously" what is expected of actors "in a particular set of circumstances," precision "narrows the scope for reasonable interpretation." *Delegation* means "that third parties have been granted authority to implement, interpret, and apply the rules; to resolve disputes, and (possibly) to make further rules" (Ibid., 401). The characteristic form is legal delegation to a third-party dispute settlement mechanism. There is a remarkable variety of international legalization, and we assume that this also holds true for PPPs. Hence, we apply this concept of legalization to PPPs and distinguish a continuum from high to low "degrees of institutionalization" (Beisheim et al. 2005). Instead of focusing solely on legal obligation, we focus on language and other indicators of intent to be bound by the rules of a PPP. When analyzing the obligation within PPP, we do not focus solely on the *legal* bindingness—as we hardly find legally binding rules within private regimes—but more on the overall level of bindingness, also including other forms such as social commitments or various types of employed conditionality. Instead of focusing on delegation to a court, we focus on the delegation to an external monitoring agency. In doing so, we link the idea of delegation to findings of the enforcement theory to compliance, that is, the relevance of monitoring and sanctions (Downs et al. 1996).

Taking all three elements together (see table 5.4), our hypothesis on the effectiveness of PPP (H1) reads: the higher the overall degree of institutionalization, the more effective the partnership and the higher the compliance with its rules.

TABLE 5.4 Degree of Institutionalization

	Obligation (Bindingness and Conditionality)	Precision of Norms	Delegation (Monitoring, Evaluation, Implementation)
High (3)	Binding rules (e.g., contract between PPP partners), conditionality	Determinate rules: no or only narrow issues of interpretation	External monitoring, centralized enforcement
Medium (2)	Contingent obligations and escape clauses	Areas of discretion and issues of interpretation	Internal or external monitoring and publicity
Low (1)	Rules not binding	Broad rules: impossible to determine whether conduct complies	No monitoring or confidential monitoring

Process Management and Capacity Building

Following the managerial approach to compliance, we contend that the effectiveness of PPPs depends on an institutional design that reflects and addresses the material and cognitive capacities of norm addressees. The managerial approach rejects the assumption that actors violate a rule because of a lack of enforcement and argues that actors have a propensity to comply with rules: "The strongest circumstantial evidence for the sense of an obligation to comply with treaties is the care that states take in negotiating and entering into them" (Chayes and Chayes 1993, 186). According to the Chayes, noncompliance often stems from a lack of or limitations in capacity (Chayes and Chayes 1993, 188). Lack of capacity refers to a lack of "scientific, technical, bureaucratic, and financial wherewithal" (Chayes and Chayes 1993, 194;

cf. Chayes et al. 1998). Consequently, proponents of the managerial school recommend "managed compliance" (Raustiala and Slaughter 2002, 542).

Applied to PPPs, we look at what we call "process management" as a crucial design feature of effective PPPs. We expect that a partnership's effectiveness depends on an efficient and professional management of the PPP itself.[4] For example, the partnership secretariat should be able to work independently. Professional full-time staff should have the means to establish an efficient communication infrastructure and information management. While the communication between the partners must be continual, reliable, and transparent, transaction costs need to be kept low. Other indicators for good process-management are efficient and transparent decision-making rules and procedures, professional fund-raising, and staff recruitment. If conflicts or problems arise, there should be tools for conflict management and mediation (Hemmati et al. 2002). Red tape bureaucracy and organizational dysfunctions, in contrast, might hinder the effectiveness of PPPs (Schäferhoff 2008d). Thus, our second hypothesis (H2) reads: the more professional and efficient the process management, the more effective the PPP.

Given the absence or lack of capacities in many developing countries, we furthermore assume that PPPs must ensure productive capacity building measures for their partners and addressees in areas of limited statehood. According to this new consensus in the literature on aid effectiveness, PPPs and other initiatives must contribute to the development of local capacities (OECD-DAC 2006; Guhar-Sapir 2005). Thus, our third hypothesis (H3) reads: the more a PPP invests in the development of local capacities and the longer the time frame for these measures, the more effective the PPP, particularly in terms of outcome and impact.

Learning and Legitimacy

Following the literature on socialization and compliance, we assume that compliance can be the result of processes of arguing and socialization, which may lead to learning and internalization. According to Koh (1997), states comply with international rules, not because of enforcement but because of internalization of the underlying norms. Internalization processes may be initiated and sustained by norm entrepreneurs and issue-specific networks (Risse and Sikkink 1999), by deliberation (Risse 2000; Ulbert and Risse 2005), or by social learning (Checkel 2001). The constructivist literature assumes that social interaction—rather than pressure or cost-benefit assumptions—leads to compliance because social learning is "a process whereby agent interests and identities are shaped through and during interaction" (Checkel 2001, 560). Applied to PPPs, we distinguish two causal chains: we expect higher degrees of effectiveness through organizational learning (H4) as well as through the inclusion of stakeholders (H5).

Much of the broader literature on organizational learning links the effectiveness of organizations to their ability to adapt to changing environments and new challenges (Dirks et al. 2002; Siebenhüner 2003). Here the focus is applied to a change in the knowledge of an organization that paves the way to modified practices of the organization and its members. Institutional learning takes place when innovative and consensual knowledge is provided by the PPP so that members may use it for improving their projects. Evaluations play a pivotal role in this. Even more important is the follow-up process within the PPP—there should be an established process on how to react to criticism, for example, within evaluations. Accordingly, we hypothesize that if processes of institutional learning are embedded in the design of a partnership, this will increase the PPP's effectiveness, and thus our fourth hypothesis (H4) reads: the more institutionalized a process of organizational learning, the more effective the PPP.

Furthermore, a sociological perspective on compliance and the research on policy implementation would expect compliance to depend on whether norm addressees were involved in the process of norm setting (Mayntz 1983; Börzel and Risse 2002). It is controversial whether more inclusion and participation in fact leads to more effectiveness. While some authors assume that the success of governance is linked, at the very least, to its perception as legitimate (Reinicke et al. 2000; Zürn 2004), others argue the opposite and stress the potential tradeoff between (time-consuming) normative procedural demands and actual performance (Dahl 1994; Keohane and Nye 2001; Scharpf 1999). We take up the former position and hypothesize that the involvement of stakeholders and rule addressees increases compliance (outcome). We do so for various reasons: if stakeholders are involved in the process of rule setting, norms are the result of reasoned consensus with stakeholders rather than bargained compromise. This may increase ownership and hence compliance (Beisheim and Dingwerth 2010). In addition, broad participation may induce a higher level of social learning and thus a reshaping of member's interests. In a bottom-up fashion, stakeholders may bring in (local) knowledge and thus shape rules, so that they fit the actual conditions on the ground and meet a higher level of acceptance when applied. Moreover, we use accountability mechanisms as another indicator for the substantial involvement of stakeholders. Thus, our fifth hypothesis (H5) reads: the higher the involvement of stakeholders in establishing, steering, and holding the PPP accountable, the more effective the PPP.

Applying the Framework to the Cases

COMPARATIVE ANALYSIS

How can we explain the different degree of effectiveness? Before we start to discuss our results, we have to introduce a typology of PPPs, which helps to identify patterns and to better understand the covariation of independent variables. In the literature on PPPs, many authors attempt to categorize the various types of PPPs, mostly according to their main objectives or functions (Tesner 2000, 73–77; Witte et al. 2003; Nelson 2002). *Service-providing partnerships* fill operational gaps by distributing resources and services in areas of limited statehood. Especially in the area of development cooperation, many PPPs were initiated to provide services, such as the distribution of antiretroviral therapies to combat HIV/AIDS (like the Global Fund), or the construction of water and energy supply systems in urban slums (such as the Water and Sanitation for the Urban Poor PPP). *Standard-setting partnerships* establish new rules, for example by drafting minimum standards and in some cases implementing them via a certification scheme (like SA 8000). *Knowledge-transfer partnerships* seek to generate new expertise, provide a forum for exchange of the best practices, and transfer this knowledge to governmental or nongovernmental actors in developing countries (like the Global Water Partnership). While we did not use such a heuristic in designing our sample, we now see patterns along the lines of three different types of partnerships, that is, variation according to the main type of output the PPP produces. Indeed, one main finding of our research is that the factors contributing to the effectiveness of PPPs covary with regard to the specific function or type of PPPs. As our discussion of results will show, some independent variables matter for all types of PPPs—others matter only for a specific type.

Having this in mind, we will now turn to explaining the different degree of effectiveness described in section three. Table 5.5 shows the results of our

TABLE 5.5 Results

	PPP	Type	DV Effect	IV1 Institutionalization O	IV1 P	IV1 D	IV2 Management	IV3 Capacity	IV4 Learning	IV5 Inclusion
1.	GAVI	Service	3	3	3	3	3	2→3	3	2
2.	GF	Service	3	3	3	3	3→2	2	2	2
3.	WSUP	Service	2	3	3	2	3	2	2	2
4.	GAEL	Service	2	2	2	1	2	1	1	1
5.	IAVI	Knowledge→Service	2	1→3	1→3	1→2	3	2→3	3	1
6.	4C	Standard	2	3	3	3	3	2	2	3
7.	SA 8000	Standard	2	3	3	3	2	2	2	2
8.	GNESD	Knowledge	2	1	1	1	3	2	2	2
9.	GAIN	Service	2	3	1	2	3	2	1	2
10.	WCD	Standard	2	1	2	1	3	1	1	2
11.	GC	Knowledge	2	2	2	2	1	2	2	2
12.	BPD	Knowledge/Service	2	1	1	1	2	2	3	2
13.	PPPHW	Knowledge	2	1	2	1	2→1	2	1	1
14.	REEEP	Service/Knowledge	2	3	2	2	2	2	2	2
15.	GWP	Knowledge	1	1	1	1	1	1	2	2
16.	GAWC	Service	1	1	1	1	2	1	1	1
17.	GVEP	Knowledge→Service	1	1→2	1→1	1→2	1→2	1	1	1
18.	RBM	Service	1	1	1	1	1	2	2	2
19.	IAAH	Knowledge	1	1	1	1	1	1	1	2
20.	WCTE	Standard	1	1	1	1	1	1	1	1
21.	CVI	Service	1	1	1	1	1	1	1	1

Note: 3 = high; 2 = medium; 1 = low; → = change over time to.

twenty-one case studies for the aforementioned five hypotheses. It lists the abbreviation of each PPP, the type, and the categories for the dependent (DV) and the independent variables (IV).

The degree of institutionalization matters for most PPPs. We find a striking correlation between high levels of effectiveness and a high degree of institutionalization. This provides strong support for our first hypothesis. Overall, eight PPPs score high on the most important dimension — obligation — and all those show at least medium effectiveness. And all PPPs with low effectiveness share a rather low degree of institutionalization. These PPPs commit members only voluntarily; there are no binding rules or conditions. They lack enforcement mechanisms, third party monitoring, and they only vaguely define obligations and secondary rules. For example, the dissolved Children Vaccine Initiative (CVI) only broadly sets the target to "vaccinate the world's children" and fails to establish rules or obligations for its members (Schäferhoff 2008a). Even in the case of the World Committee on Tourism Ethics (WCTE), where a dispute settlement body was established, obligation and delegation remain low, because members can significantly limit the authority of the body by refusing to give the required permission on individual cases (cf. Kaan 2007b). Another example is the GWP's many purely nominal members — a sign that there is no obligation at all. Moreover, most of these low effective PPPs have a weak process management and often also lack measures for capacity building and institutional learning.

Standard-setting and service-providing PPPs with a low degree of institutionalization and a weak process management (RBM, WCTE, CVI, see table 5.2) have been hardly able to reach their output goals and did not achieve desired outcomes and impact. Knowledge-transfer partnerships seem to be the exception. Overall, they display lower degrees of institutionalization: International AIDS Vaccine Initiative (IAVI; 1996–99), Global Network on Energy for Sustainable Development (GNESD), GWP, and the International Alliance Against Hunger (IAAH) score low on all dimensions. Nevertheless, the knowledge network GNESD is relatively successful although obligation, precision, and delegation are very low. Also, IAVI was extremely successful in its first phase as knowledge-transfer PPP. Apparently, the pure exchange of knowledge does not necessarily need a high degree of institutionalization — this task is different from the provision of services, which brings with it an enormous management of resources, distributive effects, and problems of free riding or misuse. If the latter problems arise, PPPs need a high degree of institutionalization and good management procedures to be successful.

The degree of institutionalization is of less importance for the task of knowledge creation and awareness-raising. Instead, the effectiveness of knowledge-transfer PPPs seems to depend on opportunities for organizational and social learning.

While the more effective partnerships provide for capacity building, we do not find support for the hypothesis that capacity building is a necessary condition for effectiveness. In particular, several of the moderately effective PPPs, such as Social Accountability (SA) 8000, lack capacity building initiatives. External evaluations, however, suggest that capacity building is essential to achieve long-term sustained success on the ground.

The relevance of organizational learning and inclusion is even less clear. We find no positive correlation between organizational learning and effectiveness; however, none of the PPPs with low effectiveness show signs of high responsiveness and institutionalized learning. With regard to the inclusion of stakeholders, successful and moderately effective PPPs score medium or higher.[5] However, the PPPs with low effectiveness vary from low to high degrees of inclusion. If we take a closer look at the three subgroups, inclusion matters most for the standard-setting PPPs. Moreover, relatively effective standard-setting PPPs such as the Common Code for the Coffee Community (4C) and SA 8000 have set precise norms and delegated monitoring functions to external organizations (i.e., display a higher degree of institutionalization) and show good process management.

DETAILED DISCUSSION OF SELECTED CASES

In this section, we will provide a more detailed discussion of selected cases. We compare a relatively effective, a moderately effective, and a relatively ineffective PPP of each identified type. We will initially focus on the relevance of the degree of institutionalization as defined earlier and then add other explanations if appropriate.

A typical case for a very effective service PPP in the health sector is the GAVI Alliance. This PPP is highly institutionalized (Schäferhoff 2008b): obligation is high and recipient countries have to comply with several technical and procedural rules if they want to obtain funding. If countries do not achieve the immunization targets or if cases of mismanagement are reported, there is the risk that the funding will not be continued. At the time of application, they must have already established an Interagency Coordination

Committee, in which bilateral and multilateral donors, NGOs, and the private sector are represented. The degree of precision is also high, although somewhat mixed: several rules are very precise, while others are not. GAVI Alliance funding and support are conditional on the development of substantive plans and the acceptance of performance goals. Delegation is also high: GAVI's financing mechanism is performance based; countries must demonstrate that goals are being met and must also show progress toward sustainability. Country performance is externally monitored through a data-quality audit by external consultants, among them McKinsey. This supports our idea that the degree of institutionalization is crucial for an effective service PPP. GAVI is, however, also good in management and learning.

As discussed earlier, another case in point is the International AIDS Vaccine Initiative (IAVI), a PPP that had to become much more institutionalized when its focus changed from advocacy and knowledge dissemination to service provision. As they now had to take care of an increased resource management, they had to introduce legally binding Memoranda of Understanding with their partners and monitoring procedures (Schäferhoff 2008c).

In contrast, the now terminated health partnership Children's Vaccine Initiative (CVI) lacked strong obligations for its members and precise rules and was hardly effective. The aim to establish a heat-stable polio vaccine could not be reached because their public partners, notably the World Health Organization (WHO), were not willing to commit themselves to purchase new developments by the pharmaceutical industry. Furthermore, process management was weak: CVI never managed to raise substantial funds and had no competences to mediate the resource conflict with the WHO, which wanted to maintain its influence in immunization activities. The low degree of institutionalization is puzzling, but could reflect "world-time," as CVI was already established in 1990, when PPPs were a relatively new phenomenon and the partners were reluctant to engage in binding obligations (Schäferhoff 2008a).

A typical case for a moderately effective standard-setting PPP in providing CSR norms is the Common Code for the Coffee Community (4C), whose degree of institutionalization is high. Obligation can be ranked as high: in order to become a member of the code, companies have to submit a self-assessment of compliance with the code (Kaan 2007a). On the basis of this report, a work plan is drafted, which determines the obligation of the company. The performance is reevaluated after two years and, if successful, every four years thereafter. The code employs conditionality, at least for the group of producers; moreover, if they fulfill the requirements of the code they increase their chance to contract with the producers that are 4C members. Precision is also high: rules are precisely operationalized, and measurement instruments are provided for each indicator (4-C Secretariat 2004, 14–18). The level of delegation is high as well: self-assessments about performance are evaluated externally. For standard-setting PPP, we observe that, apart from the degree of institutionalization, the level of participation is crucial for their effectiveness. Participation in 4C is fairly high: the first two years were used to involve all relevant stakeholders in the creation of the code (Kaan 2007a). While the multistakeholder process has been criticized for not adequately presenting the small farmers (Hamm 2004, 22–23), the number of representatives increased significantly during the norm-setting process. Today, 4C conducts stakeholder fora in several producer countries.

Similarly, the relatively successful Social Accountability (SA) 8000 has a high degree of institutionalization, consisting of high degrees of obligation, precision, and delegation. While SA 8000 is a voluntary standard, companies still lose their certificate if they do not comply with the standard and its rules (Kaan 2008a). Accordingly, we rank obligation as high. The degree of precision is also high: the provisions are modeled along the ISO's standards and provide clear criteria for the fulfillment of any requirement. The auditors consider SA 8000 to provide a consistent system of rules (DeRuisseau 2002, 229). The degree of delegation is high: companies have to commission an external auditor, mostly firms specialized in social rights or firms involved in ISO monitoring. Once a company has been successfully audited, it commits to allow semiannual inspections over the course of the next three years. If inspectors detect instances of noncompliance, they are recorded and used to design a remediation plan (DeRuisseau 2002, 228). Social Accountability International, which developed the standard and administers its functioning, has outsourced the accreditation to auditors, that is, they have delegated this function to the independent Social Accountability Accreditation Services. The inclusion of stakeholders is quite good (and coded as medium); the ownership of companies, NGOs, trade unions, and participating public agencies is seen as one of the major success factors although bringing in the voices of worker's representatives from the south failed.

In contrast to these partnerships, the World Committee on Tourism Ethics (WCTE) is a rather ineffective standard setting PPP. The main addressee of the code, the private sector, has rarely heard about it (Kaan 2007b). It has a very low degree of institutionalization. The underlying code is not

legally binding and the broad principles for sustainable tourism are imprecise. Although dispute settlement competences were agreed upon, delegation is low, because the right to sue requires a unanimous decision by both
parties. Furthermore, WCTE also scores low with regard to process management, learning, capacity building, and inclusion.

A typical case for a relatively effective knowledge-transfer PPP is the
Global Network on Energy for Sustainable Development (GNESD).
GNESD is reasonably effective, although it does not display a high degree
of institutionalization. There are two reasons for that: first, it may be due to
the fact that the interests of partners largely converge, and second, the task
at hand—the exchange of mainly immaterial resources—does not require an
elaborate institutional structure. The efficient facilitation of communication
and exchange—a feature of its process management—is seen by all partners
as its decisive asset (Campe 2008b).

When measured against its ambitious goals, Global Compact (GC) had
been only moderately effective during the first years of its existence (1999 until
2006). On purpose and against much criticism, the degree of institutionalization had been kept at a low level in the beginning: "Critics wish it were something that it is not: a regulatory arrangement, specifically a legally binding
code of conduct with explicit performance criteria and independent monitoring and enforcement of company compliance" (Ruggie 2001, 372). Obligation
is rated medium; while the principles which stem from several U.N. conventions and soft law are binding for participating companies, they could choose
to report on only one of the ten principles in their progress report—that is,
there was no unconditional obligation to report on all principles. At first, there
was no penalty, such as a delisting or exclusion, for noncompliance with the
reporting procedure. Moreover, precise secondary rules concerning the communication of progress (COP) were predominantly lacking. This has recently
changed; we thus rate precision as medium now. The same applies to the degree of delegation. The COPs are now posted on Global Compact's website—
mainly with the intent to promote learning. This step, however, also brings
in some degree of social control, as a company is now marked as "noncom-
municating" or "inactive" in the participant database of the Global Compact
website if it fails to deliver the COP on time. Also obligations have been tightened: reports have to be handed in annually and a company will be excluded
if it fails to comply with this requirement three times. All of these measures
improve compliance. One could argue that recently—in contrast to Ruggie's

statement in 2001—the nature of Global Compact has evolved to some extent in the direction of a standard-setting PPP.

Virtually no output is produced by the International Alliance Against Hunger (IAAH)—a very low institutionalized knowledge-transfer partnership—founded to advocate efforts for the eradication of hunger worldwide. Tasks and rules remain ambivalent; it is the task of the national stakeholders to come up with ideas and projects. Due to a lack of resources, process management is hardly possible and the IAAH does not even provide tools for the otherwise successful national twinning projects against hunger.

Conclusions

Drawing on theories on international institutions and compliance, we analyzed causes for transnational PPP effectiveness—output, outcome, and impact—or the lack thereof. By comparing case studies of twenty-one transnational PPPs in the areas of health, social, and environmental governance, we explained under which conditions these PPPs successfully provide collective goods in developing countries. As to explanatory factors, we focused on the degree of a PPP's institutionalization, the quality of its process management, its capacity development measures, given opportunities for organizational learning and the extent of the inclusion of its stakeholders.

Our analysis reveals several results. We find that theories on international institutions and compliance are indeed applicable to transnational public-private partnerships. Their assumptions, however, fit some specific "types" of PPPs better than others. First, we find strong empirical support for our first hypothesis: Our comparison indicates that the degree of institutionalization significantly affects the effectiveness of partnerships. However, its relevance varies according to the type of PPP. While the degree of institutionalization is very relevant for PPPs in service provision and standard setting, it is less important for those partnerships engaging in knowledge transfer. Obviously, a high level of obligation, precise rules, and independent monitoring provisions improve the effectiveness of transnational PPPs that need to raise funds and distribute resources or commit different partners to changes in their behavior. For knowledge transfer, strong institutions do not seem to be a necessary prerequisite as third-party monitoring is absent even in the most successful cases.

Second, we find process management to influence the effectiveness of service-providing and standard-setting partnerships. Here, a time component
comes in. During the first years, most PPPs experience significant challenges;
it is during this time that they are required to manage institutional changes in
their governance structure. Moreover, in those cases when public and private
"partners" start their collaboration against the background of highly diver-
gent organizational cultures, a lack of communication or conflict management has proven to be detrimental. Especially after negative evaluations, we
also find organizational learning to be relevant.

Third, although we cannot support the assumption that capacity development always matters, we cannot dismiss it entirely. While capacity development apparently matters less for output (especially at the transnational level),
it seems to have an effect on outcome and impact on the country level. We
will further test this revised hypothesis once more detailed data on country-
level performance of PPPs is available.

Fourth, there is hardly any empirical evidence for a positive correlation
between the inclusion of stakeholders and partnership's effectiveness. Only
for our standard-setting partnerships is the level and quality of participation
relevant. During the drafting of norms, debates may be more cumbersome,
but in the end a high level of inclusion seems to improve the identification and ownership with the PPP's standard. In contrast, service-providing
PPPs tend to rely on their output-legitimacy. In general, most PPPs strive
to establish a governance structure that attempts to meet at least the basic
requirements of legitimacy or that combines them with considerations for
effectiveness. On the transnational level, many PPPs have a relatively small
board, often dominated by the most important donors and supported by an
independent secretariat, and complemented by a broader council for relevant stakeholders, though giving the latter only limited participation rights.
This governance structure pays tribute to the need for lean management
and seeks to meet the minimum requirement of some sort of stakeholder
participation.[6]

In sum, we found substantial support for the assumption that the institutional design of PPPs matters. If transnational PPPs would choose to
invest more resources in evaluating their governance structure and process
management, they would very likely achieve more of the goals they have
set for themselves regarding the provision of governance in areas of limited
statehood. These improvements in PPP-design are all the more relevant, as
recent reports warn that most countries will fall short on the United Nation's

Millennium Development Goals. Future studies should also analyze more data on the relevance of the local conditions in areas of limited statehood for PPP effectiveness. Next to developing their own capacities, PPPs might also need to invest more in local capacity development to achieve sustainable results on the ground.

NOTES

1. We thank Sabine Campe, Christopher Kaan, Thomas Risse, Marco Schäferhoff, and Cornelia Ulbert for ongoing discussions and input and Jessica Bither, Tanja Börzel, Tanja Brühl, Hannah Janetschek, and Bernhard Zangl for comments on earlier versions of this chapter.

2. We developed the database during the first funding period of our research project (2006–2009). Currently, we are in the process of adding more data on local effectiveness and on local conditions for effectiveness.

3. In the case of mainly output-oriented PPPs, our focus on goal attainment is less ambitious than using a concept of effectiveness such as problem solving.

4. There is a huge body of literature on the relevance of managerial qualities for performance. For an overview see Ingraham and Lynn 2004.

5. With the exception of the Handwashing Partnership (PPPHW).

6. For explanations of this convergence or isomorphism see Campe 2008a.

REFERENCES

Abbott, Kenneth W., Robert O. Keohane, Andrew Moravcsik, Anne-Marie Slaughter, and Duncan Snidal. 2000. "The Concept of Legalization." *International Organization* 54, no. 3:401–19.

Beisheim, Marianne, Sabine Campe, and Marco Schäferhoff. Forthcoming. "Global Governance Through Partnerships." In *Handbook on Multi-Level Governance*, edited by Michael Zürn, Sonja Wälti, and Hendrik Enderlein. Cheltenham: Edward Elgar.

Beisheim, Marianne, and Klaus Dingwerth. 2010. "The Link Between Standard Setting NGO's Legitimacy and Effectiveness: An Exploration of Social Mechanisms." In *Evaluating Transnational NGOs: Legitimacy, Accountability, Representation*, edited by Jens Steffek and Kristina Hahn, 74–99. New York: Palgrave Macmillan.

Beisheim, Marianne, Andrea Liese, Thomas Risse, and Cornelia Ulbert. 2005. *Erfolgsbedingungen transnationaler Public Private Partnerships in den Bereichen Umwelt,*

Gesundheit und Soziales. Antrag zum Projekt D1 im Sonderforschungsbereich 700 "Governance in Räumen begrenzter Staatlichkeit". Berlin: unpublished grant application.

Börzel, Tanja, and Thomas Risse. 2002. "Die Wirkung internationaler Institutionen. Von der Normanerkennung zur Normachtung." In *Regieren in internationalen Institutionen*, edited by Markus Jachtenfuchs and Michèle Knodt, 141–81. Opladen: Leske + Budrich.

——. 2005. "Private-Public Partnerships: Effective and Legitimate Tools of International Governance?" In *Complex Sovereignty: Reconstituting Political Authority in the Twenty-First Century*, edited by Edgar Grande and Louis W. Pauly, 195–216. Toronto: University of Toronto Press.

Brühl, Tanja. 2007. "Partnerships: Unlike Partners? Assessing New Forms of Regulation." In *Globalization: State of the Art and Perspectives*, edited by Stefan A. Schirm, 143–61. London: Routledge.

Bull, Benedicte, Morten Bøås, and Desmond McNeill. 2004. "Private Sector Influence in the Multilateral System: A Changing Structure of World Governance?" *Global Governance* 10, no. 4:481–98.

Campe, Sabine. 2008a. "Complex Problems, Easy Failures: Why Transnational Water PPP Move to the Next Phase." Paper presented at the Forty-Ninth Annual ISA Conference, San Francisco, March 26–29.

——. 2008b. "The Global Network for Energy for Sustainable Development (GNESD): PPP Mapping (as of 13 January 2008)." Berlin: SFB 700, unpublished manuscript.

Chayes, Abram, and Antonia Handler Chayes. 1993. "On Compliance." *International Organization* 47, no. 2:175–205.

Chayes, Abram, Antonia Handler Chayes, and Ronald B. Mitchell. 1998. *Managing Compliance: A Comparative Perspective*. Cambridge, Mass.: MIT Press.

Checkel, Jeffrey 2001. "Why Comply? Social Learning and European Identity Change." *International Organization* 55, no. 3:553–88.

Dahl, Robert A. 1994. "A Democratic Dilemma: System Effectiveness Versus Citizen Participation." *Political Science Quarterly* 109, no. 1:23–34.

DeRuisseau, Douglas. 2002. "Social Auditing: An Auditor's Perspective." In *Globalisierung und Sozialstandards*, edited by Andreas Georg Scherer, Karl-Herrmann Blickle, Daniel Dietzfelbinger, and Gerhard Hütter, 223–33. Munich: Hampp.

Dirks, Jan, Andrea Liese, and Eva Senghaas-Knobloch. 2002. "International Regulation of Work in the Era of Globalization: Policy Changes of the International Labour Organization (ILO) in the Perspective of Organizational Learning." Artec working paper 94, Research Centre Work—Environment—Technology, Bremen.

Downs, George W., David A. Rocke, and Peter Barsoom. 1996. "Is the Good News About Compliance Good News about Cooperation?" *International Organization* 50, no. 3:379–406.

Easton, David. 1965. *A Systems Analysis of Political Life*. New York: Wiley.

4-C Secretariat. 2004. "Common Code for the Coffee Community." Accessed Nov. 25, 2010. www.4c-coffeeassociation.org/en/verification.

Global Fund. 2007. "Partners in Impact: Results Report." www.theglobalfund.org/documents/publications/progressreports/ProgressReport2007_en.pdf.

———. 2009. "Scaling Up for Impact: Results Report." www.theglobalfund.org/documents/publications/progressreports/ProgressReport2008_en.pdf.

———. 2010. "Innovation and Impact." www.theglobalfund.org/documents/replenishment/2010/Global_Fund_2010_Innovation_and_Impact_en.pdf.

Guhar-Sapir, Debarati. 2005. "What Have We Learned? Capacity Building for Health Responses in Disasters." *Prehospital and Disaster Medicine* 20, no. 6:480–82.

Hamm, Brigitte. 2004. *Evaluation des Multistakeholderprozesses des Common Code for the Coffee Community aus zivilgesellschaftlicher Sicht.* Duisburg: INEF.

Hemmati, Minnu, Felix Dodds, Jasmin Enayati, and Jan McHarry. 2002. *Multi-Stakeholder Processes for Governance and Sustainability: Beyond Deadlock and Conflict,* London: Earthscan Publications.

Hurd, Ian. 1999. "Legitimacy and Authority in International Politics." *International Organization* 53, no. 2:379–408.

Ingraham, Patricia W., and Laurence E. Lynn Jr. 2004. *The Art of Governance: Analyzing Management and Administration.* Washington, D.C.: Georgetown University Press.

Kaan, Christopher. 2007a. "Common Code for the Coffee Community: PPP Mapping (as of November 26, 2007)." Berlin: SFB 700, unpublished manuscript.

———. 2007b. "Global Code on Ethics in Tourism: PPP Mapping (as of November 23, 2007)." Berlin: SFB 700, unpublished manuscript.

———. 2008a. "Social Accountability 8000: PPP Mapping (as of May 7, 2008)." Berlin: SFB 700, unpublished manuscript.

———. 2008b. "United Nations Global Compact: PPP Mapping (as of January 7, 2008)." Berlin: SFB 700, unpublished manuscript.

Keohane, Robert O., and Joseph S. Nye. 2001. "The Club Model of Multilateral Cooperation and Problems of Democratic Legitimacy." In *Efficiency, Equity, and Legitimacy: The Multilateral Trading System at the Millennium,* edited by Roger B. Porter, Pierre Sauvé, Arvind Subramanian, and Americo Beviglia Zampetti, 264–94. Washington, D.C.: Brookings Institution Press.

Koh, Harold H. 1997. "Why Do Nations Obey International Law?" *Yale Law Journal* 106, no. 8:2599–2659.

Linder, Stephen D., and Pauline Vaillancourt Rosenau. 2000. "Mapping the Terrain of the Policy Partnership." In *Policy Partnerships,* edited by Pauline Vaillancourt Rosenau, 1–18. Cambridge, Mass.: MIT Press.

Martens, Jens. 2007. "Multistakeholder Partnerships. Future Models of Multilateralism?" FES Occasional Paper 29, Friedrich Ebert Stiftung, Berlin.

Mayntz, Renate. 1983. *Implementation politischer Programme II. Ansätze zur Theoriebildung.* Opladen: Westdeutscher Verlag.

McKinsey&Company. 2003. "Assessing the Global Compact's Impact." www.unglobalcompact.org/docs/news_events/9.1_news_archives/2004_06_09/imp_ass.pdf.

Mohaupt, Franziska, Katharina Schmitt, and Christian Hochfeld. 2005. "Global

Compact—Global Impact? Stand und Perspektiven der Initiative der Vereinten Nationen." Öko Institut e.V. www.oeko.de/publikationen/dok/883.php?id=&do kid=275&anzeige=det&ITitel1=&IAutor1=Mohaupt&ISchlagw1=&sortieren=& dokid=275.

Nelson, Jane. 2002. "Building Partnerships: Cooperation between the United Nations System and the Private Sector." Report commissioned by the United Nations Global Compact Office, United Nations, New York.

Nelson, Jane, and Simon Zadek. 2000. *The Partnership Alchemy: New Social Partnerships in Europe*. Copenhagen: The Copenhagen Centre.

OECD-DAC. 2006. "The Challenge of Capacity Development: Working Towards Good Practice." Accessed Nov. 25, 2010. www.oecd.org/dataoecd/4/36/36326495 .pdf.

Posner, Daniel N. 2004. "Civil Society and the Reconstruction of Failed States." In *When States Fail: Causes and Consequences*, edited by Robert I. Rotberg, 237–55. Princeton: Princeton University Press.

Randeria, Shalini. 2007. "The State of Globalization: Legal Pluralities, Overlapping Sovereignties, and Ambiguous Alliances Between Civil Society and the Cunning State in India." *Theory, Culture, and Society* 24, no. 1:1–33.

Raustiala, Kal, and Anne-Marie Slaughter. 2002. "International Law, International Relations, and Compliance." In *Handbook of International Relations*, edited by Walter Carlsnaes, Thomas Risse, and Beth A. Simmons, 538–58. London: Sage.

Reinicke, Wolfgang H., Francis Deng, Jan Martin Witte, Thorsten Benner, Beth Whitaker, and John Gershman. 2000. *Critical Choices: The United Nations, Networks, and the Future of Global Governance*. Ottawa: International Development Research Centre.

Richter, Judith. 2003. "'We the Peoples' or 'We the Corporations'?" Geneva: IBFAN-GIFA. www.gifa.org/files/wearethepeople.pdf.

Risse, Thomas. 2000. "'Let's argue!' Communicative Action in World Politics." *International Organization* 54, no. 1:1–39.

Risse, Thomas, and Ursula Lehmkuhl. 2006. "Governance in Areas of Limited Statehood—New Modes of Governance?" SFB 700 Working Paper Series, Berlin.

Risse, Thomas, and Kathryn Sikkink. 1999. "The Socialization of International Human Rights Norms Into Domestic Practices: Introduction." In *The Power of Human Rights: International Norms and Domestic Change*, edited by Thomas Risse, Stephen Ropp, and Kathryn Sikkink, 1–38. Cambridge: Cambridge University Press.

Ruggie, John Gerard. 2001. "Global_governance.net: The Global Compact as a Learning Network." *Global Governance* 7, no. 4:371–78.

Schäferhoff, Marco. 2008a. "The Children's Vaccine Initiative (CVI): PPP Mapping (as of January 12, 2008)." Berlin: SFB 700, unpublished manuscript.

——. 2008b. "GAVI Alliance (formerly Global Alliance for Vaccines and Immunization): PPP Mapping (as of January 8, 2008)." Berlin: SFB 700, unpublished manuscript.

——. 2008c. "International AIDS Vaccine Initiative (IAVI): PPP Mapping (as of 13 January 2008)." Berlin: SFB 700, unpublished manuscript.

——. 2008d. "Organizational Dysfunctions and the Effectiveness of Transnational Partnerships." Paper presented at the Annual Convention of the International Studies Association, San Francisco, March 26–29.

——. 2009. "Global Health Partnerships and the Challenge of Limited Statehood—How Much State Is Enough?" Paper presented at the Fifth ECPR General Conference, September 10–12, Potsdam.

Schäferhoff, Marco, Sabine Campe, and Christopher Kaan. 2009. "Transnational Partnerships in International Relations: Making Sense of Concepts, Research Frameworks, and Results." *International Studies Review* 11, no. 3:451–74.

Scharpf, Fritz W. 1999. *Governing in Europe: Effective and Democratic?* Oxford: Oxford University Press.

Siebenhüner, Bernd. 2003. *International Organisations as Learning Agents in the Emerging System of Global Governance.* Potsdam, Berlin, and Oldenburg: The Global Governance Project.

Tesner, Sandrine (with George Kell). 2000. *The United Nations and Business: A Partnership Recovered.* New York: MacMillan.

Ulbert, Cornelia. 2008. "The Effectiveness of Global Health Partnerships: What Determines Their Success or Failure?" Paper presented at the Forty-ninth Annual ISA Conference, San Francisco, March 26–29.

Ulbert, Cornelia, and Thomas Risse. 2005. "Deliberately Changing the Discourse: What Does Make Arguing Effective?" *Acta Politica* 40, no. 3:351–69.

Vaillancourt Rosenau, Pauline. 2000. "The Strength and Weaknesses of Policy Partnerships." In *Policy Partnerships*, edited by Pauline Vaillancourt Rosenau, 217–42. Cambridge, Mass.: MIT Press.

Witte, Jan Martin, Charlotte Streck, and Thorsten Benner. 2003. "The Road from Johannesburg: What Future for Partnerships in Global Environmental Governance?" In *Progress or Peril? Partnerships and Networks in Global Environmental Governance: The Post-Johannesburg Agenda*, edited by Jan Martin Witte, Charlotte Streck, and Thorsten Benner, 59–84. Washington, D.C.: Global Public Policy Institute.

Young, Oran R. 1992. "The Effectiveness of International Institutions: Hard Cases and Critical Variables." In *Governance Without Government: Order and Change in World Politics*, edited by James N. Rosenau and Ernst-Otto Czempiel, 160–95. Cambridge: Cambridge University Press.

——. 1994. *International Governance: Protecting the Environment in a Stateless Society.* Ithaca, N.Y.: Cornell University Press.

——, ed. 1999. *The Effectiveness of International Environmental Regimes: Causal Connections and Behavioral Mechanisms.* Cambridge, Mass.: MIT Press.

Zammit, Ann. 2003. *Development at Risk: Rethinking UN-Business Partnerships.* Geneva: The South Centre and UNRISD.

Zürn, Michael. 2004. "Global Governance and Legitimacy Problems." *Government and Opposition* 39, no. 2:260–87.

6

Racing to the Top?

Regulatory Competition Among Firms

in Areas of Limited Statehood

Tanja A. Börzel, Adrienne Héritier,

Nicole Kranz, and Christian Thauer

CONVENTIONAL WISDOM HOLDS THAT ECONOMIC internationalization leads to a regulatory race to the bottom among countries.[1] Global competition induces firms to invest in countries that minimize regulations, taxes, and other issues affecting the costs of production. Likewise, firms will press governments of highly regulated countries to lower regulatory standards in order to avoid competitive disadvantages (Bhagwati and Hudec 1996; Murphy 2000; Lofdahl 2002). However, there are numerous instances in which we find corporate behavior revealing just the opposite: imposing strict self-regulatory standards and even pressing governments to issue stricter public regulations (Vogel and Kagan 2004; Flanagan 2006; Mol 2001). Why would firms operating in a similar market engage in regulatory race to the top and voluntarily subject themselves to costly regulatory requirements or demand governments to issue stricter regulations? The governance literature has identified the threat of state legislation as a key incentive for firms to engage in self-regulation (cf. Mayntz and Scharpf 1995; Scharpf 1997; Héritier and Lehmkuhl 2008). Yet, areas of limited statehood lack by definition the capacity to cast such a credible "shadow of hierarchy" because governments are not capable, and often not willing, to set legislation and to enforce it, respectively (Risse in this volume; cf. Börzel and Risse 2010).

In this chapter, we explore under which conditions firms seek higher rather than lower regulatory standards despite weak regulatory capacities of the state, either by engaging in self-regulation or by exerting pressure on governments to tighten regulation.

Drawing from insights of rational choice institutionalism and bargaining theory, we put forward a number of hypotheses specifying conditions under which we expect firms to seek higher levels of self-regulation or public regulation in countries with weak regulatory capacities. We argue that firms may engage in a regulatory race to the top (1) if the quality of the brand-name product they market benefits from observing strict regulatory provisions; (2) if they have an economic advantage by seeing strict regulatory conditions imposed on foreign competitors; (3) if they are under pressure from nongovernmental organizations' campaigns that may damage their reputation; and finally, (4) if they are under regulatory pressure from their country of origin.

We conduct an empirical plausibility probe of our hypotheses by analyzing the behavior of firms in South Africa. More specifically, we will explore when and how firms in the automobile, food and beverage, and textile sectors engage in a regulatory race to the top in environmental regulation.

Racing to the Bottom or Racing to the Top?

While nonstate actors have gained prominence in research on global governance, companies have received little attention. The bulk of the literature has concentrated on the role of civil society organizations (Reinicke 1998; Clark et al. 1998; Fox and Brown 1998; Waterman 2001). There are studies, which have explored the rise of "private authority," exploring the opportunities and constraints of private self-regulation (Cutler et al. 1999; Ronit and Schneider 2000; Hall and Bierstecker 2002; Bohle 2008). Yet, the impact of companies on governmental regulation is still contested. In an increasingly globalized economy, companies are assumed to escape strict national regulation by relocating their production sites to areas of limited statehood where regulation is low and enforcement is weak. While countries with high levels of regulation will respond by lowering their standards, countries with weak regulatory capacities are prevented from tightening regulation in order not to threaten direct foreign investments. Thus, the behavior of firms drives states into a "race to the bottom," leading to the degradation of natural resources and the compromising of social standards for the sake of potential economic growth or the attraction of short-term foreign investment.[2] On a more general level, transnational corporations are found to systematically undermine the regulatory capacities of states resulting in the "retreat" (Strange 1996) or even the "end" (Ohmae 1995) of the state as the main provider of governance functions (cf. Ruggie 1998).

However, avoiding strict governmental regulation is only one form of a firms' behavior. Companies can also be "drawn into playing public roles to compensate for governance gaps and governance failures at global and national levels" (Ruggie 2004, 13). Empirical evidence abounds on companies, which voluntarily commit themselves to social and environmental standards and adopt private self-regulatory regimes—even in the absence of a regulatory threat by the state.[3] Thus, some studies no longer doubt that companies can contribute to the provision of public goods and services, but rather ask "under what circumstances and to what extent companies can be expected to provide regulatory governance functions in the public interest" (Wolf et al. 2007, 295).

Why Firms Compete for Regulation

Why should we expect companies to engage in regulation and thereby perform governance functions? Unlike states and civil society actors, firms are not committed to the public good but pursue private interests. We argue that under certain conditions private for-profit actors are inclined to actively engage in the fostering of regulation. The governance literature posits that the shadow of hierarchy cast by the state is a key incentive in this respect. In order to avoid state regulation, firms may choose voluntarily to commit themselves to reaching a regulatory outcome closer to their preferences. Moreover, the possibility of state intervention reduces the incentive to renege on a voluntary commitment (cf. Mayntz and Scharpf 1995; Scharpf 1997; Héritier and Lehmkuhl 2008).

Yet, if the shadow of hierarchy is a key premise for the regulatory engagement of firms, this results in a dilemma, if not a paradox, for regulators in areas of limited statehood. Failed and failing states are not only too weak to credibly threaten companies with regulatory intervention; often they do not even provide sufficient stability to allow for collective self-organization of market actors. Nevertheless, we do find corporate regulatory engagement in areas of limited statehood. Multinational companies police local communities, voluntarily implement environmental protection standards, provide HIV/AIDS-related services, or agree to use sustainable energy (Deitelhoff and Wolf 2010; Flohr et al. 2010). In some instances, they even seek to foster state regulation by pressuring for stricter legislation and helping to strengthen the enforcement capacity of state actors (Vogel and Kagan 2004; Flanagan 2006; Mol 2001). How can we explain these findings?

Strategic choice and bargaining approaches allow us to derive a series of hypotheses on when firms are likely to engage in strict self-regulation or press governments to issue public regulation in states, which are too weak to credibly enact or enforce legislation. These approaches assume that competing firms that operate in the same reference market prefer no regulation over weak regulation over strict regulation.[4] However, under certain conditions, the situational preferences of firms favor strict self-regulation if the imposed regulatory standards enhance the market value of the product offered. Under these circumstances firms have an incentive to increase the strictness of their self-regulation to augment the product quality and increase their prospects of successfully marketing this product (Ammenberg and Hjelm 2003; Anton et al. 2004; Parker 2002). By engaging in product competition with other firms targeting the same market, firms may trigger off a regulatory race to the top: once a firm starts engaging in self-regulation, increasing the quality of its products, competitors will have strong incentives to follow suit for fear of losing market shares.[5]

Firms interact in the context of specific environmental conditions, which pose additional demands to be taken into account when calculating the costs and benefits of their regulatory choices (Brousseau and Fares 2000; Wolf, Deitelhoff, and Engert 2007, 299–300). In our case, the relevant environmental conditions that we consider of particular importance are (1) the existence or absence of NGO campaigns affecting firms' attitudes toward an increase in regulatory stringency, and (2) the existence of strict public regulation in the country of origin of a firm.

Conducting a systematic variation of either environmental conditions or actors' preferences, we predict particular outcomes as regards firms engaging in self-regulation or pressing for public regulation. We argue that the causal mechanism linking environmental conditions to outcomes is a process of economic incentives and implicit bargaining among the concerned actors. Actors instrumentally learn from competing actors and thereby increase their benefit. If they do not instrumentally learn from their competitors, they lose out in markets. It reflects a bargaining situation in which the choice of actors will determine the allocation of some values, and in that the outcome of each participant is a function of the behavior of the other actors (Young 1975, 3).

A distributive power-based bargaining approach allows us to conceptualize the second underlying causal mechanism linking the explanatory factors to the outcomes. The relevant actors engage in an implicit bargaining process (Sebenius 1992), in which, depending on their relative power, they are able to influence the distribution of the surplus of the bargaining process in their favor. The relative power of the involved actors derives from their time horizon, the institutional rules governing the bargaining process—such as the sequence of actions and the preexisting regulatory provisions—as well as actors' resources (Faure and Rubin 1993).

Given these assumptions and the underlying bargaining models, we employ a strategic choice approach. We begin by varying actors' preferences— that is, the preferences of firms—and holding environmental conditions constant.

The first important factor that may prompt a willingness to engage in a regulatory race to the top is a firm's brand name and high-market orientation. If a firm blatantly neglected regulatory standards to protect the environment and public health in its productive activities, it would lose business and the marketing prospects of its products would deteriorate as compared to other firms observing these standards (Haufler 2001b; Mol 2001, 97–100; Blanton and Blanton 2007). Moreover, obvious violations of social or environmental standards may result in public shaming and consumer boycotting. Thus, reputational incentives may account for firms' strict self-regulation or pressing governments to issue strict regulatory standards.

1. Brand-name firms targeting the same high-end market are more likely— *ceteris paribus*—to engage in a regulatory race to the top than non-brand-name firms not targeting a high-end market ("brand-name/high-end market hypothesis").

We further assume the existence of an incumbent firm with high regulatory standards that is faced with a foreign competitor with low regulatory standards targeting the domestic market. In this situation, the established firm will seek to press its government to issue strict regulation binding for both the established firm and new market entrants. By imposing strict regulation upon foreign competitors, the home firm will improve its commercial position in the home market, maintain its competitive advantage, and even manage to force out its opponents (Rugman, Soloway, and Kirton 1999; Garcia-Johnson 2000; Porter and van der Linde 1995; Kolk, van Tulder, and Welters 1999). To successfully negotiate such measures, the established firm has to be able to credibly threaten its government, for example, by menacing to leave (cf. Hönke et al. 2008).

2. If an established firm is faced with a strong foreign competitor adhering to low regulatory standards, it will—*ceteris paribus*—press its government for stricter regulation of goods targeting the home market ("keeping-competitors-out hypothesis").

We systematically vary political environmental conditions while holding firms' preferences (competing firms that operate in the same reference market prefer no regulation over weak regulation over strict regulation) constant. Our first environmental factor of interest is the existence or nonexistence of an NGO campaign that puts firms under pressure to engage in self-regulation. The reputation of a company and the loyalty of its clients constitute a key corporate asset (Spar and LaMure 2003). Firms that are targeted by NGO campaigns that condemn their process of production and product quality risk reputational costs, consumer boycotts, loss of market shares, falling stock prices, and criticism by their shareholders (Waygood 2006; Hendry 2006; Wheeler 2001). Thus, they will seek to meet this criticism by adopting self-regulatory standards that alleviate the negative external effects of their mode of production (Schepers 2006; Trullen and Stevenson 2006; Hoffmann 2001; Halfteck 2008).

3. If firms are subject to strong NGO campaigns, they are—*ceteris paribus*—more likely to engage in strict self-regulation ("NGO campaign hypothesis")

The strictness of regulation in a firm's country of origin may be crucial in accounting for its willingness to subject itself to strict self-regulation. International firms tend to transport their regulatory standards abroad if investing in foreign countries (Murphy 2000; Skjaerseth and Skodvin 2003; Hall and Soskice 2001; Xing and Kolstad 2002). If these regulatory standards—often a result of complying with national regulatory requirements—are applied in foreign countries, these firms will contribute to an increase in regulatory standards in the country of investment.

4. A firm that originates in a country with strict regulation is more likely to seek strict regulatory standards in the foreign country of investment and, therefore, exert pressure for higher regulatory standards ("home country regulation hypothesis").

Fostering Regulation? Corporate Engagement in South Africa

A fostering of regulation has occurred when regulatory standards and procedural prescriptions improve: new substantive or procedural rules are introduced or tightened with regard to their precision, obligation, and substantive scope. Additionally, corporate engagement may help improve the implementation of these measures by contributing material, human, or knowledge resources and providing for monitoring and sanctioning devices of implementation. The fostering of regulation by companies can take two forms. First, firms voluntarily commit themselves to introducing regulation that goes beyond public regulation in the host country. Whether firms pursue private self-regulation unilaterally, within a business association, or through multistakeholder initiatives and public-private partnerships is an interesting question. Explaining the particular patterns of private self-regulation is, however, beyond the scope of this chapter (cf. Hönke et al. 2008; Müller-Debus et al. 2009). Second, firms can seek stricter (enforcement of) public regulation in the host country. Their involvement in fostering public regulation may be the result of successful lobbying, consultations by, and negotiations with state actors in tripartite or multistakeholder arrangements. Again, explaining the form of corporate engagement lies outside the scope of this chapter. Both private self-regulation and public regulation can entail (tighter) standards on the quality of products (e.g., food or textiles) or on the production process (e.g., environmentally friendly means of production).[6]

Our four hypotheses specify various conditions under which we may expect companies to enter a regulatory race to the top pushing for stricter public regulation and engaging in private self-regulation, respectively. In order to explore their explanatory power, we focus on corporate engagement in regulatory governance in South Africa. South Africa is a newly industrializing country whose legal standards are fairly well developed in most policy areas, while the administrative capacity for implementing regulations and securing compliance is rather weak. If companies foster regulation in South Africa, their impact should be even bigger in developing countries whose regulatory capacities are much more limited. We will analyze the regulatory behavior of several companies in the automotive, food and beverage, and textile sectors. These three manufacturing sectors comprise a significant number of foreign as well as local companies that cater to different market segments within South Africa and that are exposed to varying pressure from NGOs and foreign competitors. Choosing different firms of these sectors as cases allows us to systematically assess our hypotheses.

The chapter focuses on environmental product and process regulation. Over the past years, South Africa has enacted comprehensive legislation on the protection of several environmental goods, including water, biodiversity, and recently also air. While legal requirements are demanding, details pertaining to the specific behavior of firms are often not specified. Moreover, overlapping responsibilities of several government departments persist, which leads to regulatory confusion, contradictions, and implementation gaps. Most importantly, the implementation of regulations is in many cases deficient since local state agencies often lack the capacity and willingness to effectively monitor and sanction corporate malpractice. Compliance with environmental standards tends to entail significant costs, which firms are reluctant to bear. The next section will identify factors that provide incentives for firms to foster (self-) regulation despite the costs involved.

Protecting the Brand Name in High-End Markets

Our first hypothesis expects brand-name companies to voluntarily introduce new product and process standards and tighten existing ones if self-regulation increases the market value of their products. This particularly holds for companies that operate in high-end markets where product prices are above average, consumer controls are tight, and companies perceive each other as competitors in the same reference market. A comparison within the automotive and the food retail sectors helps us empirically assess whether brand-name firms targeting high-end markets are more likely to compete as regards tightening regulation of products and production processes. On the side of our explanatory factors, we vary brand-name high-end market firms with non-brand-name low-end market firms by scrutinizing the aspects of product price, customer control, and perceived competitors. In order to assess the outcomes—that is, the strictness of firms' self-regulation—we evaluate the degree of obligation of self regulation, the degree of precision, the degree to which a regulation is demanding and the scope of the regulation applied by firms. In addition, we take into account the resources allocated for the implementation of the regulation. Policies may either be developed in-house or delegated to third-party certification schemes.

FOOD RETAIL SECTOR

The food retailing sector in South Africa allows us to explore the extent to which high-end brand-name companies are likely to engage in a regulatory race to the top.

In this sector we compare food retailers that cater to different market segments, ranging from comparably high-priced market segments to those catering to the mass market. At the same time, we also compare companies with a strong brand to those with less established brands. We expect that companies catering to high-priced markets and therefore having a clear interest to protect their brand-names will also engage in higher self-regulation in terms of environmental standards. By contrast, firms catering to lower price segments will pay considerably less attention to regulating environmental impacts.

Woolworths is a food retailer that mostly caters to the high-priced market segment, which amounts to about 5 to 10 percent of the South African households. In recent years, the growing black middle class, who constitutes up to 40 percent of the consumer base, has become more and more important. Woolworths has been able to achieve a premium for its products by paying higher attention to product quality and production standards; responding to an emerging demand from consumers, it has introduced self-regulation on organic food as well as ethical retail in general. In the absence of any South African legislation in this area, Woolworths is clearly viewed as the forerunner in this segment.

In order to assure the quality of its products, Woolworths employs a variety of self-regulatory measures along the food value chain, regarding the products themselves as well as packaging and transport. For example, the company has developed packaging that is easy to recycle, avoids genetically modified organisms, and decreases water usage during production. Like its other self-regulatory activities, packaging is audited against the standard set by the Global Reporting Initiative (GRI). The regulatory targets require the company to continually work with its suppliers on maintaining product quality and closely monitors adherence to internally set standards. Woolworths introduced an organic product labeling scheme in order to communicate product qualities to customers. Their organic food is strictly governed by international organic standards and independent certifying bodies. Next to enhancing the quality of its products, Woolworths also seeks to reduce the carbon footprint of its production. This is to be achieved by cutting transport and relative electricity usage by up to 30 percent, making carbon-neutral sourcing decisions and helping with the setup of carbon-friendly production sites. For the voluntary tightening of both product and process-regulation, the company received the Responsible Retailer of the Year award in 2008. The company's market share grew by 25 percent in 2007.

The frontrunner strategy is likely to pay even more in the future since the sales of organic food is expected to rise significantly over the next three years, with a growth rate of up to 30 percent expected over the next five years. As a result, some of the larger competitors in the food retailing sector started to capitalize on the rising popularity of organic and ethically produced food both at the national and the global level. Pick&Pay is probably the closest follower and has increased the range of organic products on offer by 50 percent over the last years, which supports the company's overall commitment to social responsibility as part of their overall strategy. Shoprite as well as Massmart have also undertaken significant efforts to improve the environmental footprint of their products by working with their suppliers; still, their corporate engagement is less consistent and concerted than the self-regulation of Woolworths (Reichardt 2008). Also in the area of organic food, their activities are still rather limited. By contrast, companies catering to the 45 percent of South Africans, whose purchasing power is limited because they still live in more or less severe poverty, seek to capitalize on high sales volumes with relatively low margins rather than enhanced product quality. They impose comparably less stringent requirements on their suppliers. There also appears to be a difference between those retailers specializing in branded product versus those selling mostly bulk products, such as rice or maize (mealie).

In sum, the evidence from the South African food retail sector shows that brand-name food retailers engage in self-regulation to increase the market value of their products and that competing firms targeting the same type of market tend to follow suit. Among those companies targeting low-end markets, however, the tendency to self-regulation is much less developed.

AUTOMOTIVE INDUSTRY

The automotive sector of South Africa corroborates the importance of brand-name and high-end markets as major incentives to engage in self-regulation. The sector is dominated by seven international brands that operate production sites in South Africa: BMW, Ford, General Motors, Nissan-Renault, Mercedes Benz, Toyota, and VW. Generally speaking, two to three out of these seven brands—BMW, Mercedes Benz, and Toyota—are brands targeting a premium segment of the automotive market. Ford, General Motors, Nissan-Renault, VW, and Toyota produce cars for a middle-class mass segment. Toyota is in many ways an exception as its strategy is the most comprehensive of all automotive producers. The company strives for market dominance in all market segments and is thus listed as a mass and a premium segment producer.

To validate our claim, we compare two firms targeting a premium segment of the consumer market to a firm that focuses on the mass market with respect to average prices, consumer control, and perception of competitors in the same reference market. The difference in the target market is reflected in the fact that the firms aiming at the premium market sell their products at higher average prices than the one firm targeting a mass market (Kirmani et al. 1999). Managers of the two high-end-market firms stated that they rely less on economies of scale than other automotive firms and are able to add markups to end prices. The difference in the target market is further reflected in the importance of consumer control. The latter plays a more important role in the case of the two luxury brands, less so in the case of the mass-market firm. Especially as regards quality, the two high-end-market firms are faced with much higher consumer expectations than the mass-market firm. Hence, they are more vulnerable in this respect. Moreover, the high-end-market producers stated that they do not perceive themselves as competitors of the low-end-market firm. That is, they do not operate in the same consumer markets.

How do these differences in target markets impact upon the self-regulatory endeavors of the three firms? As expected, we find a variation in the extent of self-regulation of the three automotive producers. The differences, however, occur at a relatively high level of regulation: All three automotive manufacturers apply high levels of self-regulation as regards strictness of rules and the resources allocated to implement these rules. All three firms operate ISO 14001 and ISO 9001 certificated management systems. These systems come to bear within a firm *and* within the supply chain. All three producers request both kinds of management systems from their first-tier suppliers: ISO 14001 is an environmental management system; ISO 9001 is a quality management system with environmental components. The two certification schemes demand high-level standards, such as independent legal compliance audits and certificates. Since South African environmental legislation is quite demanding as regards formal provisions (even though implementation is not satisfactory) this means that the environmental policies of the three manufacturers are quite strict. Moreover, the implementation of self-regulation is subject to an auditing process and systematic control. Noncompliance is sanctioned by noncertification. In other words, the certification schemes not only provide for monitoring, but also for enforcement.

Beyond these similarities in the application of ISO-certified management systems, there are also some differences in the self-regulation of the three firms. The high-end-market producers operate, in addition to the ISO management systems, particularly strict and demanding in-house environmental and quality management systems. These systems are company-specific and prescribed by their global headquarters. As regards the degree to which rules are demanding, their scope and strictness, they go beyond both the standards of the ISO management systems and of South African legislation. In fact, these specific in-house systems require full compliance with all relevant European environmental process and product regulation, and go even beyond European legislation. The mass producer, in addition to the ISO-certified systems, also provides its own in-house policies. These policies are, however, less strict when compared to the premium producers. Moreover, the mass producer's practice focuses almost exclusively on quality standards, rather than requiring more stringent environmental self-regulation.

In sum, the self-regulatory standards of the mass producer are less demanding than those of the premium producers. This difference, however, only exists with respect to in-house self-regulation. Self-regulation with respect to the supply chain is very similar in all three firms: all automotive manufacturers only require ISO-certified management systems from their first-tier suppliers.

One possible explanation for this finding partially disconfirming our first hypothesis is that a similar and standardized approach in the supply chain guarantees "vertical compatibility" (Farrell 2007, 378). It reduces the degree to which large automotive buyer firms are dependent on specific suppliers, thereby reducing the risk of becoming victims of "hold ups" and excessive rent-seeking behavior in their relationship with suppliers (Héritier et al. 2009; Farrell 2007).

Keeping Competitors Out

While our attention so far has focused on corporate commitment to self-regulation, our second hypothesis focuses on firms pressing governments to regulate. We claim that companies that are faced with a strong foreign competitor adhering to only low regulatory standards will pressure their governments to tighten regulation.

The South African automotive sector provides a good testing ground for the extent to which such companies indeed seek to level the playing field by lobbying for stricter public regulation. We compare an automotive firm faced with an attempt at market entry by a low-regulating foreign competitor with firms that are not confronted with such an attempt. We identify a low-regulating foreign competitor by examining the level of regulation it has to comply with in the country of origin, and the implementation of these requirements. Attempts at market entry are specified as holding sales contracts with a South African car dealer and the perception of established South African firms that a low-regulating competitor strives for market entry. We assess whether our expectation holds by identifying the lobbying activities of car manufacturers within the national association. More specifically, we investigate who initiates and drives the lobbying activities within the association and whether a fostering of governmental regulation results from these activities.

The South African car-sales market is dominated by the same seven large brands that also hold prominent positions on OECD markets (see previous section). While South Africa is a high-price, high-quality car market comparable to Europe, Japan, and North America, the uneven income distribution, high rates of unemployment, mass poverty, and a relatively small middle-class population result in a mismatch between demand and supply. Car manufacturers from low-regulating countries, such as China, India, and South America, producing low-price cars increasingly seek to enter the South African market and to satisfy the South African demand for cheap cars. Chinese automakers Chery and Brilliance signed contracts with South African car dealers to gain access to the South African market. The foreign offer of cheap cars poses a significant threat to South African mass producers, such as Ford, General Motors, Nissan-Renault, and VW; it will make it much more difficult for them to sell their relatively costly cars to the average South African consumer. The premium segment (BMW and Mercedes Benz), by contrast, would not be affected since the new competitors do not target the same high-end market. Toyota constitutes a special case since it is the only company that strives for dominance in all market segments—middle class, premium and, long term, also in the Third World segment.

According to our "keeping competitors out" hypothesis, we expect the South African car producers focusing on the mass market to lobby the government for stricter regulation that effectively raises the bar for market entry of emerging-economies car producers. By contrast, the premium-segment producers and Toyota should refrain from such lobbying activities.

Our empirical evidence shows that, indeed, the National Association of Automobile Manufacturers of South Africa (NAAMSA) is actively lobbying the South African government to issue stricter emissions regulations for newly registered vehicles. These lobbying activities have been quite successful so far. In response to pressure from NAAMSA, the South African government raised emissions standards to the EURO 3 norm emissions control level. In addition, it announced that it would raise the standard to the EURO 4 level within the next two years. These stricter regulatory requirements have the effect of keeping the competitors from China, India, and South America out of the South African market since their cars observe only lower emissions standards and cannot be easily upgraded.

Additional confirming evidence for our hypothesis is offered by the fact that the "Fuel and Emissions Committee" of NAAMSA is chaired by one of the mass producers; vice chairs are held by representatives of two other mass producers. In fact, all six car firms that were interviewed stated that three out of the four mass producers were, and still are, driving the lobbying activities. In contrast, the premium producers as well as Toyota and the fourth mass producer have refrained from engaging in the issue.

In short, our evidence shows that all firms, with the exception of one mass producer, participate in the lobbying activities. This exception may arise from the fact that this producer sells one product line in South Africa that does not comply with the shortly to be imposed emissions norm. One of this producer's product lines would thereby become illegal. The other South African car producers, by contrast, all comply with the highest international standards, not surprising, since large parts of their production are exported to the high-regulating markets of the European Union, Australia, New Zealand, Japan, and the United States. They are therefore complying with emissions standards of these export markets, which are above the existing South African standards. As a result, their interest in stricter regulation is much more pronounced.

NGO Campaigns

The protection of a brand-name targeting a high-end market provides an important incentive for companies to engage in self-regulation. Another factor inducing a firm to engage in self-regulation is being exposed to public criticism by an NGO campaign.

TEXTILES

To empirically assess our NGO pressure hypothesis, we first compare two firms within the textile sector. One has been subject to an NGO campaign, the other has not. Both firms, SF and TP,[7] are lower-tier suppliers to big South African and international brands. SF produces specialized Nylon products (yarns, fabrics, and tapes). The other textile firm, TP, is selling finished and unfinished fabrics. As the production processes of both firms involve toxic chemicals and excessive energy consumption, their effluent waste and other emissions in particular have a potential negative environmental impact. Both companies have become the object of increased inspections and stricter environmental regulations over the past years, as the province of the Western Cape and especially the municipality of Cape Town have upgraded their environmental regulatory capacities. What sets both companies apart, however, is that SF has been constantly targeted over the past years by local, grassroots NGO protests concerning its environmental performance, while TP has not drawn the attention of NGO activists. The NGO campaigns exposing SF were predominantly organized by the local population, that is, local property owners and concerned citizens, who pointed to the air pollution and the effluents of SF as a health and environmental hazard and a factor impinging upon the value of their properties. The protests and petitions of these grassroots civil society organizations put pressure on local government to take up the issue with SF. Responding to public pressure, the company founded the Bellville South Environmental Forum. This forum developed into a council within which local residents and civic organizations negotiated with SF the step-by-step reduction of its pollution. The most pressing problems were tackled and targets for the reduction of the pollution were decided upon.

SF has developed and implemented environmental measures that are much more ambitious and detailed than those of TP. It has focused on the most critical areas of emissions reduction and effluent waste management. Thus, in the past, SF was burning coal for its energy supply and thereby contributed significantly to local air pollution. In the meantime they have systematically reduced the on-site burning of coal by changing their overall energy supply system. Similar improvements were achieved as regards the reduction of effluents. In the past, effluents were simply released into the environment. Today, SF collects its effluents and treats them until they meet the legally prescribed wastewater standards. Moreover, the company has implemented an environmental management system and started the ISO 14000 certification process. The certification process is expected to be completed within the next two years.

TP has also developed various environmental measures over the past years. It has mainly focused on energy consumption reduction; for example, it has replaced regular electric bulbs for energy-efficient neon-bulbs and introduced a switching-off-lights-and-machines policy after work. Yet, TP has not yet tackled the problems related to their biggest pollution, their highly polluting toxic effluents. According to the environmental manager, this does not appear be a priority for the top management. TP is not planning to acquire an ISO 14000 environmental certification. As a consequence, with respect to the effluents, "most of it just ends up in the sea, so we kill all our whales."[8]

In short, the empirical evidence confirms the "NGO campaign" hypothesis. As expected, the company targeted by NGO campaigns, SF, has introduced much stricter environmental measures than the company not targeted by such campaigns. The community forum established together with the local NGOs significantly contributed to the deploying of these measures.

FOOD AND BEVERAGE

Assessing the hypothesis within the food and beverage industry sector points to some important qualifications of our NGO hypothesis. We selected two firms from the South African sugar industry. Tongaat Hulett and Illovo Sugar are diversified companies with a focus on agribusiness, who dominate the South African market and also maintain operations in several other countries. Both operate out of the Durban area in KwaZulu-Natal. The sugar production can be differentiated in the growing process and the milling process, both with their own very specific environmental impacts. We focus in this case study on the industrial refining process.

Tongaat Hulett and Illovo Sugar operate sugar mills in the South Durban Industrial Area. They are under extensive scrutiny by the South Durban Community Environmental Alliance (SDCEA), as sugar mining next to oil refining and paper milling constitutes the main source of pollution in this region (Alstine 2007). The SDCEA is a community-based NGO with local reach and composition. In the past, the NGO together with other local citizen groups has criticized effluents from these operations as contaminating water resources as well as impacting local air quality through the use of coal for energy generation. Both firms have responded to this intense pressure. Illovo announced the launch of a program to curb their sulfur dioxide emissions from coal-burning activities. Tongaat, in turn, established a consultative process, in which they invite affected citizens, NGOs as well as relevant government departments, to engage in an open dialogue about their environmental impact. The multistakeholder forum brings together community and government representatives in sixth-month intervals to discuss issues, such as monitoring and reporting on operations' spills. Yet, the newly established municipal air-quality monitoring systems demonstrates that there has been no reduction in air pollution. Moreover, Illovo withdrew from plans to switch to other energy sources. Since the environmental measures taken by the two firms are clearly insufficient, SDCEA and other NGOs have resumed their protests.

The findings on the sugar sector point to an important qualification to the impact of NGO campaigns in the environmental field. While NGO campaigns might result in some immediate action by corporate actors, the measures taken might be unsustainable or result in a situation where some concessions are made, but which do not result in any fundamental improvements. One problem revealed by our case study may be that NGO campaigns do not always single out one polluter, but direct their campaigns against several firms, which reduces their leverage. Also, the local government addressing the problem has followed a coordinative approach toward polluters, which has further diminished the leverage of NGO campaigns. All in all, NGOs have not been able to summon sufficient pressure to overcome the strategic decisions of the two sugar mills to use cheap coal for energy generation. And even if they did, Illovo and Tongaat appear to have a viable exit option since they could move their production to less stringently regulated African countries, like, for example, Zambia and Malawi.

Country of Origin

Our last hypothesis argues that multinational companies subject to strict regulation in their country of origin tend to comply with these standards in their host country, too, even if the latter requires less stringent regulation. Using the same organizational production setup as in the country of origin helps save transaction costs. Thereby, these firms contribute to a strengthening of regulation in their host country. We expect companies that have their headquarters in high-regulating countries to introduce or tighten their product and process-related standards and pressure the government of their host country to raise its regulations accordingly.

AUTOMOTIVE INDUSTRY

In the automotive sector, we compare three lower-tier automotive supplier firms. They produce automotive parts and are neither one of the seven big international brands that dominate the South African car market nor direct suppliers for them. Instead, lower-tier suppliers deliver indirectly to these brands by supplying the direct suppliers. One of the lower-tier automotive suppliers selected for comparison is a company with headquarters in Germany, who, therefore, comes from a country with particularly strict legislation and implementation concerning environmental and quality standards. The company produces filter textiles and directly supplies catalytic converter producers in South Africa, which, in turn, supply several of the big Western brands dominating the South African car market. By contrast, the country of origin of the two other lower-tier suppliers is South Africa, where enforcement capacities are weak. One of these South African lower-tier suppliers manufactures textile filters and (like the German producer) supplies the South African catalytic converter industry. The other one produces specialized nylon yarns for the South African tire industry. We expect that the lower-tier suppliers originating in South Africa will be engaged in less self-regulation than the lower-tier supplier originating in Germany.

The lower-tier supplier with a home base in Germany, a high-regulating country, indeed has stricter quality and environmental controls than the South African suppliers. The German-based supplier is ISO 14001 and ISO 9001 certified and demands its suppliers to achieve ISO 14001 and ISO 9001 environmental and quality management certification. The two lower-tier suppliers originating in South Africa also have implemented some in-house environmental management systems. For example, the nylon yarn producer engaged itself in a local multistakeholder initiative in which emissions reduction measures are discussed and negotiated with local stakeholders. Because of this commitment, the company has implemented some substantial environmental policies. However, it so far failed to pass ISO 14001 certification. The textile filter producer originating in South Africa has achieved ISO 14001 certification. Most importantly, however, both South African suppliers—contrary to the German-based supplier—do not demand any environmental standards from their suppliers and do also not require ISO 9001 quality management certification from them. Indeed, both South African suppliers reported to observe only weak standards and even no standards at all in their respective supply chains.

FOOD AND BEVERAGE

In the food and beverage sector, we compare large multinational food and beverage companies—Unilever, Nestlé, Coca-Cola, Cadbury, and SAB Miller—that originate from or are listed in countries with high regulatory standards with large well-known South African food companies Pioneer Foods, Premium Foods, and Clover Danone. We would expect the first group to engage in stricter environmental self-regulation while the South African firms should apply lower standards.

In terms of supply-chain management, those companies originating from or listed in highly regulating countries take a much more proactive approach in terms of controlling the environmental impacts of their own operations as well as their suppliers. Coca-Cola and Cadbury are looking into using management systems developed for addressing the environmental impact of sugar production, one of their main ingredients. Similarly, SAB Miller and Nestlé are promoting environmentally friendly farming practices among their suppliers. Furthermore, they mandate their suppliers to adopt either an internationally accepted or in-house environmental management program. While these efforts might not be comprehensive, multinationals clearly deal more openly with supply-chain issues and seek to exert their influence than South African companies. The companies surveyed, while adherent to the complex South African food regulations, are less proactive in this respect. Clover Danone constitutes an exception, but it aims for international markets and thus shows a strong inclination to engage in strict self-regulation, which is then also expanded to the supply chain to some extent.

Unlike in the automobile industry, we have also found evidence on multinationals lobbying the South African government for stricter environmental standards. Coca-Cola and SAB Miller actively participated in the consultative process leading up to the new waste management act. Seeking to promote their own international best practice in terms of bottle recycling, their lobbying efforts went well beyond the activities of the respective industry associations.

The food and beverage sector by and large supports our last hypothesis. However, the internationalization of standards among multinationals and the export orientation of local firms might be more important as a driver for fostering regulation than the regulatory standards imposed by the home country.

Conclusions

Why would firms foster regulation in areas where the state is too weak to set and enforce social and environmental standards? This chapter identified factors that motivate firms to subject themselves to costly self-regulatory regimes or to demand stricter regulation from governments in the absence of a state with sufficient regulatory capacity to cast at least a credible shadow of hierarchy. Reputational costs and benefits linked to the protection of a brand name and yielded by the higher market value of products, respectively, as well as external pressures by foreign competitors and their country of origin may induce firms to engage in (self-) regulation. Moreover, we argue that the voluntary adoption of stricter product and process regulation may induce competing firms operating in the same market to follow suit. The example of the South African automotive producers shows that a regulatory race to the top may not only emerge among (international) brands competing in the same premium segment of a market; a self-regulatory race to the top with respect to supply-chain regulation may also occur across market segments if a standardization yields positive coordination effects among buyers. Such "spill-over" effects are all the more important in a country like South Africa, where capitalizing on the premium segment of retail markets is severely limited by mass poverty, high unemployment, and a small middle class. However, fostering regulation by firms in low-price markets can also have adverse effects. The South African association of automobile manufactures (NAAMSA) successfully lobbied the South African government to issue stricter environmental regulation to keep low-regulating competitors from China, India, and South America and their very cheap cars out of the market. The "California effect" (Vogel and Kagan 2004) may also work in areas of limited statehood—if countries have reached a certain level of socioeconomic development. After all, South Africa as well as its major competitors belong to newly industrializing countries. At the same time, this example illustrates the hidden politics behind standardization processes. On the one hand, enhanced standards improve the environmental performance of South Africa. On the other hand, this establishes obstacles to free trade and a price barrier for the South African poor masses for their access to mobility.

Beside economic incentives, firms are induced to engage in a regulatory race to the top if they are subject to (a threat of) public legislation. The "shadow of hierarchy" tends to be weak in areas of limited statehood where governments are often not capable or willing to credibly threaten regulation. Yet, the example of the South African textile sector shows that NGO campaigns do not only cause reputational damage. They can also yield pressure on (local) governments to take legal action. The shadow of hierarchy, however, is weakened, as in the case of the South African sugar industry, where (transnational) firms may have an exit option and can divert their commercial activities to areas where regulatory pressures by NGOs and governments are weaker. Such race-to-the-bottom dynamics can be countered by an "external shadow of hierarchy" (Börzel 2007) cast on transnational companies by the strict regulation in their country of origin. It may also affect local firms seeking to export their products to foreign markets subject to stricter regulation (Hönke et al. 2008).

In sum, firms do engage in a regulatory race to the top, even in areas of limited statehood. To what extent their performance of governance functions is sustainable and, hence, may compensate for weak or nonexisting public regulation, remains an open question. The approach developed here, however, avoids a normative bias in this respect. From the outset, it grasps standardization as a process of "implicit bargaining" and is therefore compatible with, and interested in, the hidden politics, conflicts, and potentially adverse effects of corporate self-regulation. Our findings suggest furthermore that economic incentives alone are not sufficient to ensure the fostering of regulation by firms. Somewhat paradoxically, corporate self-regulation may require a shadow of hierarchy to be effective (cf. Börzel 2008; Héritier and Lehmkuhl 2008).

NOTES

1. We thank Lisa Thormälen for her excellent research assistance. We are also grateful to Jana Hönke, Anna Müller-Debus, and Thomas Risse for their helpful comments on previous versions of this chapter.

2. Cf. Chan and Ross 2003; Brühl et al. 2001; Kaufmann and Segura-Ubiergo 2001; Lofdahl 2002; Rudra 2002; Xing and Kolstad 2002; Andonova et al. 2007.

3. Hall and Bierstecker 2002; Haufler 2001a; Ronit and Schneider 2000; Espach 2006; Neumayer and de Soysa 2005.

4. We further assume that the preferences of governments in the country of investment with weak regulatory capacity favor weak regulation over strict regulation. Governments of the countries of origin, in contrast, prefer strict regulation over weak or no regulation. So do NGOs, which seek to pressure both firms and governments toward stricter standards.

5. This is a modification of the argument about "competitive diffusion" developed by Simmons, Dobbin and Garett that the authors apply to governmental policies (Simmons et al. 2006, 793). Cf. Vogel 1995; Potoski and Prakash 2005.

6. The following is based on extensive field research in South Africa. For documentation of interview materials and other sources see Hönke et al. 2008; Thauer 2010; Hönke 2010; Kranz 2010; Müller-Debus 2010.

7. Both firms made strict confidentiality a precondition for their agreement to interviews. Hence, the companies will be called SF and TP.

8. TP 2007. Interview with Corporate Manager, Cape Town, April 2, 2007.

REFERENCES

Alstine, James van. 2007. "Institutions for the Environmental Governance of Multinational Corporations: The SAPREF Oil Refinery in Durban, South Africa." Paper presented at the Amsterdam Conference on the Human Dimensions of Global Environmental Change, Amsterdam, May 24–26.

Ammenberg, Jonas, and Olof Hjelm. 2003. "Tracing Business and Environmental Effects of Environmental Management Systems—a Study of Networking Small- and Medium-sized Enterprises Using a Joint Environmental Management System." *Business Strategy and the Environment* 12, no. 3:163–74.

Andonova, Liliana B., Edward D. Mansfield, and Helen V. Milner. 2007. "International Trade and Environmental Policy in the Postcommunist World." *Comparative Political Studies* 40, no. 7:782–807.

Anton, Wilma Rose Q., George Deltas, and Madhu Khanna. 2004. "Incentives for Environmental Self-Regulation and Implications for Environmental Performance." *Journal of Environmental Economics and Management* 48, no. 1:632–54.

Bhagwati, Jagdish, and Robert Hudec. 1996. *Fair Trade and Harmonization: Prerequisites for Free Trade?* Cambridge, Mass.: MIT Press.

Blanton, Robert G., and Shannon Lindsey Blanton. 2007. "Human Rights and Trade: Beyond the 'Spotlight.'" *International Interactions* 33, no. 2:97–117.

Bohle, Dorothee. 2008. "Race to the Bottom? Transnational Companies and Reinforced Competition in the Enlarged European Union." In *Neoliberal European Governance and Beyond—the Contradictions and Limits of a Political Project*, edited by Bastiaan Van Apeldoorn, Jan Drahokoupil, and Laura Horn, 163–86. London: Palgrave.

Börzel, Tanja A. 2007. "Regieren ohne den Schatten der Hierarchie. Ein modernisierungstheoretischer Fehlschluss?" In *Regieren ohne Staat? Governance in Räumen begrenzter Staatlichkeit*, edited by Thomas Risse and Ursula Lehmkuhl, 41–63. Baden-Baden: Nomos.

——. 2008. "Der Schatten der Hierarchie—Ein Governance Paradox?" In *Governance in einer sich wandelnden Welt*, edited by Gunnar Folke Schuppert and Michael Zürn, 118–31. Wiesbaden: Politische Vierteljahresschrift.

Börzel, Tanja A., and Thomas Risse. 2010. "Governance Without a State—Can It Work?" *Regulation and Governance* 4, no. 2:1–22.

Brousseau, Eric, and M'hand Fares. 2000. "Incomplete Contracts and Governance Structures." In *Institutions, Contracts and Organizations: Perspectives From New Institutional Economics*, edited by Claude Ménard, 399–421. Cheltenham: Edward Elgar.

Brühl, Tanja, Tobias Debiel, Brigitte Hamm, Hartwig Hummel, and Jens Martens, eds. 2001. *Die Privatisierung der Weltpolitik. Entstaatlichung und Kommerzialisierung im Globalisierungsprozess*. Bonn: Dietz.

Chan, Anita, and Robert J. Ross. 2003. "Racing to the Bottom: Industrial Trade Without a Social Clause." *Third World Quarterly* 24, no. 6:1011–28.

Clark, Ann Marie, Elisabeth Friedman, and Kathryn Hochstetler. 1998. "The Sovereign Limits of Global Civil Society: A Comparison of NGO Participation in UN World Conferences on the Environment, Human Rights, and Women." *World Politics* 51, no. 1:1–35.

Cutler, Claire A., Virginia Haufler, and Tony Porter, eds. 1999. *Private Authority and International Affairs*. Albany: State University of New York.

Deitelhoff, Nicole, and Klaus-Dieter Wolf, eds. 2010. *Corporate Security Responsibility?* Basingstoke: Palgrave Macmillan.

Espach, Ralph. 2006. "When Is Sustainable Forest Sustainable? The Forest Stewardship Council in Argentina and Brazil." *Global Environmental Politics* 6, no. 2:55–84.

Farrell, Joseph. 2007. "Should Competition Policy Favour Compatibility?" In *Standards and Public Policy*, edited by Shane Greenstein and Victor Stango, 372–89. Cambridge: Cambridge University Press.

Faure, Guy Oliver, and Jeffrey Z. Rubin. 1993. "Organizing Concepts and Questions." In *International Environmental Negotiation*, edited by Gunnar Sjöstedt, 17–26. London: Sage.

Flanagan, Robert J. 2006. *Globalization and Labour Conditions*. Oxford: Oxford University Press.

Flohr, Annegret, Lothar Rieth, Sandra Schwindenhammer, and Klaus Dieter Wolf. 2010. *The Role of Business in Global Governance: Corporations as Norm-Entrepreneurs*. Basingstoke: Palgrave Macmillan.

Fox, Jonathan A., and David L. Brown. 1998. *The Struggle for Accountability: The World Bank. NGOs, and Grassroots Movements*. Cambridge, Mass.: MIT Press.

Garcia-Johnson, Ronnie. 2000. *Exporting Environmentalism*. Cambridge, Mass.: MIT Press.

Halfteck, Guy. 2008. "Legislative Threats." *Stanford Law Review* 61. Available at SSRN: http://ssrn.com/abstract=1113173.

Hall, Peter A., and David Soskice. 2001. *Varieties of Capitalism: The Institutional Foundations of Comparative Advantage*. Oxford: Oxford University Press.

Hall, Rodney Bruce, and Thomas J. Biersteker, eds. 2002. *The Emergence of Private Authority in Global Governance*. Cambridge: Cambridge University Press.

Haufler, Virginia. 2001a. "Globalization and Industry-Self-Regulation." In *Governance in a Global Economy*, edited by Miles Kahler and David Lake, 226–54. Princeton: Princeton University Press.

——. 2001b. *A Public Role for the Private Sector—Industry Self-Regulation in a Global Economy*. Washington, D.C.: Carnegie Endowment for International Peace.

Hendry, Jamie. 2006. "Taking Aim at Business." *Business and Society* 45, no. 1:47–86.

Héritier, Adrienne, and Dirk Lehmkuhl. 2008. "Introduction. The Shadow of Hierarchy and New Modes of Governance." *Journal of Public Policy* 38, no. 1:1–17.

Héritier, Adrienne, Anna Müller-Debus, and Christian Thauer. 2009. "The Firm as an Inspector: Private Ordering and Political Rules," *Business and Politics* 11, no. 4: article 2.

Hoffmann, Andrew. 2001. *From Heresy to Dogma: An Institutional History of Corporate Environmentalism*. Palo Alto, Calif.: Stanford University Press.

Hönke, Jana. 2010. "Liberal Discourse and Hybrid Practice in Transnational Security Governance: Companies in Congo and South Africa in the Nineteenth and Twenty-first Centuries." Ph.D. diss., Department of Political and Social Sciences, Freie Universität Berlin, Berlin.

Hönke, Jana, Nicole Kranz, Tanja A. Börzel, and Adrienne Héritier. 2008. "Fostering Environmental Regulation? Corporate Social Responsibility in Countries with Weak Regulatory Capacity. The Case of South Africa." SFB-Governance Working Paper Series No. 9. Berlin: Freie Universität Berlin.

Kaufmann, Robert R., and Alex Segura-Ubiergo. 2001. "Globalization, Domestic

Politics, and Social Spending in Latin America: A Time-Series Cross-Section Analysis, 1973–97." *World Politics* 53, no. 4:553–87.

Kirmani, Amna, Sanjay Sood, and Sheri Ridges. 1999. "The Ownership Effect in Consumer Responses to Brand Line Stretches." *Journal of Marketing* 63, no. 1:88–101.

Kolk, Ans, Rob van Tulder, and Carlijn Welters. 1999. "International Codes of Conduct and Corporate Social Responsibility: Can TNCs Regulate Themselves?" *Transnational Corporations* 8, no. 1:143–80.

Kranz, Nicole. 2010. "What Does It Take? Engaging Business in Addressing the Water Challenge in South Africa." Ph.D. diss., Department of Political and Social Sciences, Freie Universität Berlin.

Lofdahl, Corey L. 2002. *Environmental Impact of Globalization and Trade: A Systems Study*. Cambridge, Mass.: MIT Press.

Mayntz, Renate, and Fritz W. Scharpf. 1995. "Steuerung und Selbstorganisation in staatsnahen Sektoren." In *Gesellschaftliche Selbstregulierung und politische Steuerung*, edited by Renate Mayntz and Fritz W. Scharpf, 9–38, Frankfurt/Main: Campus.

Mol, Arthur P. J. 2001. *Globalization and Environmental Reforms: The Ecological Modernization of the Global Economy*. Cambridge, Mass.: MIT Press.

Müller-Debus, Anna. 2010. "Collective Action of Firms. Motivation, Facilitation, Social Engagement: A Comparative Analysis of Industry Behaviour in South Africa." Ph.D. diss., Department of Political and Social Sciences, Freie Universität Berlin, Berlin.

Müller-Debus, Anna, Christian Thauer, Jana Hönke, and Nicole Kranz. 2009. "Governing HIV/AIDS in South Africa. The Role of Firms." SFB-Governance Working Paper Series No. 20. Berlin: Freie Universität Berlin.

Murphy, Dale. 2000. *The Structure of Regulatory Competition: Corporations and Public Policies in a Global Economy*. Oxford: Oxford University Press.

Neumayer, Eric, and Indra de Soysa. 2005. "Trade Openness, Foreign Direct Investment, and Child Labour." *World Development* 33, no. 1:43–63.

Ohmae, Kenichi. 1995. *The End of the Nation State: The Rise of Regional Economies*. New York: Free Press.

Parker, Christine. 2002. *The Open Corporation: Effective Self-regulation and Democracy*. Cambridge: Cambridge University Press.

Porter, Michael, and Claas van der Linde. 1995. "Toward a New Conception of the Environment-Competitiveness Relationship." *Journal of Economic Perspectives* 9, no. 4:97–118.

Potoski, Matthew, and Aseem Prakash. 2005. "Green Clubs and Voluntary Governance: ISO 14001 and Firms' Regulatory Compliance." *American Journal of Political Science* 49, no. 2:235–48.

Reichardt, Markus. 2008. "Ethical Shopping: South Africa's Middle Class Goes Green." *Ethical Corporation*, June 9, 2008.

Reinicke, Wolfgang H. 1998. *Global Public Policy: Governing Without Government?* Washington, D.C.: Brookings Institute.

Ronit, Carsten, and Volker Schneider, eds. 2000. *Private Organizations in Global Politics*. London: Routledge.

Rudra, Nita. 2002. "Globalization and the Decline of the Welfare State in Less-Developed Countries." *International Organization* 56, no. 2:411–45.

Ruggie, John G. 1998. *Constructing the World Polity*. London: Routledge.

——. 2004. "How to Marry Civic Politics and Private Governance." In *The Impact of Global Corporations on Global Governance*, edited by Carnegie Council on Ethics and International Affairs, 10–15. New York: Carnegie Council on Ethics and International Affairs.

Rugman, Alan, Julie Soloway, and John Kirton. 1999. *Environmental Regulations and Corporate Strategy: A NAFTA Perspective*. Oxford: Oxford University Press.

Scharpf, Fritz W. 1997. *Games Real Actors Play: Actor-Centered Institutionalism in Policy Research*. Boulder, Colo.: Westview.

Schepers, Donald H. 2006. "The Impact of NGO Network Conflict on the Corporate Social Responsibility Strategies of Multinational Corporations." *Business and Society* 45, no. 3:282–99.

Sebenius, James K. 1992. "Challenging Conventional Explanations of International Cooperation: Negotiation Analysis and the Case of Epistemic Communities." *International Organization* 46, no. 1:323–65.

Simmons, Beth, Dobbin, Frank, and Geoffrey Garrett. 2006. "Introduction: The International Diffusion of Liberalism." *International Organization* 60, no. 4:781–810.

Skjaerseth, Jon Birger, and Tora Skodvin. 2003. *Climate Change and the Oil Industry: Common Problems, Varying Strategies*. Manchester: Manchester University Press.

Spar, Deborah L., and Lane T. LaMure. 2003. "The Power of Activism: Assessing the Impact of NGOs on Global Business." *California Management Review* 45:78–101.

Strange, Susan. 1996. *The Retreat of the State: The Diffusion of Power in the World Economy*. Cambridge: Cambridge University Press.

Thauer, Christian. 2010. "Corporate Social Responsibility in the Regulatory Void—Does the Promise Hold? Self-Regulation by Business in South Africa and China." Ph.D. diss., Social and Political Science Department, European University Institute, Florence.

Trullen, Jordi, and William B. Stevenson. 2006. "Strategy and Legitimacy: Pharmaceutical Companies' Reaction to the HIV Crisis." *Business and Society* 45, no. 2:178–210.

Vogel, David. 1995. *Trading Up: Consumer and Environmental Regulation in a Global Economy*. Cambridge, Mass.: Harvard University Press.

Vogel, David, and Robert Kagan, eds. 2004. *Dynamics of Regulatory Change: How Globalization Affects National Regulatory Policies*. Berkeley: University of California Press.

Waterman, Peter. 2001. *Globalization, Social Movements, and the New Internationalism*. London: Continuum.

Waygood, Steve. 2006. *Capital Market Campaigning: The Impact of NGOs on Companies, Shareholder Value, and Reputational Risk*. London: Risk Books.

Wheeler, David. 2001. "Racing to the Bottom? Foreign Investment and Air Pollution in Developing Countries." *Journal of Environment and Development* 10, no. 3:225–45.

Wolf, Klaus Dieter, Nicole Deitelhoff, and Stefan Engert. 2007. "Corporate Security Responsibility." *Cooperation and Conflict* 42, no. 3:294–320.

Xing, Yuqinq, and Charles Kolstad. 2002. "Do Lax Environmental Regulations Attract Foreign Investment?" *Environmental and Resource Economics* 21, no. 1:1–22.

Young, Oran R., ed. 1975. *Bargaining: Formal Theories of Negotiation*. Urbana-Champaign: University of Illinois Press.

7

Governance in Sovereign Debt Crises

Analyzing Creditor-Debtor Interactions

Henrik Enderlein, Laura von Daniels,

and Christoph Trebesch

M ANY DEVELOPING COUNTRIES RELY HEAVILY ON financial resources provided by private creditors. Consequently, in situations of financial distress, governments and private creditors often enter into a complex strategic interaction. This type of interaction takes place in an "area of limited statehood" in the sense that debtor governments show a limited ability to provide a crucial governance good: macroeconomic stability. Creditor-debtor negotiation fora thus serve as "functional equivalents" of sovereign macroeconomic management. Rather than crisis management by the government we find a specific and temporally limited form of public-private partnership (PPP).

Given the absence of an international regulatory organization or statutory regime to solve sovereign debt crises, the public-private partnership evolves in a context that lacks a "shadow of hierarchy." Instead, debt negotiations between sovereigns and foreign commercial banks and bondholders generally represent a type of nonhierarchical governance. The governance mode resembles an informal bargaining in which private and public actors are likely to have conflicting interests (cf. Risse 2008). For a public-private partnership to develop, both sides have to be interested in reaching financial stability, the key *governance good* to be provided.

From the perspective of governments, the key focus of this interaction is the provision of macroeconomic stability in the developing country under the constraint of servicing external debt. From the perspective of private creditors, the key focus is to limit losses from potential defaults. The resulting outcomes can take different forms: at one extreme, the private sector can be completely bailed out through official financing of a country's sovereign debt (e.g., through the IMF); at the other extreme, the private sector—as the "residual claimant"—can be forced to renegotiate its debt at a high cut in face value. In this chapter we explore how governments and private creditors engage in PPPs and what form such interactions take during different phases of a crisis.

To this date, this type of interaction is still insufficiently understood in the crisis literature and a stronger conceptual focus is needed to uncover its nature. For a long time, the debate on public-private coordination centered on the question of how much effort from the private sector was needed. After the Mexican crisis in 1995 was solved by a large official rescue package, leaders of the G7 countries initiated a new debate on the topic, pushing for greater "burden sharing" of private creditors. In this context, "private sector involvement" (PSI) became a policy buzzword even if its exact meaning remained blurred.

For a better understanding of PPP and the role of economic governance in areas of limited statehood, it is crucial to analyze patterns of behavior on both sides—the private and the public. In this chapter we therefore follow two main goals. The first is to describe archetypal crisis devolution and identify what instruments are generally employed during different phases. We find that governments by far play a more dominant role than creditors in shaping crisis resolution patterns and setting up PPP negotiation for a for crisis resolution. Given this finding, our second goal is to analyze the behavior of governments during crises systematically, in particular the role of governance institutions in for predicting. A key insight from our empirical analysis is that debtor governments with better governance institutions are more cooperative on average. This hints at a possible link between governance effectiveness and the patterns of crisis resolution. Good governance institutions go hand-in-hand with good creditor-debtor relations and improve the prospects for successful PPPs to resolve a crisis and provide macroeconomic stability in middle-income countries.

This chapter proceeds as follows: First, pursuing the objective to build a concept of PPP during financial crises, it reviews and critically evaluates the existing literature on the interaction between creditors and governments, particularly the recent contributions on PSI, which we see as a subtype of PPP. We propose a new, more functional concept and definition of PSI based on earlier approaches, developing them further. Next, we compare our approach to the empirical reality of crisis negotiations as perceived by financial, legal, and policy experts. The second part of the chapter takes a deeper look at the behavior of debtor governments on the brink of and during debt crises. We provide a unique new categorization of government policy choices, dubbed the "Index of Government Coerciveness," which was developed by our research team (Enderlein et al. 2010). We then use this data to provide new evidence on the role of governance in debt crisis resolution. We conclude with an agenda for future research on government-creditor bargaining processes during crises.

Creditor-Debtor Interactions in Sovereign Debt Crises

This section discusses creditor-debtor interactions in sovereign debt crises and provides a critical review of the related academic and political debate. As a starting point, we present the broad literature on creditor and investor behavior in financial distress episodes. We then turn to a number of more specific articles that explicitly focus on a key concept in the debate, namely that of "private sector involvement" (PSI) in crisis resolution. In a third step, we depart from the existing literature and propose a new timeline approach to public-private interactions in sovereign debt crises.

The Broad Literature on Private Creditor Behavior in Crises

The last decades have brought about a large body of research on financial crises in general and sovereign debt and default in particular.[1] Here, we provide a broad overview of the contributions analyzing the role of private sector behavior during distress episodes. This literature can be grouped into two categories: (1) literature related to the policy debate on a new international financial architecture, including studies on creditor moral hazard; (2) articles that analyze the determinants of capital flows during debt crises, including those on the catalytic effect of IMF lending.

LITERATURE ON REFORM PROPOSALS
FOR CRISIS RESOLUTION

Since the mid-1990s, a controversial debate has been taking place and many legal or institutional reform proposals have been floated.[2] A core issue in these discussions was how to mitigate adverse creditor behavior such as co-ordination failures, moral hazard, or a "rush to the exit" by investors facing a crisis. The policy debate was accompanied by a large analytical literature.

A series of authors have proposed theoretical models to evaluate the merits of competing policy proposals. Gai et al. (2004) analyze how different official sector interventions affect investors and the efficient prevention and resolution of crises. Their results and those of Morris and Shin (2004) underline the crucial role of proper information on fundamentals for private creditor behavior, that is, through public sector monitoring and surveillance efforts. Haldane et al. (2005) examine the welfare implications of competing policy proposals distinguishing between liquidity and solvency crises. Among other findings, they conclude that coordinated lending by private creditors is only a second-best solution for liquidity crises, while in solvency crises debt write-downs should be preferred to IMF bailouts. They also find that a statutory mechanism and third-party intervention is only necessary in case of serious coordination problems between the debtor and private creditors. For this reason—failed creditor coordination—Ghosal and Miller's (2004) analytical article argues in favor of a formal sovereign bankruptcy procedure. Related work has also focused on the role of collective action clauses (CACs) in sovereign bond contracts—a legal feature facilitating debt restructurings and limiting creditor coordination problems (Eichengreen and Mody 2004).

Further contributions have explicitly tested for creditor moral hazard during crisis episodes, mainly by examining the reaction of market participants to official bailout announcements. Most of these articles focus on the private sector's behavior after official bailout announcements. Lane and Phillips (2000) analyze the bond spread effect of news about the potential size of IMF emergency lending, but find little indication for moral hazard, except in the Russian crisis case. Based on a comparably large news sample, Haldane and Scheibe (2003) test the same by employing stock market data of major emerging market creditor banks, which, they conclude, provide some evidence of moral hazard. Zhang (1999) and Kamin (2004) focus on the Mexican crisis bailout in 1995 to test moral hazard, finding only weak evidence. However, an article by Dell'Ariccia et al. (2002) strongly criticizes relying on the Mexican case. In their much perceived event study, they focus on the Russian crisis instead, providing robust evidence for investor moral hazard.

LITERATURE ON PRIVATE CAPITAL FLOWS IN CRISIS EPISODES

Another body of research on the private sector's role in crises focuses on capital flows.[3] Capital movements, that is, the composition, size, and direction of private investment flows, are key factors for the success or failure of crisis resolution. If creditors "rush to the exit" in situations of financial distress, they are likely to make things worse. In contrast, fresh money inflows, such as the spontaneous lending during the Mexican crisis, can help to avoid serious adverse consequences of a crisis.

One crucial determinant of creditor actions during crises is the behavior of the IMF. The literature on catalytic finance has focused on this, examining if and how private capital flows toward distressed countries are influenced by official lending announcements (See Morris and Shin 2004 and Corsetti et al. 2006 for analytic models). Díaz-Cassou et al. (2006) provide a comprehensive review of the empirical literature and summarize the following main determinants of such catalytic flows: (1) the macroeconomic and political conditions in the crisis countries; (2) the kind of the IMF program (long versus short term, conditional versus unconditional); and (3) the program's total volume. Overall, the evidence suggests that the catalytic effect is large only in countries that have "intermediate" fundamentals and those that have not been hit excessively by the crisis (Eichengreen and Mody 2001; Mody and Saravia 2003). Bad performers appear to receive less catalytic flows (Bordo et al. 2004). Additionally, Eichengreen et al. (2006) and Díaz-Cassou et al. (2006) provide some evidence that programs for crisis prevention have a particularly positive effect on private flows.[4]

The second strand of literature that should be considered is articles on contagion, analyzing herd behavior of private creditors in withdrawing capital from crisis countries. A number of theoretical studies illustrated how rumors or unexpected changes in fundamentals can lead to such contagious behavior and the occurrence and spread of financial crises (see the overview in Pericoli and Sbracia 2003). Others, such as Goldstein et al. (2000) and Kaminsky et al. (2004), provide empirical evidence for contagion, showing that private creditors, such as international banks and mutual funds, play a crucial role in transmitting of crises. Regarding banks, both Heid et al. (2005) and Van Rijckeghem and Weder (2003) show clear evidence for contagion during the Russian crisis. Similarly, Gande and Parsley (2005) show for the bond market that a change in the sovereign credit rating of one crisis country can have a contagious effect on the credit spreads of other emerging markets (see also Eichengreen et al. 2001). As a general tendency, an interesting article by Mauro et al. (2002) finds that in recent times, investors appear to pay less attention to an individual country's characteristics than in earlier decades. Instead, today's investors appear to invest and divest in groups of countries simultaneously. Given the rich and convincing evidence on the topic, it seems quite obvious that contagion and herd behavior may have a considerable impact on the likelihood of private-public cooperation in debt crises.

The Specific PSI Literature

When referring to the "specific" PSI literature, we mean three quite distinct categories of articles, which have one thing in common: they explicitly refer to the debate on and the concept of PSI or bail-in. The first category comprises the many policy reports on PSI published by the official sector. The second contains a number of more analytical studies on the PSI debate published in academic journals. Finally, there are contributions that make efforts to define and categorize the concept of PSI.

POLICY REPORTS ON PSI: THE OFFICIAL SECTOR VIEW

PSI has been a "hot topic" in the international public debate since 1995 (Haldane 1999). Accordingly, over the years many reports and statements on PSI were published by different official players. Among the more important documents in this debate are the reports by the Group of 10 (Group of 10 1996), the Group of 22 (Group of 22 1998), the Group of 7 (Group of 7 2000), the contributions by the Bank of England and the Bank of Canada (Haldane and Kruger 2001), the many IMF reports on the issue (IMF 1999b; 2000; 2001; 2003) as well as the voices from the U.S. Treasury (Rubin 1998; Taylor 2002).

As Roubini and Setser (2004) pointed out: 7 PSI became the "accepted jargon" for a new policy followed by international organizations and Western governments to reduce official funding in crisis resolution by "binding-in" private investors, essentially by sharing crisis costs in a significant amount. With such a definition in mind, the political message behind the propagation of PSI is clear: creditors and investors rather than the general tax payer in the United States or Europe should "bear the consequences of their decisions as fully as possible" (U.S. Treasury Secretary Rubin in a speech on January 21, 1998). At this point, it seems important to emphasize that the official understanding of PSI as a policy goal remains rather unspecific. Hence, it differs from an understanding of PSI as a coherent theoretical concept of public-private partnerships as a governance mode in crises.

ANALYTICAL LITERATURE ON THE PSI DEBATE

Parallel to the policy debate, some authors have analyzed prospects of PSI from a more academic point of view. In essence, Eichengreen and Rühl (2001) argue that official announcements to forcefully bail-in the private sector are not credible and will thus not affect investor behavior. Tillmann (2005) and McBrady and Seasholes (2000) oppose this view. In their empirical contributions, they show that the market actually reacts to PSI policy announcements through changes in prices and risk perceptions. Quite different is the argument put forth by Lipworth and Nystedt (2001) who use a theoretical model to show that past experiences are generally not well suited to evaluate the future efficacy of PSI initiatives. The authors emphasize the role of forward looking adaptation of market participants.

Surprisingly, none of these more analytical articles clearly and explicitly defines PSI or bail-in—even though these terms are deliberately used and at the core of the research question. Apparently, given the lack of a clear-cut general consensus, the authors have implicitly adopted the official sector's "accepted jargon."

MORE FUNCTIONAL ATTEMPTS FOR A DEFINITION OF PSI

Only a few authors have proposed helpful attempts to define the concept of PSI. In an important contribution, William Cline (2004) classifies modes of PSI as a function of the degree of private creditor willingness to engage in crisis resolution. Cline takes a private creditor perspective, opposed to the earlier official sector view, and puts forth three main categories of PSI:

spontaneous, quasi-voluntary, and involuntary PSI. He then goes on and attributes a series of past crises and their resolution instruments to each of these categories.[5] As Leiderman emphasizes (2004), Cline's most valuable contribution is probably that he discusses a series of measurement issues and provides first rough estimates on the size of PSI in past crises.

In a similar vein, Roubini (2004, 101–2) categorizes PSI on a spectrum of voluntary and more involuntary types of private sector burden sharing. He states that defaults such as in Argentina, Russia, or Ecuador should be regarded as very coercive PSI, while cases with large bailouts (Mexico in 1995) or semivoluntary rollover agreements (Brazil in 1999, Turkey in 2001) were "softer" types of PSI. Similarly, Roubini and Setser (2004, 373) categorize PSI and ways to enforce private crisis financing into "voluntary and catalytic means," "semi coercive" steps, and "fully coercive" steps. In their view, PSI is essentially equal to the volume of debt that was rolled over or restructured (148). No further differentiation or discussion on measuring PSI is provided.

The focus on private sector efforts and financial burden sharing is also reflected in a comprehensive study by Thiemann et al. (2005, 6) at the European Central Bank (ECB) who define PSI as "the contributions or efforts of private sector creditors to the crisis resolution process." Note that as it stands, this definition is much more general than the earlier one. In their analysis, however, Thiemann et al. mainly limit private sector involvement to financial burden sharing.

A review of the policy debate on PSI shows that the term is not easy to define and actual crises are difficult to categorize. The official sector view of PSI as a "policy goal" is ill suited for systematic analysis and in a bulk of contributions and reports PSI remains a catch-all category, avoiding the politically delicate concrete specification of types of instruments or contributions that would count as private sector involvement or bail-in.

Cline (2004) and Roubini (2004) provide more specific categorizations. However, the categories proposed lack a clear systematic foundation. For example, Cline's dividing line between "voluntary" and "quasi-voluntary" remains blurry. His categories are built inductively, based on his own extensive knowledge and judgement of past debt crises. He does not offer objective criteria to distinguish and delimit the categories and subcategories he presents.

Summarizing, there is no convincing definition of PSI, nor an appropriate categorization of crisis cases. Also, there are only very few contributions that do provide a functional definition of "PSI" or "bail in." Most often, PSI or bail-in and burden sharing are simply used as a self-explanatory buzzword.

However, the concept is much less self-explanatory than it might seem at first. In fact the perspectives on, and the understanding of, PSI differ considerably between authors. It is remarkable that a standard publication in this field simply postulates that no consensus on the concept of private sector involvement and commitment in debt crises appears to exist (Roubini and Setser 2004, 140). Our first goal in this paper is thus to develop a more concise definition of PSI and its subcategories.

THE IDEAL-TYPE CRISIS: THREE PHASES OF PUBLIC PRIVATE INTERACTIONS

As was shown earlier, what the few existing attempts to define PSI have in common is that they conceptualize PSI as a variable that can be separated into several categories, degrees, or phases (Cline 2004; Ghosal and Miller 2004; Haldane et al. 2005; Roubini 2004; Roubini and Setser 2004). Although we share this view, our main point of critique of the respective approaches is that they remain implicit about what characterizes each phase. Building on the approach of Thiemann et al. (2005), we define PSI as any kind of intentional, informal, or formal forms of cooperation between debtor governments and the private sector starting at that point in time when a debt crisis becomes likely. However, whereas the ECB authors constrain the concept to financial costs on the creditor side, we go beyond this definition, including also the not directly measurable actions of preventing crises (such as informally agreeing to keep money in a distressed country).

In contrast to this literature we try to conceptualize crises as processes. We propose a new perspective on PSI as a form of private public interaction with the goal to resolve a crisis. Essentially, we portray how an "ideal type" of a crisis would look and categorize the related instruments used by public and private actors in the course of a crisis. Figure 7.1 presents our timeline approach including three phases of interactions: phase 1 entailing "preventive efforts," phase 2 "moderate losses," and phase 3 "significant losses."

The first phase of PSI in a debt crisis is mostly characterized by informal policy efforts. More specifically, we define phase 1 on the basis of (1) a presentiment of a debt crisis or default; (2) an intentional effort by the private sector to solve the distress situation; and (3) some kind of informal agreement between debtor and creditors to prevent a crisis. Phase 1 may include any promise of creditors to maintain credit lines or maintain the overall level

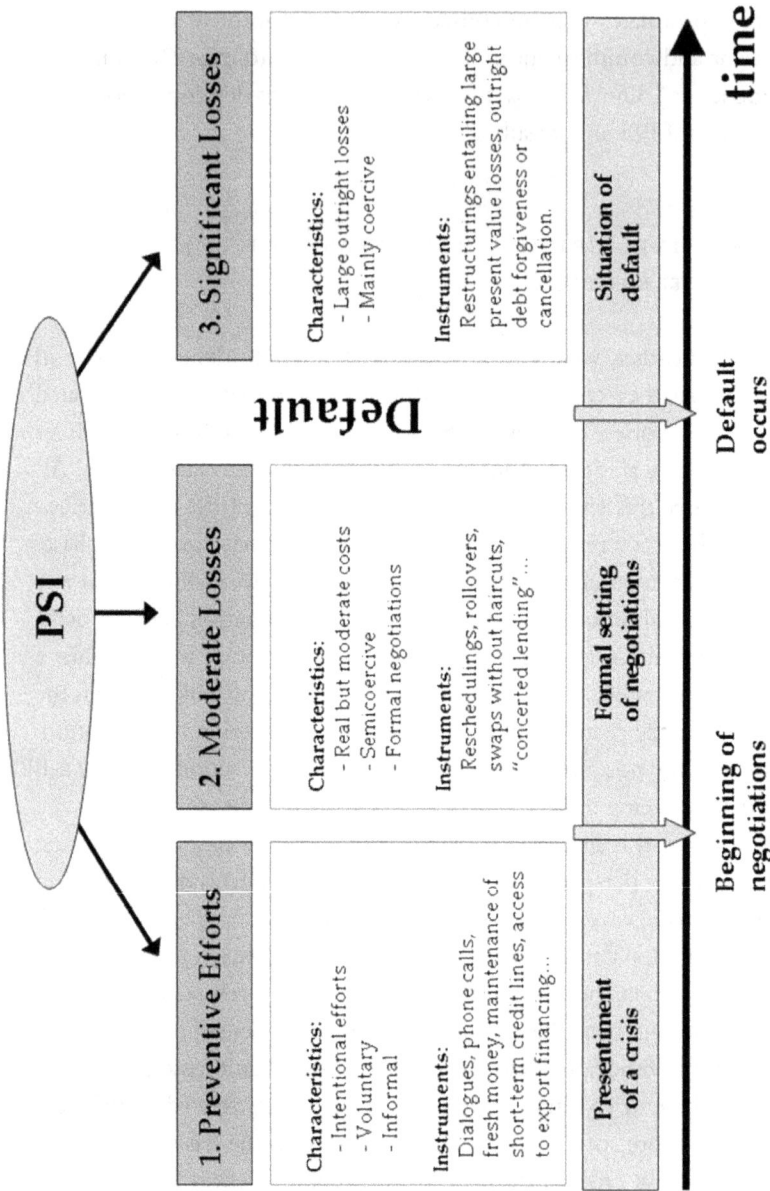

FIGURE 7.1. Timeline approach to private-sector involvement.

of capital inflows. It is important to note, however, that this includes only voluntary and intentional efforts. One type of "private sector preventive efforts" would be attentive calls by chief executives of foreign banks or financial intermediaries to finance ministries in EMEs. Another example would be the promise to increase or maintain export credits.

Phase 2 is characterized by a more formal negotiation setting between a sovereign and its creditors and involves classic policy measures to address a liquidity problem. More specifically, we define phase 2 on the basis of (1) a formal negotiations between a government and its creditors; and (2) the emergence of debt agreement entailing losses—beyond mere symbolic costs—for private creditors. In this phase, both sides realize that informal agreements are not sufficient and that further steps need to be taken to avoid a more severe crisis. While the interaction in phase 1 was largely informal, negotiations in phase 2 have an official character. One distinctive criterion to identify such formal negotiations is the existence of a written agreement signed by both sides. Crisis resolution instruments applied in this phase can be rollovers, debt standstills, or short- or medium-term debt rescheduling without a cut in face value. Overall, creditor losses in this second phase remain comparatively low.

We define phase 3 on the basis of (1) the presence of a context of "default" with all or part of the debt payments not being serviced any longer; (2) debt renegotiations aimed at substantially reducing the debt burden faced by the debtor government; and (3) a debt restructuring leading to significant present value losses for private creditors. The dividing line between phase 2 and phase 3 of crisis workouts is the degree of losses following default. Once the crisis has reached phase 3, private investors have to accept losses beyond rollovers or maturity extensions, which could be considered as opportunity costs.

The three phases—Preventive Efforts, Moderate Losses, Significant Losses—describe the theoretically distinct forms of "involvement" of the private sector in relation to debtor governments.

From Theory to Practice and Back: Evidence on Public-Private Partnerships in Crises

To find out if this scheme is consistent with the empirical reality we first chose to discuss it with financial market, legal, and policy experts in New

York and Washington, D.C., who had been actively involved in past debt workouts over the past thirty years. In a series of semistructured interviews we were trying to find out if our suggested "timeline approach" matched with the insights of former "architects" of major deals between debtor governments and their private creditors. The interviews largely supported our three phases and the efforts taken by both sides during each of the phases. At the same time, the discussions emphasized our initial impression that it is extremely difficult to track informal contributions by the private sector based on publicly available records of past crises.

Another insight from the interviews stands out. All experts agreed on the leading role of governments in debt crises and the power they have to either initiate public-private cooperation or to actively reject it. In other words, when it comes to interactions between private creditors and governments, the latter seem to be sitting in the driver's seat whereas the creditors tend to merely react to what they find. Even more notably, the majority of our interview partners come to the conclusion that there is considerable variance in government behavior toward creditors. We therefore decided to start by focusing on government behavior if we want to get a better understanding of creditor-government cooperation. The idea is to analyze the process of debt negotiations by concentrating on patterns of government behavior and, in the next step, to search for determinants for these patterns.

For this purpose we engaged in extensive case study research of all major debt restructuring episodes between governments and their private creditors since 1980. We base our analysis on more than 20,000 pages of secondary information from financial press archives, relevant academic contributions, and policy reports on past crises. The approach we chose for evaluating the debt negotiation process was to categorize government behavior and track particular types of actions in each of the crises episodes. We thus coded an "Index of Government Coerciveness," which measures the degree of aggressiveness in government actions in nine separate categories.

The index is based on but goes beyond the previous attempts to categorize debt crises (Cline 2004; Roubini 2004) and the criteria of "fair debt restructuring" and "good faith efforts" in crisis resolution outlined in key policy reports in the past decade (IIF 2006; IMF 1999a; 2002). Each of the nine subindicators of our "Index of Government Coerciveness" captures observable coercive actions that governments impose on their international creditors (banks and bondholders). The index consists of four criteria of payment behavior and five criteria of negotiation behavior.[6]

Overall, this approach yielded a large number of new insights and stylized facts on government actions (summarized in Enderlein et al. 2010). Government behavior and rhetoric show a large variability, ranging from very uncooperative to very smooth crisis resolution processes. In particular, we found serial patterns of coercive government behavior and conflict during crisis resolution. Countries with governments that adapted a conflictive stance in the 1980s debt crises also tended to show unilateral government behavior in restructurings of the 1990s and in more recent cases (e.g., Argentina or Peru). This finding confirms and extends the prominent concept of serial defaults proposed by Reinhart et al. (2003).

All in all, we found that debtor governments are the key actors in enabling PPPs in the context debt crises. If they chose to act unilaterally, for example by declaring a stop on external debt payments, little room remains for a constructive private sector involvement. The next question is why some governments adopt a cooperative attitude toward their international creditors, while others show a very aggressive stance. In the second part of this chapter we therefore go on to explain the difference between a conflict-riddled debt restructuring process such as Argentina (2001–2005), where the government refused to engage in negotiations, froze payments for four years, and enforced a fully unilateral debt restructuring deal, and a cooperative crisis resolution case such as Uruguay (2003), where the government was able to restructure its debt in only three months, in agreement with creditors and without missing any payments. With a view to the theme of this collected volume, the key focus here lays on the quality of governance.

The Role of Governance Institutions for Debt Crisis Resolution

In this section, we explore the particular role of governance institutions for crisis resolution. For this purpose, we rely on the widely used governance indicators provided by the World Bank's annual "Governance Matters" publication (Kaufmann et al. 2009). Their indicators provide a picture of six different aspects of governance including: (1) Voice and Accountability, (2) Political Stability and Absence of Violence, (3) Government Effectiveness, (4) Regulatory Quality, (5) Rule of Law, and (6) Control of Corruption. Based on this data, we provide a first tentative analysis of on the link between the quality of governance and the patterns of crisis resolution and macroeconomic stabilization in areas of limited statehood.

Hypotheses

Looking at the literature, it remains an open question if and how governance institutions affect crisis and crisis resolution processes (see Acemoglu et al. 2003; Du forthcoming; Van Rijckeghem and Weder 2009). To provide new insights and a new perspective on this question we present four working hypotheses and test them using our novel data on government behavior during debt crises.

Hypothesis 1: Weak regulatory quality and low government effectiveness lead to more coercive government behavior. Strong domestic regulatory bodies can be seen as guaranteeing the fulfillment of international debt contracts. And low governance effectiveness will translate into less effective crisis handling.

Hypothesis 2: States with a weak rule of law and high corruption are more likely to act coercively. If contracts are not abided at home, they are also likely to be less respected abroad.

Hypothesis 3: Stronger degrees of voice and accountability are related with more coercive external debt policies. States in which citizens have more voice are more likely to act aggressively.

Hypothesis 4: Less political stability and more violence in debtor countries increase the likelihood of aggressive government behavior toward international creditors. Political instability and violence inhibits economic policymaking and effective crisis resolution.

These hypotheses can be linked to a broader literature on the role of governance and institutions for economic policymaking in developing countries (Knack and Keefer 1995).

Data and Econometric Approach

In the analysis, the additive Index of Government Coerciveness is used as a dependent variable so that our sample comprises crisis countries only. Specifically, we use the agreement-based dataset described by Enderlein et al. (2010). The time frame is 1980 to 2005, a period for which we coded 103 individual debt restructurings in thirty-six developing countries. Each of these agreements has an individual index value indicating how many of the nine subindicators of coerciveness have been fulfilled during the restructuring process. In other words, the dependent variable captures the degree of coercive actions that governments impose on their foreign creditors in the negotiations preceding each agreement. The minimum index value is 1 (very cooperative debtor behavior) and the maximum is 10 (very coercive). Across all 103 cases, the average index value is 3.58. Interestingly, the standard deviation is quite high (2.01) underlining the large variability in debtor behavior across countries and time.

To test our hypotheses systematically, we use the governance indicators by Kaufman et al. as key explanatory variables. More specifically, we group the indicators as follows: Hypothesis 1 will be tested based on the indicators "Government Effectiveness" and "Regulatory Quality." Hypothesis 2 is tested using the "Rule of Law" and "Control of Corruption" indicators. Hypothesis 3 is based on the measure of "Voice and Accountability," while Hypothesis 4 is tested using the indicator on "Political Stability and Absence of Violence." Higher values for each of the indicators reflect a higher quality of governance.

The governance indicators were first released for the year 1996 and are available on an annual basis only since 2002. Given these constraints, we simply construct average values of each of the six indicators based on the available data from 1996 to 2005. The rationale for using these time-invariant average indicator values is that we are mostly interested in cross-country differences in governance levels. This will unveil general empirical regularities, while we explicitly disregard within-crisis dynamics. However, we do include year fixed effects to capture some of the variation in our dependent variable and to improve the preciseness of estimation.

Given the categorical character of our dependent variable (ranging from 1 to 10), we estimate an ordinal probit model. Ordinal probit models are a generalization of the simple two-outcome probit model. In a first step, we therefore regress our coerciveness index for each of the restructurings on the six governance indicators and a set of cutpoints.

Results

Table 7.1 presents the main results of our explorative analysis. We find strong evidence supporting hypothesis 1. Both variables (columns 1 and 2) have statistically significant coefficients and a negative sign, indicating that higher levels of government effectiveness and regulatory quality are associated with less coercive government behavior in crises. We also find indication that debtor countries with a better rule of law and less corruption show a more cooperative (less coercive) stance on average. This gives some support to hypothesis 2. In contrast, we find no significant effects with regard to "Voice and Accountability" and, surprisingly, no significant coefficient for the indicator "Political Stability and Violence."

One obvious concern with the results in table 7.1 is that we do not control for the level of economic development and the degree of debt distress of the sovereign. A country's per capita income and its level of indebtedness are likely to be crucial for crisis resolution. We therefore gather data for these two variables from the World Bank's World Development Indicators. More specifically, we use per capita GNI (gross national income) in PPP terms (purchasing power parity) and the share of total external debt to GNI and construct their average values for the years 1980 to 2005. As stated, we also include time dummies on an annual level.

Table 7.2 shows that our results hold with time-fixed effects and even when controlling for the level of indebtedness and economic development of countries. This gives some support to our findings mentioned earlier. Only the indicator on "Control of Corruption" turns borderline significant (at the 10% level only). Overall, we therefore find governance to matter, especially with regard to regulatory quality, the rule of law, and the state's capacity to implement effective policies.

A caveat is in order at this point: while we do unveil interesting correlations between our index and the set of governance indicators, the results should not be misinterpreted. We have not shown any causal effect nor have we identified specific mechanisms for our findings. In particular, it should be highlighted that the governance indicators are outcome variables and partly based on expert opinions. This raises the concern of reverse causality, as debtor governments that adopt a particularly aggressive stance toward Western creditors may also be perceived and evaluated as having lower levels of governance. Additionally, there might be measurement error. One explanation for the insignificant effect of "political instability and violence" could, for example, be that these factors have strong short-term effects, which are clouded by our use of time-variant explanatory variables. Further analysis, possibly on a year-by-year level, is needed to address some of these concerns.

TABLE 7.1 Results on Governance and Crisis Resolution (100 Restructurings)

	Government Effectiveness (coef/se)	Regulatory Quality (coef/se)	Rule of Law (coef/se)	Control of Corruption (coef/se)	Voice and Accountability (coef/se)	Political Stability and Violence (coef/se)
Government Effectiveness	−0.492** (0.210)					
Regulatory Quality		−0.380* (0.211)				
Rule of Law			−0.446** (0.193)			
Control of Corruption				−0.449** (0.199)		
Voice and Accountability					−0.301 (0.205)	
Political Stability and Absence of Violence						−0.196 (0.193)
/cut1	−1.082*** (0.171)	−1.133*** (0.170)	−1.014*** (0.173)	−1.037*** (0.168)	−1.143*** (0.170)	−1.038*** (0.176)
/cut2	−0.200 (0.152)	−0.261* (0.156)	−0.131 (0.158)	−0.150 (0.152)	−0.279* (0.155)	−0.180 (0.167)

TABLE 7.1 Results on Governance and Crisis Resolution (100 Restructurings) *(continued)*

	Government Effectiveness (coef/se)	Regulatory Quality (coef/se)	Rule of Law (coef/se)	Control of Corruption (coef/se)	Voice and Accountability (coef/se)	Political Stability and Violence (coef/se)
/cut3	0.116	0.051	0.187	0.170	0.031	0.128
	(0.149)	(0.149)	(0.157)	(0.151)	(0.154)	(0.167)
/cut4	0.588***	0.517***	0.658***	0.644***	0.491***	0.582***
	(0.164)	(0.158)	(0.173)	(0.174)	(0.163)	(0.180)
/cut5	0.918***	0.842***	0.987***	0.975***	0.815***	0.901***
	(0.169)	(0.161)	(0.183)	(0.190)	(0.161)	(0.184)
/cut6	1.372***	1.290***	1.439***	1.425***	1.266***	1.346***
	(0.201)	(0.196)	(0.205)	(0.219)	(0.194)	(0.205)
/cut7	1.748***	1.662***	1.820***	1.800***	1.639***	1.718***
	(0.189)	(0.185)	(0.181)	(0.195)	(0.187)	(0.186)
/cut8	1.987***	1.900***	2.066***	2.040***	1.878***	1.959***
	(0.264)	(0.257)	(0.270)	(0.279)	(0.253)	(0.264)
Number of observations	100	100	100	100	100	100

Results of ordered probit estimation. The dependent variable indicates the degree of government coerciveness related to each sovereign debt restructuring on a scale of 1 (very low coerciveness) to 10 (very high coerciveness). ***/**/* denote significance at a 1/5/10 percent level respectively. Country-clustered standard errors in parentheses.

	Government Effectiveness (coef/se)	Regulatory Quality (coef/se)	Rule of Law (coef/se)	Control of Corruption (coef/se)	Voice and Accountability (coef/se)	Political Stability and Violence (coef/se)
GDP per capita (in PPP)	10.801*	6.652	9.265	6.738	2.786	5.360
	(6.004)	(5.960)	(6.204)	(6.432)	(8.742)	(7.727)
	0.717	0.512	0.954	0.494	0.256	0.483
Ext. Debt / GDP	(1.070)	(1.076)	(1.111)	(1.102)	(1.124)	(1.161)
Year Fixed Effects	Yes	Yes	Yes	Yes	Yes	Yes
Government Effectiveness	−0.830***					
	(0.320)					
Regulatory Quality		−0.616**				
		(0.282)				
Rule of Law			−0.690**			
			(0.317)			
Control of Corruption				−0.570*		
				0.320		
Voice and Accountability					−0.300	
					(0.429)	
Political Stability and Absence of Violence						−0.422
						(0.366)
Number of observations	80	80	80	80	80	80

Results of ordered probit estimation. The dependent variable indicates the degree of government coerciveness related to each sovereign debt restructuring on a scale of 1 (very low coerciveness) to 10 (very high coerciveness). ***/**/* denote significance at a 1/5/10 percent level respectively. Debt/GNI and GDP p.c. are averaged for the period 1980–2005. Country-clustered standard errors in parentheses. Coefficients of cutpoints not reported.

Conclusions

Under extreme financing pressures debtor governments find themselves in a critical dilemma. On the one hand, a lack of macroeconomic governance capacities forces them to turn to their (private) creditors for financial assistance. On the other hand, they face increased domestic political pressures when they enter international debt negotiations. If their governance institutions are weak—they lack effectiveness and are characterized by low respect of the rule of law—governments tend to act more aggressively toward their international private creditors. Their lack of institutional capacities makes them less likely to implement important adjustment measures necessary to continue debt service.

In situations of debt distress we often find that creditor-debtor negotiation fora serve as "functional equivalents" to sovereign macroeconomic management. The PPP that develops, consisting of governments and their private creditors, is temporally limited to the crisis period. The chapter aimed to critically evaluate the chances of macroeconomic co-governance between governments and the private creditors during sovereign debt crises. What forms of creditor-debtor negotiations do appear and how do they evolve over time—that is, in the advent and during crises? A broad review of the literature on "private sector involvement" does not provide functional concepts on how to categorize debtor-creditor interactions and types of debt crises.

We therefore develop a more concise definition of PSI and put this concept to the empirical test. Expert interviews and a large number of case studies indicated that creditors generally are the reactive element in government-creditor relations: debtor governments set the agenda and terms of the negotiations. Consequently, we shift our focus on the behavior of governments in crisis resolution. We capture debtor policies with a newly developed Index of Government Coerciveness, explained in detail by Enderlein et al. (2010). Using this novel data, we analyze the role of governance institutions in managing crises and debt renegotiations. This provides interesting new insights on the role of governance institutions for crisis resolution. In particular, we find that higher levels of "Government Effectiveness," "Regulatory Quality," and a better "Rule of Law" are associated with a lower degree of government coerciveness vis-à-vis private foreign creditors. Further work is needed to identify the related mechanisms at play.

Looking forward, it may be promising to focus on the obstructive role of creditors in financial distress situation. As stated, we find little evidence for constructive, deliberate private sector efforts to resolve a crisis. However, there is increasing evidence that creditors hinder crisis management processes.

One example is the increasing incidence of holdout creditor and litigation cases, that is, creditors initiating legal actions against sovereign governments. "Runs" to the courthouse are an increasingly important instrument used by private creditors after debt restructurings and in the run-up to debt relief initiatives in the poorest countries. Litigation is the main fallback solution for private creditors not willing to accept a default on their claims or a debt exchange proposed by governments. It is also increasingly being used as a way to extract government resources directly, thus affecting government finances and the availability of public goods to the benefit of private commercial actors.

The provision of governance in areas of limited statehood is likely to be affected by these developments. What is the role of creditors in establishing and maintaining debtor-creditor negotiation fora as functional equivalents to sovereign macroeconomic governance? This constitutes an agenda for future research, as there is barely any empirical work on the causes and consequences of creditor litigation against developing country governments.

NOTES

1. See Eaton and Fernandez (1995) and Panizza et al. (2009) for reviews. The empirical research on debt crises has mainly focused on the determinants of default and the construction of early warning systems (see, for example, Manasse et al. 2003 or Detragiache and Spilimbergo 2001; on the predictive power of credit ratings see Reinhart 2002 or Sy 2004). Similarly, a large number of theoretical contributions have identified and discussed possible factors for the occurrence and characteristics of sovereign default. (See, for example, chapters 2 and 3 in Roubini and Setser [2004] for a good overview.)

2. In essence, proponents of a more "statutory approach" to crisis resolution—i.e., through the establishment of an international bankruptcy procedure for sovereigns—stood in opposition to advocates of a more market-based, case-by-case approach—i.e. through the introduction of collective action clauses in bond contracts. For a detailed discussion of the debate see Eichengreen (2003), Kenen (2002) or Roubini and Setser (2004).

3. Note that there is also a large literature on the general determinants of capital

flows to emerging markets, which is not directly related to crisis episodes. For a recent overview see Daude and Fratzscher (2006) or Alfaro et al. (2005).

4. Interestingly, bond issuance seems to respond more to IMF interventions than bank lending, which is attributed to the fact that the IMF's role as a "delegated monitor" is much more important in bond markets than for banks, which frequently have their own surveillance divisions (Eichengreen and Mody 2001 and Eichengreen et al. 2006).

5. The PSI instruments, in descending order of voluntariness and linked to past crises, are the following: Spontaneous lending (Mexico 1994–95), Foreign direct investment, Maintenance of bank credit lines (Brazil 1999), Medium-term conversion of bank credit lines (Korea 1998), London-club rescheduling (1980s debt crisis), London-club concerted lending/new money (1980s debt crisis), Bond exchange maintaining value (Pakistan 1999, Ukraine 2000, Argentina 2001), Brady bond debt reduction (1980s debt crises), Bond exchange and forgiveness (Russian GKOs, 1998, Ecuador 1999), Bonds rescheduled through collective action clauses, Officially approved Standstill (Ecuador 1999), Outward capital controls (Malaysia 1997–98), Default and Arrears (Latin America in the late 1980s, Indonesia 1998, Russia and Ecuador 1999, and Argentina 2002).

6. See Enderlein et al. (2010) for details. The subindicators are (1) payments missed; (2) unilateral payment suspension; (3) full payment suspension, including interest payments; (4) freeze on assets of nonresidents; (5) breakdown or refusal of negotiations; (6) explicit moratorium or default declaration; (7) explicit threats to repudiate on debt; (8) data disclosure problems and outright data related disputes; (9) forced and nonnegotiated restructuring.

References

Acemoglu, Daron, Simon Johnson, James Robinson, and Yunyong Thaicharoen. 2003. "Institutional Causes, Macro-economic Symptoms: Volatility, Crises, and Growth." *Journal of Monetary Economics* 50, no. 1:49–123.

Alfaro, Laura, Sebnem Kalemi-Ozcan, and Vadym Volosovych. 2005. "Capital Flows in a Globalized World: The Role of Policies and Institutions." NBER Working Paper, 11696.

Bordo, Michael D., Ashoka Mody, Nienke Oomes. 2004. "Keeping Capital Flowing: The Role of the IMF." *International Finance* 7, no. 3:421–50.

Cline, William R. 2004. "Private Sector Involvement in Financial Crisis Resolution: Definition, Measurement, and Implementation." In *Fixing Financial Crises in the Twenty-first Century*, edited by Andrew G. Haldane, 61–94. London: Routledge.

Corsetti, Giancarlo, Bernardo Guimaraes, and Nouriel Roubini. 2006. "International Lending of Last Resort and Moral Hazard: A Model of IMF's Catalytic Finance." *Journal of Monetary Economics* 53, no. 3:441–71.

Daude, Christian, and Marcel Fratzscher. 2006. "The Pecking Order of International Financial Integration." ECB Working Paper, 590.

Dell'Ariccia, Giovanni, Isabel Schnabel, and Jeromin Zettelmeyer. 2002. "Moral Hazard and International Crisis Lending: A Test." IMF Working Paper, WP/02/181.

Detragiache, Enrica, and Antonio Spilimbergo. 2001. "Crises and Liquidity: Evidence and Interpretation." IMF Working Paper, WP/01/2.

Díaz-Cassou, Javier, Alicia García-Herrero, and Luis Molina. 2006. "What Kind of Capital Flows Does the IMF Catalyze and When?" Banco de Espana Working Paper, 617.

Du, Julan. Forthcoming. "Institutional Quality and Economic Crises: Legal Origin Theory Versus Colonial Strategy Theory." *Review of Economics and Statistics*.

Eaton, Jonathan, and Raquel Fernandez. 1995. "Sovereign Debt." NBER Working Paper, 5131.

Eichengreen, Barry. 2003. "Restructuring Sovereign Debt." *Journal of Economic Perspectives* 17, no. 4:75–98.

Eichengreen, Barry, Galina Hale, and Ashoka Mody. 2001. "Flight to Quality: Investor Risk Tolerance and the Spread of Emerging Market Crises." In *International Financial Contagion*, edited by Stijn Claessens and Kristin Forbes, 129–55. Norwell: Kluwer Academic Publishers.

Eichengreen, Barry, Kenneth Kletzer, and Ashoka Mody. 2006. "The IMF in a World of Private Capital Markets." *Journal of Banking and Finance* 30, no. 5:1335–57.

Eichengreen, Barry, and Ashoka Mody. 2001. "Bail-Ins, Bailouts, and Borrowing Costs." *IMF Staff Papers* 47, special issue: 155–87.

——. 2004. "Do Collective Action Clauses Raise Borrowing Costs?" *Economic Journal* 114, no. 495:247–64.

Eichengreen, Barry, and Christof Rühl. 2001. "The Bail-In Problem: Systematic Goals, Ad Hoc Means." *Economic-Systems* 25, no. 1:3–32.

Enderlein, Henrik, Laura von Daniels, and Christoph Trebesch. 2010. "Sovereign Debt Disputes." Hertie School of Governance, mimeo.

Gai, Prasanna, Simon Hayes, and Hyun Song Shin. 2004. "Crisis Costs and Debtor Discipline: The Efficacy of Public Policy in Sovereign Debt Crises." *Journal of International Economics* 62, no. 2:245–62.

Gande, Amar, and David C. Parsley. 2005. "News Spillovers in the Sovereign Debt Market." *Journal of Financial Economics* 75, no. 3:691–734.

Ghosal, Sayantan, and Marcus Miller. 2004. "Co-ordination Failure, Moral Hazard, and Sovereign Bankruptcy Procedures." In *Fixing Financial Crises in the Twenty-first Century*, edited by Andrew G. Haldane, 313–20. London: Routledge.

Goldstein, Morris, G. Kaminsky, and Carmen Reinhart. 2000. "Assessing Financial Vulnerability: An Early Warning System for Emerging Markets." Washington, D.C.: Institute for International Economics.

Group of 7. 2000. "Statement of G-7 Finance Ministers and Central Bank Governors and Action Plan." Washington, D.C.: International Monetary Fund.

Group of 10. 1996. "The Resolution Liquidity Crises: A Report to the Ministers and Governors Prepared Under the Auspices of the Deputies." Bank for International Settlements, May 1996, Basel.

Group of 22. 1998. "Report of the Working Group on International Financial Crises." Washington, D.C.: International Monetary Fund.

Haldane, Andrew. 1999. "Private Sector Involvement in Financial Crisis: Analytics and Public Policy Approaches." *Bank of England Financial Stability Review* 7:184–202.

Haldane, Andrew G., and Mark Kruger. 2001. "The Resolution of International Financial Crises: Private Finance and Public Funds." Bank of Canada Working Paper, 01–20.

Haldane, Andrew G., Adrian Penalver, Vicky Saporta, and Hyun Song Shin. 2005. "The Analytics of Sovereign Debt Restructuring." *Journal of International Economics* 65, no. 2:315–33.

Haldane, Andrew G., and Jörg Scheibe. 2003. "IMF Lending and Creditor Moral Hazard." Bank of England Working Paper, 216.

Heid, Frank, Thorsten Nestmann, Natalja von Westernhagen, and Beatrice Weder. 2005. "German Bank Lending During Financial Crises: A Bank Level Analysis." CEPR Discussion Paper, 5164.

IIF. 2006. "Principles for Stable Capital Flows and Fair Debt Restructuring In Emerging Markets: Report on Implementation by the Principles Consultative Group." Washington, D.C.: Institute of International Finance

IMF. 1999a. "IMF Policy on Lending into Arrears to Private Creditors." Washington, D.C.: IMF Policy Development and Review and Legal Departments.

——. 1999b. "Involving the Private Sector in Forestalling and Resolving Financial Crises." Washington, D.C: International Monetary Fund.

——. 2000. "Involving the Private Sector in the Resolution of Financial Crises—Standstills—Preliminary Considerations." Washington, D.C.: IMF Policy Development and Review and Legal Departments.

——. 2001. "Involving the Private Sector in the Resolution of Financial Crises: Restructuring International Sovereign Bonds." Washington, D.C.: IMF Policy Development and Review and Legal Departments.

——. 2002. "Fund Policy on Lending into Arrears to Private Creditors: Further Consideration of the Good Faith Criterion." Washington, D.C.: IMF Policy Development and Review and Legal Departments.

——. 2003. "Crisis Resolution in the Context of Sovereign Debt Restructuring: A Summary of Considerations." Washington, D.C.: IMF Policy Development and Review Department.

Kamin, Steven B. 2004. "Identifying the Role of Moral Hazard in International Financial Markets." *International Finance* 7, no. 1:25–59.

Kaminsky, Graciela L., Richard K. Lyons, and Sergio L. Schmukler. 2004. "Managers, Investors, and Crises: Mutual Fund Strategies in Emerging Markets." *Journal of International Economics* 64, no. 1:113–34.

Kaufmann, Daniel, Aart Kraay, and Massimo Mastruzzi. 2009. "Governance Matters VIII: Aggregate and Individual Governance Indicators, 1996–2008." World Bank Policy Research Working Paper, 4978.

Kenen, Peter B. 2002. "The International Financial Architecture: Old Issues and New Initiatives." *International-Finance* 5, no. 1:23–45.

Knack, Stephen, and Philip Keefer. 1995. "Institutions and Economic Performance: Cross-Country Tests Using Alternative Institutional Measures." *Economics and Politics* 7, no. 3:207–27.

Lane, Timothy, and Steven Phillips. 2000. "Does IMF Financing Result in Moral Hazard?" IMF Working Paper, WP/00/168.

Leiderman, Leonardo. 2004. "Comments on 'Private Sector Involvement in Financial Crisis: Definition, Measurement, and Implementation.'" In *Fixing Financial Crises in the Twenty-first Century*, edited by Andrew G. Haldane, 95–98. London: Routledge.

Lipworth, Gabrielle, and Jens Nystedt. 2001. "Crisis Resolution and Private Sector Adaptation." *IMF Staff Papers* 47, special issue: 188–214.

Manasse, Paolo, Nouriel Roubini, and Axel Schimmelpfennig. 2003. "Predicting Sovereign Debt Crises." IMF Working Paper, WP/03/221.

Mauro, Paolo, Nathan Sussman, and Yishay Yafeh. 2002. "Emerging Market Spreads: Then versus Now." *Quarterly Journal of Economics* 117, no. 2:695–733.

McBrady, Matthew R., and Mark S. Seasholes. 2000. "Bailing In." *Journal of Restructuring Finance* 1, no. 1:1–29.

Mody, Ashoka, and Diego Saravia. 2003. "Catalyzing Private Capital Flows: Do IMF-Supported Programs Work as Commitment Device?" IMF Working Paper, WP/03/100.

Morris, Stephen, and Hyun Song Shin. 2004. "Coordination Risk and the Price of Debt." *European Economic Review* 48, no. 1:133–53.

Panizza, Ugo, Federico Sturzenegger, and Jeromin Zettelmeyer. 2009. "The Economics and Law of Sovereign Debt and Default." *Journal of Economic Literature* 47, no. 3:651–98.

Pericoli, Marcello, and Massimo Sbracia. 2003. "A Primer on Financial Contagion." *Journal of Economic Surveys* 17, no. 4:571–608.

Reinhart, Carmen M. 2002. "Default, Currency Crises, and Sovereign Credit Ratings." *World Bank Economic Review* 16, no. 2:151–70.

Reinhart, Carmen M., Kenneth Rogoff, and Miguel A. Savastano. 2003. "Debt Intolerance." *Brookings Papers on Economic Activity* 1:1–70.

Risse, Thomas. 2008. "Regieren in Räumen begrenzter Staatlichkeit: 'Zur Reisefähigkeit' des Governance-Konzepts." In *Governance in einer sich wandelnden Welt*, edited by Gunnar Folke Schuppert and Michael Zürn, 149–70. Wiesbaden: VS Verlag für Sozialwissenschaften.

Roubini, Nouriel. 2004. "Private Sector Involvement in Crisis Resolution and Mechanisms for Dealing with Sovereign Debt Problems." In *Fixing Financial Crises in the Twenty-first Century*, edited by Andrew G. Haldane, 101–42. London: Routledge.

Roubini, Nouriel, and Brad Setser. 2004. *Bailouts or Bail-Ins? Responding to Financial Crises in Emerging Economies*. Washington, D.C.: Institute for International Economics.

Rubin, Robert E. 1998. "Statement at the Special Meeting of Finance Ministers and Central Bank Governors." U.S. Treasury, Washington, D.C, January 30.

Sy, Amadou N. R. 2004. "Rating the Rating Agencies: Anticipating Currency Crises or Debt Crises?" *Journal of Banking and Finance* 28, no. 11:2845–67.

Taylor, John B. 2002. "Sovereign Debt Restructuring: A US Perspective." Sovereign Debt Workouts: Hopes and Hazards, Institute for International Economics, Washington, D.C., April 1–2. www.iie.com/publications/papers/paper. cfm?ResearchID=455.

Thiemann, Christian, Regine Wölfinger, Thierry Bracke, Rita Bessone Basto, Ole Hollensen, Stephan van Stenglin, Santiago Fernández de Lis, Pierre-Francois Weber, Marco Committeri, Rolf Pauli, Christian Just, Minna Nikitin, and John Drage. 2005. "Managing Financial Crises in Emerging Market Economies: Experience with the Involvement of Private Sector Creditors." ECB Occasional Paper, 32.

Tillmann, Peter. 2005. "Private Sector Involvement in the Resolution of Financial Crises: How Do Markets React?" *Journal of Development Economics* 78, no. 1:114–32.

Van Rijckeghem, Caroline, and Beatrice Weder. 2003. "Spillovers Through Banking Centers: A Panel Data Analysis of Bank Flows." *Journal of International Money and Finance* 22, no. 4:483–509.

——. 2009. "Political Institutions and Debt Crises." *Public Choice* 138, no. 3:387–408.

Zhang, Xiaoming Alan. 1999. "Testing for Moral Hazard in Emerging Markets Lending." Institute of International Finance Research Paper, 99–1, Washington, D.C.

III

State Building and Good Governance

The Role of External Actors

8

International Legal and Moral Standards
of Good Governance in Fragile States

BERND LADWIG AND BEATE RUDOLF

F RAGILE STATES ABOUND IN THE WORLD TODAY. The reasons for state fragility vary greatly, from ethnic tensions, social unrest, or increased migration caused by economic or environmental factors to interstate conflicts over territory or resources. As a result, numerous entities that are considered to be "states" under public international law are unable to exercise power over all their territory or in all policy fields. Yet, even if a state, by its fragility, verges on dissolving or being a "failing" or "failed" state, it remains a state in the legal sense. This characterization hardly squares with the traditional requirement of the definition of a state according to which its authorities must exercise effective power over its population and territory. Yet, through this legal fiction, international law protects "failed" states from becoming *terra nullius* and hence the object of military conflicts for its annexation.

Nevertheless, the legal fiction does not mean that sovereignty is an impenetrable shield and that statehood is recognized unconditionally. Today, sovereignty has become a normatively laden concept. States are bound, in their actions, by human rights, the rule of law, and the obligation to be responsive to the needs of their populations and to ensure their political participation. These demands stand in tension with the fact just mentioned that fragile states are unable to fulfill even the basic function of states—securing internal peace—let alone the more ambitious normative standards of good governance.

In discussing solutions to this tension, we will proceed as follows: we will show that the rather ambitious standards of good governance are already part of positive law, and that they also can be justified by a rights-based approach of political morality. Applied to conditions of fragile statehood, the criteria pose problems of legitimacy on two logically distinct levels. We argue that this gives reason to focus primarily on a responsibility to rebuild, which is already recognized by international law. It encompasses, in particular, the obligation to establish institutional structures and social cohesion that may necessitate taking nonstate actors into account. We conclude by finding that not only states, but nonstate actors and the international community are bound by international legal standards of good governance.

In our contribution, we develop a normative concept of good governance based on public international law and political morality that is built on the analytical concept of governance as explained in the introduction. Our focus is on fragile states, that is, areas of limited statehood nearing the end of the continuum, where governance is rarely, if at all, achieved by the state. For this reason, the question of normative standards for governance by nonstate actors and the international community is particularly urgent.

Normative Dimensions of Sovereignty Under Public International Law

Sovereignty

Under present-day public international law, sovereignty is not what it used to be[1]: during the "classical" period of international law, sovereignty meant the exclusive legal power of a state to regulate matters within its own territory according to its own will (Lauterpacht 1997, 140). Since the end of the First World War and with an ever increasing speed and substantive scope, states have concluded international treaties by which they limit their freedom of action, both within and outside their own territories. While some conclude, therefore, that "sovereignty on the international plane . . . must be seen largely as a myth" (Lauterpacht 1997, 149), others rightly propose that the meaning of sovereignty has not changed (Schrijver 1999, 98). Sovereignty today still means what it meant since the beginning of the Westphalian system: the legal—not factual—equality of states. Because of this "sovereign equality of states" (article 2.1, U.N. Charter), a state cannot be bound under international law by a treaty concluded between other states against its will (article 34, Vienna Convention on the Law of Treaties), even if these states are more powerful than itself.

Although sovereignty has not changed conceptually, its appearance differs from earlier times. Most relevant for present purposes is the extent to which states have limited themselves through international law. In particular the states' reserved domain was reduced considerably through rules that regulate the internal actions of states. As a consequence, the scope of application of the prohibition of (nonmilitary) intervention shrank enormously: other states and international organizations are allowed to take an interest in state actions in areas hitherto within the reserved domain of states. With these subject-matters turning into objects of international concern, the absolute protection of states through the prohibition of the use of force became increasingly problematic. This development is reflected in the debate on "humanitarian intervention," whether unilateral or based on a decision of the U.N. Security Council under chapter 7 of the charter.

A second important change of sovereignty occurred through the acceptance of states that certain rules of public international law are peremptory norms (*ius cogens*) and hence cannot be changed by agreements between individual states (article 53, Vienna Convention on the Law of Treaties). These rules of *ius cogens* embody the fundamental values of the international legal order. Consequently, any exercise of state power in contravention of these norms constitutes a grave assault on the international legal order. Moreover, and even more important in the present context, the existence of *ius cogens* proves that sovereignty is not absolute, but that, on the contrary, there are some absolute limits to sovereignty.

Good Governance

As these considerations show, standards of good governance under public international law are compatible with (international) sovereignty. They can be understood as normative dimensions of (internal) sovereignty. In addition, they have become relevant for international sovereignty in the context of recognition of new states[2] and for the determination of whether the prohibition of intervention applies.

To determine the normative dimension of sovereignty, the various public international law standards of good governance will be examined. In a narrow sense, "Good Governance" is a concept within the context of development cooperation, the meaning of which varies in different legal contexts. In a more general sense, good governance means the fulfillment of public international law rules on the way in which power must be exercised within a state. If fulfilled, governance can be considered to be "good governance." In the following, we shall examine the central components of good governance in this broad sense: human rights, the rule of law, responsiveness, and public participation.

HUMAN RIGHTS

The most important category of public international law rules on good governance are human rights, because they regulate the exercise of power within a state. On the universal level, the central sources are the International Covenant on Civil and Political Rights (ICCPR) and the International Covenant on Economic, Social, and Cultural Rights (ICESCR). Alongside these treaties, which guarantee human rights extensively (with the notable exception of the right to property), human rights under customary international law continue to exist and thus build the minimum human rights obligations worldwide—a minimum standard of good governance.

The character of human rights as a yardstick for internal governance is illustrated by the change of focus in the important policy field of development, where a "rights-based approach" is now commonly accepted.[3] It requires states, both in their internal actions for their own development and in any development cooperation, to devise an agenda and strategies with a view to realizing human rights. Human rights thus set the priorities for development; at the same time, development itself is understood as a process for the realization of all human rights (Rudolf 2008). Under the internal dimension of the right to development, every state is obliged to ensure development to its population.[4] Thus, a state's governance is measured against the realization of human rights. Since all human rights are "universal, indivisible, and interdependent,"[5] there is no hierarchy between civil and political rights (the "first generation" of human rights), and economic, social, and cultural rights ("second generation" rights). Nevertheless, some human rights enjoy

a higher status under public international law because they embody fundamental values of the international community. Consequently, the realization
of these rights is a matter of priority.

Some human rights are considered part of *ius cogens*. Hence, states cannot
free themselves of these obligations. It is generally recognized that the prohibition of torture and of slavery as well as the prohibition of genocide and
of racial discrimination are such peremptory norms. Arguably, a prohibition
of arbitrariness with respect to survival and basic needs also amounts to *ius
cogens*.[6] Thus, nobody may be deprived of his or her life or liberty arbitrarily.
This follows from common article 3 of the Geneva Conventions: if these
rights must be respected in an armed conflict under all circumstances, they
apply a fortiori in peacetime. The same holds true for fundamental principles
of fair trial.[7] For the same reason, the equal value of all human beings and
the right to be recognized as a person under the law constitute peremptory
rules. Consequently, no one may be denied access to means of survival only
because of his or her gender or because he or she belongs to a particular
(ethnic, social, or other) group.

Another category of higher-ranking human rights are nonderogable rights,
that is, rights that cannot be suspended in times of emergency. In addition to
the *ius cogens* rights, article 4.2 of the ICCPR considers as nonderogable the
principle of legality in the field of criminal law (*nullum crimen, nulla poena
sine lege*), and the freedom of thought, conscience, and religion. The Human
Rights Committee adds the right of persons deprived of their liberty to be
treated with respect for the inherent dignity of the human person; the prohibition against taking hostages, abductions, and unacknowledged detentions;
the prohibition of forced displacement of populations; and the obligation to
provide for effective remedies against violations of human rights.[8] *Ius cogens*
and nonderogable human rights impose obligations on states that must be
respected under all circumstances.[9]

APPLYING THE HUMAN RIGHTS STANDARD
TO THE SPECIFIC SITUATION OF FRAGILE STATES

For fragile states, the problem arises that universally applicable human rights
impose obligations they hardly can meet, either for lack of effective internal regulatory or enforcement power or for lack of sufficient means. The

ICESCR takes the latter difficulty into account through the obligation to realize economic, social, and cultural rights progressively (article 2.1).[10] Thus, the covenant does not require states to fulfill the rights immediately, but "to move as expeditiously and effectively as possible towards that goal,"[11] and "to the maximum of its available resources" (article 2.1). Even the "minimum core obligation" under each covenant right, namely "to ensure the satisfaction of, at the very least, minimum essential levels of each of the rights" is not an absolute obligation, but must take into account the resource constraints within a country.[12] However, if a state demonstrably is not able to fulfill even the core rights, it is obliged to use resources available through international cooperation and assistance.[13] Whether the international community, in turn, is obliged to provide such help—as the ICESCR Committee assumes—will be examined later.

The ICCPR does not contain a comparable provision on progressive implementation of the rights guaranteed. This difference reflects the—now outdated—understanding that civil and political rights contain "negative obligations," that is, they require mere abstention, while economic, social, and cultural rights give rise to "positive obligations," that is, they necessitate action by the state and hence the use of financial resources. Under a modern concept of human rights, all human rights encompass three dimensions of obligations—to respect, to protect, and to fulfill (Eide 1989, 37; Simma 1998, 872, with reference to Shue 1980). This means that the state has to abstain from interfering with the exercise of the right ("to respect"), it has to take measures against violations of the right by private actors ("to protect"), and it has to create the necessary social conditions for an effective exercise of the right ("to fulfill"). Even the "respect" dimension may require the state to take (costly) action; in order to respect the right to a fair trial, for example, the state must set up an independent court system. Equally, the "protect" dimension of the right to life obliges the state to establish a police force. Nevertheless, it is no oversight that the ICCPR does not limit the extent of the states' obligations to their available resources. Rather, the immediate effect of the obligations arising out of the rights guaranteed by the ICCPR reflects the premise underlying that covenant that it is the purpose of the state to ensure the Hobbesian minimum—physical security, both from willful violence and from forcible self-help. Consequently, a state's fragility alone is no reason for lowering the standards of the ICCPR.

The same conclusion holds true for human rights under customary international law. This is borne out by the fact that the Universal Declaration of Human Rights does not contain an obligation to "progressive implementation."

RULE OF LAW

A second core element of good governance is the rule of law. In numerous declarations, the international community committed itself to realizing this principle.[14] Although the rule of law as understood by common law systems differs from related European concepts, namely, *Rechtsstaat* and *état de droit*, a minimum content derives from human rights. In particular, restrictions of human rights are permissible only if provided by law, that is, if there is a prior law of general applicability that was properly enacted and is accessible for the public (Nowak 2005, article 19, marginal no. 46). Moreover, such laws and their application must respect the principle of equality before the law (article 26, ICCPR). Lastly, at least for criminal and civil matters, control through independent courts is necessary (article 14, ICCPR); in all other cases of alleged violations of a human right, there must be an effective remedy (article 2.3, ICCPR). By these minimum requirements, the rule of law ensures that the supremacy of the law is upheld and thus that restrictions of human rights are foreseeable. For states that are not bound by the ICCPR, the supremacy of law and the independence of the judiciary are binding as general principles of law (Rudolf 2006, 1024 and Rudolf 2000, 486–93, respectively). No special rules apply to fragile states because, as the Human Rights Committee emphasizes, the maintenance of the rule of law is most needed in times of emergency.[15]

RESPONSIVENESS

"Responsiveness" as an element of good governance means that governments must be "responsive to the needs and aspirations of the people."[16] The international community reaffirmed that "solid democratic institutions responsive to the needs of the people" are a key factor for economic development.[17] The concept of responsiveness can be traced back to the 1986 Declaration on the Right to Development of the U.N. General Assembly, which also acknowledges the duty of all states to pursue development policies aimed "at the constant improvement of the well-being of the entire population and of all individuals, on the basis of their active, free and meaningful partici-pation."[18] Consequently, responsiveness reflects the conviction that human beings are at the center of the development process. It is thus closely con-nected with participation: responsiveness is the purpose and—ideally—also the result of participation.

The international documents cited here do not permit the conclusion that responsiveness, in the sense of a duty to be responsive, exists under public international law. However, states are bound by law to create central preconditions of responsiveness. Freedom of opinion and freedom of as-sociation are necessary for the population to formulate its demands toward state authorities and to express its support for, or criticism of, state policies. Only if the population can express itself without fear of sanctions will state authorities learn of the people's needs and demands. Although such expres-sions are more effective if based on sound facts, states are not duty-bound to provide transparent decision making: freedom of opinion does not (yet) encompass a right of access to all information available to a state (Rudolf 2006, 1023).

Mechanisms of accountability of public authorities are a further means of realizing responsiveness. With respect to policy makers, the most promis-ing means are political sanctions—the fear of not being reelected. Although general international law does not oblige states to establish and uphold a democratic system, the human right to political participation provides a suf-ficient basis for this political sanction of nonresponsiveness.

PUBLIC PARTICIPATION

Almost all definitions of good governance used by international bodies list public participation as a constitutive element (Rudolf 2006, 1020). It is not limited to a democratic system, although democracy is often referred to as being helpful. Documents of the last decade put an emphasis on democracy as being based on participation, yet fall short of pronouncing a legal obliga-tion to democracy.[19] In this vein, the World Summit called democracy a "uni-versal value based on the freely expressed will of the people" and its "full par-ticipation in all aspects of their lives."[20] Thus, the international community did not affirm the more extensive approach of the Commission on Human Rights. In a contested resolution, the commission had declared full popular participation to presuppose that all citizens can "take part in the government of their country, directly or through freely chosen representatives," that the "will of the people shall be the basis of the authority of Government and that this shall be expressed in periodic and genuine elections," that political equality is essential to democracy, and that popular participation and control "must be realized through a framework of accessible, representative and accountable institutions subject to periodic change or renewal."[21]

Despite the reluctance of states to commit themselves to these elements, public international law already contains the legal bases for the obligation to realize them: the right of peoples to self-determination (article 25, ICCPR) and the principle of equality, as enshrined in articles 2.1 and 26 of the ICCPR. The right to self-determination is the right of a people to determine freely its political status as well as its economic and social system.[22] Today, it is recognized that it also has an internal dimension, that is, that every people has the right to participate in the decision-making process of its state (Nowak 2005, article 1, marginal no. 34). Moreover, the right to self-determination has a permanent character; therefore, it is not "consumed" by its exercise, but requires expression in a continual process (Nowak 2005, article 1, marginal nos. 17–18). Through both features, self-determination has democratic elements. Article 25 of the ICCPR is more precise in that it guarantees the right to take part in the conduct of public affairs, to vote and to be elected, and to have access to the public service of one's own state. Thus, the provision goes beyond the electoral process as a means of participation. Finally, public participation in the conduct of the state's affairs is a requirement flowing from the principle of equality: if all human beings are "born free and equal in dignity and rights" (article 1, Universal Declaration of Human Rights), if discrimination based on personal features such as race, gender, or religion is prohibited (article 2.1, ICCPR), and if all are equal before the law (article 26, ICCPR), then no person has the right to impose his or her will on others arbitrarily. Consequently, everyone must have a say in the establishment of general restrictions of a person's freedom of action and in the determination of the course of the society he or she lives in.

The obligation of states to provide for public participation exists also for states not parties to the ICCPR. This conclusion is warranted because self-determination and the basic equality of all human beings irrespective of race, gender, or religion are binding rules of customary law. However, as Article 25 of the ICCPR does not have an equivalent under customary law, these states are not obliged to ensure participation through elections, but may apply other procedures for establishing the will of the people.

Moral Justification of the Normative Dimensions of Sovereignty

Positive Law and Morality

We will now transcend the bounds of positive law and turn to normative political theory. On the one hand, this widens the scope of arguments: political philosophers should in principle feel free to make proposals for reform, even regarding basic principles of existing law. The general reason is that any law must be legitimate: although leaving open to its addressees the motives for compliance, one *possible* motive must be respect for the law itself. To that end its basic norms have to be compatible with the basic principles of morality. And nothing guarantees a priori that an existing corpus of legal rules and principles does already fulfill that demand.

On the other hand, morality itself provides us with good reasons to take positive law seriously. The ultimate reason is that to overcome any state of nature is a metanorm of political morality. Therefore, to ignore the norms of positive law in the name of a higher moral insight is morally wrong, and not only because of the fallibility of our moral reasoning. In all such reasoning we must take into consideration the integrity of positive law. This is especially important in the case of international law, because more than most national legal systems it is a law in the making. That makes it highly sensitive to political interests and power relations, but perhaps also open to moral insights. Improving international law means enhancing its coherence in accordance with valid principles of political morality (Ladwig 2000).

Now, as already shown, international law has incorporated some basic moral insights that together indicate a remarkable shift in interpreting its ultimate purpose. Sovereignty is no longer seen as absolute and inviolable; it calls for normative qualifications. In order to be justified, it must meet certain standards of good governance. We have identified four components that gain more and more acceptance in the realm of public international law: human rights, rule of law, responsiveness, and public participation. Is there a pattern of reasoned justification that can support these components and explain their internal normative relations? In the following section we will give a sketch of a rights-based approach.

We argue that all humans are entitled to access to institutions that protect their basic rights.[23] In that respect, at least, states and other structures of institutions are never ends in themselves. Political authorities are basically legitimate insofar as they are suited and necessary for guaranteeing secure, inclusive, and nondiscriminatory access to basic goods each individual is morally entitled to, provided in forms and by means that are themselves compatible with human rights standards. This seems to be a tenable starting point for explaining in a coherent manner the idea underlying the conception of good governance outlined above.

A rights-based approach has four advantages. First, it is already widely accepted in principle, and also anchored in public international law, by means of treaties and custom, some of them even being *ius cogens*. Consequently, it cannot be reproached for imposing particularistic norms on foreign cultures, at least with regard to basic human rights. Second, it provides a plausible starting point for constructing a framework of moral norms that could orientate further legal reform. Third, it rules out any purely instrumentalist approach of good governance, as favored in certain discourses on economic development. Fostering economic development might be a further reason for adopting a rights-based approach, but basically, realizing human rights is not a mere means, it is a central *criterion* for successful development (for a similar argument, see Sen 1999, esp. chap. 2). Fourth, it does not conceptually presuppose fully consolidated statehood and is therefore applicable in principle to conditions of fragile statehood as well.

From the point of view of a rights-based approach, states are mere means for the full realization of valid claims of individuals. As such, they are in principle replaceable by other structures of institutions insofar as state authorities lack the adequate means or the will to fulfill their core responsibilities. Even passing over a state's claims to sovereignty might be required if it is necessary to give individuals what they are entitled to. The international community bears a subsidiary responsibility, and even nonstate actors can be obliged to play a role in securing access to basic goods. As we argue, building and stabilizing institutions that protect basic human rights is a cosmopolitan duty binding each actor who is in an adequate position to do their share. Part of the duty is helping weak governments; another part might be acting in place of them, for example by means of multilevel governance.

Human Rights

Human rights can be justified from different moral staring points, in accordance with more than one comprehensive doctrine, religious as well as secularist ones. Following John Rawls, we can speak of an "overlapping consensus" concerning basic rights (Rawls 1993, 133ff). That fact relieves us from the requirement of extensive moral argument that would clearly exceed the scope of this chapter. Nevertheless, a few remarks concerning the philosophical background of the very idea of human rights are required.

Human rights are valid claims each individual has simply by virtue of his or her humanity. The validity of the claims results from at least one moral principle being valid itself. What principle can play such a role? There is wide acceptance now in moral philosophy as well as in international law that each individual human being is entitled to equal concern and respect (Dworkin 1978). My fundamental interests, regarding life, well-being, and personal autonomy, deserve the same consideration than those of anybody else.[24] No political authority can be legitimate, no basic structure of a society can be just, if it rests on a systematic violation of those interests. Human rights define a threshold of minimal acceptability in the realm of politics.

BASIC INTERESTS

Is global agreement on the content of human rights possible? Must not every such attempt fail in the face of the diversity of worldviews? According to reasonable pluralism (Rawls 1993, 58ff), human rights interests would have to be so general that people with very different ideas about what is a good life would be able to agree on them. In the philosophical literature, we can find three methods of determining the content of at least basic human rights.

First, we can directly look and see if we will find reasoned agreement on basic interests. These would have to concern preconditions for, or fundamental elements of, a successful life. It is not directly a good life that is at stake here, but merely a humane life with dignity. Now, it seems plausible to presuppose interests of any human regarding goods such as prevention of premature death, physical and mental integrity, worthwhile opportunities for experience and agency, attachment to significant others such as parents and those beloved, or recognition by equals.

This is not meant to rule out the possibility that persons might make reasoned decisions against some such interests. People are plainly capable of making all manner of sacrifices—even their own life—out of conviction. But they can only do this rationally if they believe that it is supported by a value of at least equal importance. If a person simply throws his or her life away on a whim, we consider that grossly irrational and tend to regard the person as a pathological case. In that sense, interests that are significant in terms of human rights are at least prima facie interests: other things being equal, they deserve universal esteem (for details, see Gert 1998). Some are even more than prima facie interests. They affect indispensable preconditions of the ability to orientate and to be a self-aware person. Satisfying such interests is good without further qualification. Otherwise, persons would be unable to lead a personal life at all.

Second, a similar sort of argument—call it "quasi-transcendentalist"—has been presented by Henry Shue (1996), but with regard to necessary enabling conditions for realizing any human right. According to Shue, some rights are basic in the sense that enjoying them is indispensable for the enjoyment of all other rights. Consequently, if a right is truly basic, abandoning it would be literally self-defeating from the point of view of human rights as such. Shue considers rights to physical security, to subsistence, and to some liberties to be basic in that sense.

Third, one can determine the content of basic human rights by asking what is essential for being able to participate as a free and equal person in human rights discourses. This route of argument has something in common with Shue's. But instead of directly identifying some rights as basic, it refers to the intersubjectivist "construction" of any system of rights (Forst 1999). Given that rights are always in need of moral arguments, and arguments are intersubjective in and by themselves, the ability to participate in human rights discourses as a free and equal person becomes crucial. We can understand that as a reflexive turn in the very idea of equal concern and respect: the basic principle out of which specific human rights normatively emerge has to be reformulated as a discourse principle (Habermas 1998, 107). This is not a purely formalist idea. We can gain some material content by realizing that without certain endowments we would be unable to participate effectively in the common construction of a sufficiently rich and determinate system of rights.

Now, instead of taking the three approaches as mutually exclusive, we prefer to see them as mutually supportive. A right that turns out to be basic in the sense of protecting and promoting interests necessary for leading one's own life as a self-aware person, for the very same reason will turn out to be necessary for consciously and effectively exercising all other rights. What is more, the approach of basic interests highlights the advantages that rights are made to protect and promote. It directs our attention to the relation between subjective rights and intrinsic goods.[25] The approach of basic rights, in contrast, can help us to determine the normative status some interests have. It gives further support to claims regarding basic interests by explaining their role in any coherent system of rights.

Regarding the third approach, basic interests and basic rights can serve as substantial restrictions within human rights discourses. They focus the participant's attention on the points of greatest urgency. To a large degree rights that are indispensable for participating effectively in human rights discourses will overlap with those needed for leading a personal life with dignity and also with those needed for enjoying any other sorts of rights. Nevertheless, it is highly likely that some rights turn out to be basic although not securing necessary conditions of discursive engagement; we may think of interests in physical integrity, in freedom from serious pain, or from forced marriages.

So much about the content of basic human rights. For the reasons just indicated, we are confident that at least some interests can be shown to be of universal importance. Being able to satisfy them is a necessary condition for, or elementary component of, a humane life with dignity, including the status of being the holder of valid claims and a free and equal coauthor of some specific systems of rights.

CORRESPONDING DUTIES

We want to finish the section on human rights theory by saying a few words about the duties that correspond to them. As indicated in the first part of the chapter, it would be misleading to reduce respect for human rights to the inhibition of state action. Even rights to "negative liberties" are fully respected only where provisions are made regarding their sufficient protection and promotion. As Shue has convincingly argued, three types of duties belong to each right: duties to avoid deprivation, duties to protect from deprivation, and duties to aid the deprived (1996, 52). Consequently, the allocation of these duties is a central task in any attempt to realize human rights. And with respect to the second and the third type, at least, a moral division of labor is required (Shue 1988; Goodin 1988).

Although ultimately only individuals can bear moral duties, they sometimes need to coordinate their actions, act collectively, and build institutions (Mellema 1997; Schlothfeldt 2007). Structures of institutions play three important roles in any approach of human rights. They improve the effectiveness of human rights actions, they specify each actor's duties (O'Neill 1996,

130–33), and they ensure that the costs are bearable for each individual person by means of their fair allocation and the prohibition of free riding. This does not simply lessen the individual's responsibility, however. In cases where sufficiently strong institutions are already lacking, that responsibility shifts toward contributions to create and to strengthen them.

Consequently, we can distinguish two levels of duties concerning human rights. On a first level, duties are directly linked to the objects of human rights—for example, the duty to refrain from violation or the duty to provide a certain good. On a second level, there are duties regarding the prerequisites of fulfilling duties on the first level. As already indicated, among these second-order duties are those to build or to improve institutions necessary for a full realization of human rights. Thus, the objection that certain rights are mere "manifesto-rights" (Feinberg 1980, 153), because no addressee of the corresponding duties does exist, can partly be countered. Insofar as we are able to establish such an addressee by means of coordination and collective action, and insofar as we are able to coordinate our actions and to act collectively, we have a second-order-obligation to transform the manifesto-right into an effective one.

If states are stable and constitutionally well-ordered, these problems are solved in principle, at least within the respective territory. Sufficiently strong states nowadays are the primary duty bearers in the realm of human rights. But neither do they have obligations only with regard to their own citizens, nor are they the only entities that can help individuals to get what they are entitled to. At least elementary norms such as avoiding torture and slavery, preventing genocide, and providing the means for subsistence are widely seen in literature as being backed by duties of humanity that do not presuppose any special relationship, be it a framework of cooperation, of interdependence and power relations, or of being the citizen of a state. The corresponding duties are ultimately those of humanity, and the international community, as a whole.[26]

Rule of Law, Responsiveness, and Participation as Components of the Rights-Based Approach

With the last remarks about duties we have stressed the importance of institutions; hence our basic norm that any human is entitled to access to institutions that protect their basic rights. But it is equally important to emphasize that institutions must guarantee secure, inclusive, and nondiscriminatory access to basic goods *in forms and by means* that are themselves compatible with human rights standards. That allows us to relate the other three components of good governance, as outlined earlier, to that of human rights. Although human rights are the core of our normative approach, they internally refer to the rule of law, to responsiveness, and to public participation.

First, it is obvious that any attempt to realize human rights presupposes the rule of law. In a minimalist sense, "rule of law" stands for preventing the Hobbesian condition of violent chaos by means of rules backed by effective sanctions. But in order to ensure that those establishing and enforcing the rules do not simply seek their own advantage by abusing their extraordinary power, no authority shall be above the law. Moreover, legal rules should be seen as codes of conduct for persons capable of taking responsibility for their actions. For both reasons, they must meet certain standards such as publicity, generality, the exclusion of ex post facto laws, due process, independence of the judiciary, and equality before the law.[27] To be sure, not any system that replaces the rule of people by those of law automatically shows proper respect for, and is ultimately based on, human rights. But no system of human rights would be feasible in a situation of violent chaos or of sheer arbitrariness in the use of power. In short, confidence based on legal rules is a necessary, yet insufficient, condition for realizing human rights.

On the same line of argument, we can introduce the component of responsiveness. Public authorities must be willing to fulfill the purpose they were conferred for, and the presumed beneficiaries must be able to control the degree of fulfillment. Consequently, responsiveness implies transparency as well as accountability (Keohane 2007, 8–9). The performance of those who are held to account must be transparent to the accountability holders. The latter must be able to gain information relevant for assessing structures and practices of governance at reasonable cost, and they must be able to address justified critique to concrete actors. The governance actors, in turn, must be willing to answer the critique and take the appropriate steps if necessary.

Finally, participation plays two roles in a rights-based approach of legitimacy. First, it is of instrumental value insofar as it raises the probability that those wielding power respect and realize human rights. Consider Amartya Sen's famous claim that democratic governance is the most effective means to prevent famines. According to Sen, famines are almost always partly a consequence of political mismanagement and democratic accountability tends to inhibit grave mismanagement (1981). Second, the right to participate as a free and equal person is itself a requirement of minimal justice, based on human rights. Given the moral principle of equal respect and concern, it is always problematic that some persons should concentrate much more power than the rest of a population. Having a right to participate as a free and equal person is an expression of the basic moral principle whenever structures of governance distribute powers unequal—as almost any structure of governance does (Christiano 1996).

Good Governance Under Conditions of Fragile Statehood

Application of the Normative Standards

Is our conception of good governance applicable to fragile states as well? At first sight, nothing seems to prevent us from an affirmative answer. The basic norm of ensuring access to institutions necessary for realizing basic human rights only serves as a minimalist standard of justice that does not conceptually presuppose strong, or even any sort of, statehood. The same is true with regard to rule of law, responsiveness, and participation. The rule of law is conceivable without a monopoly of rightful violence and a jurisdiction based on territory; responsiveness is conceivable without a government; participation is conceivable without a *demos* (it might be a totality of stakeholders, functionally defined, instead). Although some sufficiently strong constitutional governments do embody the standards of good governance paradigmatically, in and by themselves the standards are formal and flexible enough to become transferred to more troubled conditions as well. In any situation, the rights-based approach lends support to those structures of institutions that are best suited to fulfill the basic norm in forms and by means that are themselves compatible with human rights norms.

In this respect it is important to note that the rule of law, responsiveness, and participation are principles demanding that we do the best we can to make their full application possible. A principle is not abolished by the fact that it is not always possible to act in direct accordance with it. This gives sufficient room for consequentialist calculations that are especially important where the conditions of governance are far from optimal. In order to weight costs and benefits in a nonarbitrary way the following rule might be helpful:

the higher the costs of realizing basic human rights in terms of any of the other components of good governance, the greater the gain in terms of basic human rights must be to justify such a policy. To give one example, passing over demands for participation might be required as long as there is strong evidence that a majority would not respect human rights standards toward a minority. In contrast, if two policies are feasible that meet human rights standards equally, but one is much less costly in terms of another component of good governance, for example participation, this policy is preferable, other things being equal. This is an aspect of what Robert Keohane (2007, 7) calls the criterion of "comparative benefit." Insofar as the other components are necessary conditions for realizing basic human rights, we might even be justified in weighting the other way around, too: the greater the loss in terms of basic human rights, the greater the gain in terms of any of the other components must be to justify the loss. Although basic human rights place especially strong constraints on any attempt to optimize political outcomes, these constraints cannot be absolute if otherwise the entire system of rights would break down. This principle can be seen as underlying considerations concerning "humanitarian interventions," which almost always cause massive violations of basic interests, at least as unintended yet foreseen side effects. Yet, even under extreme conditions, some human rights violations, for example, intentionally punishing innocent people or institutionalizing torture, remain strictly forbidden.

Metaproblems of Legitimacy

Up to this point, we might have the impression that the problem of defining standards of good governance for fragile states is only a matter of application: we must define the norms rather abstractly in order to be able to adapt them in such a way that they make assessments of policies under nonideal conditions intelligible. One fundamental difference between sufficiently consolidated states and fragile states, however, should not be overlooked. In the latter cases, we are often confronted with metaproblems of legitimacy that are already solved in stable states. Our components of good governance already presuppose two things: the existence of a collectivity for which binding decisions can be made; and the existence of a political authority that has the ultimate responsibility for such decisions. In this second respect, the borders that divide public and private spheres must be sufficiently clear to determine the roles different actors might play with regard to structures of governance.

The collectivity must not be the people of a state, and the authority must not be a government. But in situations in which the authority is de facto absent or fundamentally contested, and the collectivity is deeply divided or its boundaries heavily disputed, a basic question of politics cannot be answered: who is responsible to whom? Following Kalevi Holsti, we can call the first sort of problems "lack of vertical legitimacy" and the second "lack of horizontal legitimacy" (1996, chap. 5). Where the latter is lacking, communicative power in Hannah Arendt's sense—understood as the capacity to joint action, built on agreement by discourse—is absent or at least very weak. And without communicative power no public can hold the authorities responsible. Where vertical legitimacy is lacking, the public misses the opposite of a jointly accepted institutional structure with clearly defined roles for achieving supremacy in the making, application, and enforcement of collectively binding rules. The situation must not be one of true state breakdown. Even hybrid and multilevel forms of governance, as well as legal pluralism, make it easy for governance actors to conceal bad performance and to shift responsibility onto other players in cases of critique (Randeria 2003).

Solving these metaproblems of legitimacy is a precondition for fulfilling our basic norm: to guarantee that each individual has access to institutions that protect their basic rights. To repeat, that norm does not call for a specific structure of institutions corresponding to a specific collectivity, but it requires *some* structure and *some* collectivity. The conceptual openness has to be filled, and filling it means solving the metaproblems of legitimacy. Most basically this requires establishing and securing a societal order as such. In order to find solutions for the metaproblems of legitimate governance, the engagement of the international community with its organizations and institutions is indispensable. Additionally, nonstate actors, from the international and local civil society as well as business enterprises, might be well suited to do their share.

Normative political theory up to now has not much to say concerning these metaproblems. This is partly so because any concrete answer will mostly depend upon pragmatic considerations. For example, there is no general answer of principle to the question of what are the proper boundaries of a state. A principled reasoning seems to allow only a very formal answer: whoever is sufficiently well suited for becoming a governance actor on the second level should try his or her best to establish or strengthen those structures of institutions and those collectivities which most likely will satisfy all four criteria of good governance. Whenever alternatives are feasible, and accessible without prohibitive transaction costs, he or she should choose the one that most likely will bring the best benefit instead of being satisfied with a solution that is clearly suboptimal (Keohane 2007). And any actor should do so in forms and by means that do themselves express commitment to the standards in terms of which they justify their engagement.

This latter requirement is a matter of integrity: acting in accordance with one's self-proclaimed procedures and major goals. It is highly likely that an actor will not foster compliance to norms by others if he or she manifestly and unnecessarily deviates from them. The decline of the United States' reputation as a consequence of its violations of human rights and international law under the guise of a "war on terrorism" is an obvious example.

But the integrity criterion is not only of instrumental importance. It is itself a matter of principle. To the degree that actors play a political role, the standards of good governance should be applied to their performance approximately. Solving the metaproblems of legitimate governance is itself a task of governance, yet on a higher level. At that level, the demand for legitimacy appears again. In the last instance, humanity as such has a stake in the quality of meta-level governance. Fragile statehood is a challenge for cosmopolitanism.

The Subsidiary Responsibility of the International Community Under Public International Law

The foregoing analysis from the perspective of political morality has shown that a uniquely state-based approach is unable to cope with the problem of governance in and by fragile states. Public international law, too, must take this finding into account. As will be shown, there are ways to do so within the existing normative structures, although the state is, and remains, the central actor for the international legal system and hence the primary duty bearer of international legal standards for good governance. For this purpose, we will now look at the three aspects just developed from the point of view of public international law: the contents and bearers of a subsidiary responsibility, the standards applicable to the fulfillment of the responsibility, and the purpose of international engagement.

CONTENTS AND BEARERS OF A
SUBSIDIARY RESPONSIBILITY

Under public international law, a subsidiary responsibility of the international community to ensure the minimum standards of good governance has gained recognition in the past two decades. It flows from the fact that sovereignty is not absolute, but qualified by obligations to protect human rights, and from the fact that human rights, as obligations *erga omnes*, are considered the object of international concern. The international community uses international organizations, particularly the U.N., to prevent and counter human rights violations. In this context, it is significant that the Security Council took binding actions under chapter 7 of the U.N. Charter in cases of massive human rights violations, even those that did not have repercussions on neighboring states,[28] and in cases where a democratically elected government was ousted by a military coup d'état.[29] In doing so, the Security Council acted upon the subsidiary responsibility of the international community in cases of severe violations of governance standards as a part of its responsibility for the maintenance of international peace and security (article 24.1, U.N. Charter). The—albeit implicit—recognition of a subsidiary collective "responsibility to protect" by the World Summit confirms this interpretation.[30]

Governance failure in fragile states does not happen overnight. Usually, two phases can be distinguished: the first during which the violation of legal standards of good governance is imminent, and the second in which these violations take place. A subsidiary responsibility to ensure the minimum standards of good governance thus requires preventive and restorative actions. Theoretically, both types of actions can be taken under chapter 7 because imminent and actual violations can both be considered threats to the peace in the sense of article 39 of the U.N. Charter if they are sufficiently grave. In practice, the Security Council uses its power to address recommendations so as to prevent imminent violations, and reserves its power to issue binding decisions to cases of actual violations.

There are no specific rules determining the conditions under which the council must fulfill the subsidiary responsibility incumbent on the international community. Such criteria were debated only with respect to a "responsibility to react," namely a responsibility to have recourse to (military) force to protect a population, but were not accepted for it by the World Summit in 2005 (Stahn 2007). A fortiori, they do not exist for a "responsibility to prevent" or a "responsibility to rebuild."[31] Therefore, from a legal perspective, the subsidiary responsibility to protect only empowers the international community to act, but does not oblige it—there is no *duty* to protect. Thus, there is a discrepancy between the moral duty to help and international law as long as the decision to have recourse to binding measures under chapter 7 remains within the political discretion of the Security Council.

In the absence of collective actions authorized by the Security Council, the question arises whether individual states or even nonstate actors such as business enterprises or NGOs may act in fulfillment of the responsibility of the international community. Individual states may act because human rights constitute obligations *erga omnes*. Yet, the sovereignty of the targeted state and the concomitant prohibitions of intervention and of the use of force largely exclude effective preventive, reactive, or restorative actions against or without the will of the former.

As preventive measures, that is, before a violation occurs, individual states can merely warn another state against impending human rights violations. This action does not violate the prohibition of intervention because the warning state has a legally recognized interest in the respect of human rights as they constitute obligations *erga omnes*. More effective proactive measures, however, such as support for capacity building, presuppose the consent of the targeted state, if the Security Council did not authorize them. Arguably, under article 2.1 of the ICESCR, states are obliged to accept international assistance if they lack sufficient means to realize economic, social, and cultural rights. It is, however, still disputed whether states are obliged to provide such assistance.[32]

As a protective measure, that is, when serious human rights violations are occurring, a nonmilitary intervention by individual states can merely take the form of a call for cessation.[33] Although basic human rights are norms *erga omnes*, individual states may not take any other unilateral nonforcible countermeasures.[34] In the absence of a Security Council authorization, military interventions and an ensuing military occupation during the rebuilding phase constitute prohibited use of force. The reluctance of the international community to react, through the Security Council, in cases of serious violations of human rights by authorizing the use of force against the perpetrator state is at the basis of the debate about the legality of unilateral, that is, unauthorized, humanitarian interventions: it can be seen as an attempt to harmonize the requirements of morality with international law by allowing individual states or particular state coalitions to act in fulfillment of the responsibility of the international community.

NATO's intervention in Kosovo marked the turning point in the debate. Before it, the proponents of such a right, mainly from the United States, invoked a right of the state to save its own nationals abroad that they considered an exception to the prohibition of the use of force preceding the U.N. Charter (Amerasinghe 2006, 16–22). Numerous European decision makers and international lawyers, who had previously rejected a unilateral humanitarian intervention, changed their position, presuming an imminent threat of genocide in Kosovo. The justification for unilateral intervention in favor of another state's population was twofold: first, it was argued that the prohibition of the use of force had to be harmonized with the other central pillar of the U.N. system, the protection of human rights (Cassese 1999, 793). Second, proponents of intervention borrowed from considerations of morality to contend that there is a right to help a population defend itself against genocide or "ethnic cleansing" (e.g., Doehring 2004, 448). Yet this approach met with considerable and consistent opposition from numerous states, such as Russia, China, and many developing states, and subsequently was not ratified by the Security Council. It, therefore, cannot be considered to have acquired the status of customary international law (Cassese 1999).

In conclusion, states are seriously constrained by law in taking up the subsidiary responsibility of the international community: in that regard, a discrepancy between international law and morality remains.

The same conclusion holds true a fortiori for nonstate actors, such as business enterprises or NGOs: if international law does not permit states to act on their own volition in the place of the international community if the Security Council is paralyzed, it is only logical that it does not empower nonstate actors to do so. These actors are subjects of international law only with respect to a specific rule that binds or entitles them, and such rule concerning a right or duty to help a state discharge its obligations of good governance is nowhere in sight.

LEGAL STANDARDS APPLICABLE TO THE FULFILLMENT OF THE SUBSIDIARY RESPONSIBILITY

By its standards for good governance within states, public international law sets the framework also for the way in which the international community fulfills its subsidiary responsibility. These standards bind all subjects of this legal order, including the U.N., if they constitute customary international law. For governance standards arising out of human rights treaties, in particular those in connection with the fulfillment of social and economic rights, a binding effect on the U.N. is brought about by two legal considerations: First, human rights treaty obligations belong to the people living in a given territory, and stay there even in case of change of government or dismemberment of the state.[35] Consequently, if governance functions are carried out not by the state but by the U.N., the latter are bound by the human rights treaties in force for that territory. This consequence has been suggested for insurgent movements (Tomuschat 2003b), but there is no reason not to extend the concept to any other actor, be it another state that is not a successor state, an international organization, or nonstate actor.

Second, this result is reached through the general principle of agency of necessity (*negotiorum gestio*), which applies when one actor (the "agent") acts in the place of another (the "principal") who is unable to take a required action. In this situation, the agent is under the duty to respect the obligations binding upon the principal (Bühring and Hüfken 2008). This concept can be found in all legal systems of the world, and serves as a basis for a claim of the agent against the principal for reimbursement of his or her costs incurred in carrying out the action (Herdegen 1989, 313–16). Such a claim presupposes the agent's respect for the principal's interests when performing the action, because otherwise the agent would force an unwanted result upon the principal. From a normative perspective, the principal's interests include observance of his or her legal obligations as these restrict the principal's choice of actions were he or she to act. Logically, the concept of agency of necessity can be transposed to interstate relations and, consequently, it can be considered a general principle of law in the sense of article 38.1.c of the ICJ-Statute, which constitutes a source of international law. If *negotiorum gestio* thus is a rule of international law, it binds all subjects of that legal order, states and international organizations alike.

Public international law also regulates the actions of nonstate actors: if nonstate actors exercise governance functions in the absence of a functioning state, for example by ensuring physical security in a territory, by exercising adjudicative functions, or providing health services, they are bound by legal standards of governance.[36] This result is not achieved by a direct applicability of human rights obligations to nonstate actors. Attempts to bind transnational corporations and other business enterprises directly to human rights have failed so far.[37] Nevertheless, nonstate actors must be considered obliged by human rights under customary and treaty law if they exercise governance functions instead of the state. This result follows from the idea that human rights stay with the people on a given territory, and from the principle of agency of necessity (*negotiorum gestio*) as explained earlier. This conclusion is reinforced by article 9 of the ILC, Draft Articles on State Responsibility: under this rule, the conduct of a person is attributed to a state "if the person . . . is in fact exercising elements of the governmental authority in the absence or default of the official authorities and in circumstances such as to call for the exercise of those elements of authority." If, by law and irrespective of the state's will, a private act is attributed to it, the state has a legal interest in that its international legal obligations are respected by the private actor.

PURPOSE OF INTERNATIONAL ENGAGEMENT

As we have shown before, considerations of political morality may require institution building so as to create the preconditions for vertical legitimacy, and "collectivity building" so as to achieve horizontal legitimacy. Public international law takes up this idea: to effectively discharge its responsibility, the international community cannot limit its restorative actions to merely stopping violence in a fragile state. As the responsibility of the international community is subsidiary to that of the state concerned, its fulfillment is geared toward the creation of conditions in which the state can live up to its primary responsibility. Consequently, the activities of the international community must aim at establishing the material, structural, and societal preconditions of consolidated statehood unless it is evident that nonstate structures are at least equally effective for the protection of human rights, equally respectful of the rule of law, equally responsive, and equally open to public participation.

Conclusions

Under public international law and according to political morality, sovereignty is restricted by requirements of good governance based on human rights. These requirements encompass basic human rights, the rule of law, and responsiveness of and public participation in the exercise of governance functions. Public international law does not contain special (lowered) standards of good governance for fragile states; it merely allows, in case of emergency, temporary nonperformance of human rights. Yet it excludes this possibility for peremptory or nonderogable human rights. In a similar vein, the concept of "core obligations" under economic, social, and cultural rights permits taking into account the particular problems of fragile states. At the same time, however, it obliges them to seek international help if they are unable to fulfill the Hobbesian minimum. These findings are corroborated by considerations of political morality according to which states are only means to fully realize human rights, and are as such replaceable in principle if other actors are better suited to do that duty.

From both perspectives, that of public international law and that of political morality, the interrelationship of human rights and institutional structures turns out to be crucial. We have argued that solving the metaproblems of horizontal and vertical legitimacy in a collectivity has logical priority. As a consequence, the subsidiary responsibility of the international community must focus primarily on establishing institutions and societal cohesion in fragile states, be it as preventive measures ("responsibility to prevent") or as restorative measures ("responsibility to rebuild," irrespective of whether there was a preceding forcible intervention or not). It is, therefore, both morally and legally insufficient to concentrate almost exclusively on a "responsibility to react." Moreover, and contrary to a widely-held conviction, solving the metaproblems of legitimacy does often militate against a "fast in—fast out" approach.

In fulfilling its responsibility, the international community is bound by international law standards of good governance. These norms apply to all actors fulfilling governance functions, including nonstate actors, irrespective of whether their exercise of these functions is legal under international law. Thus, insurgent movements as well as warlords, NGOs, or business corporations are constrained by international law. Consolidated statehood remains the model, and may be replaced only by such structures that are at least equally respectful of the legal and moral standards of good governance. At the same time, the international community must avoid aggravating existing lacks of vertical or horizontal legitimacy by measures that deepen the divide between various societal groups or that weaken a government that is seriously trying to fulfill the moral and international legal obligations of good governance. Economic structures, as well, are in need of reform if they provide bad incentives, for example for corruption or flight of capital, which most likely will weaken political authorities that are basically legitimate.

What remains open is the question of whether unilateral state action in situations of emergency, where collective solutions are not feasible, is not only morally required but also legally valid. Again, considerations of this problem should focus more on preventive and restorative measures than on military interventions alone. Moreover, international law must develop approaches to ensuring the respect of legal standards for good governance by nonstate actors. Solutions will only be effective if they take into account the different motivations and aspirations of the various types of nonstate actors, although in principle, morally justified cosmopolitan duties regarding basic human rights are binding to each actor, of whatever type, who is capable to take part in improving the situation. Nevertheless, both for political morality and for public international law, the (consolidated) state will retain its central position, if only as a point of reference in discourses concerning legitimacy and in the aspirations of peoples that up to now lack a political order they can rightfully regard as their own.

NOTES

1. There is a host of academic literature on the changing face of sovereignty. See, e.g., Alston 2007; Bothe, O'Connell, and Ronzitti 2005; Kingsbury 1998; Krasner 2001; Tomuschat 2003a.

2. Cf., e.g., the "Declaration on the Guidelines on the Recognition of the New States in Eastern Europe and in the Soviet Union" of the EC Council of Foreign Ministers, December 16, 1991.

3. The starting point was the 1990 Human Development Report of the UNDP. For a detailed analysis of the "rights-based approach to development" see, e.g., Hamm (2001) and Kirkemann, Hansen, and Sano (2006).

4. Article 2.3 of the U.N. General Assembly Declaration on the Right to Development, December 4, 1986, A/RES/41/128. Despite the ongoing debate about the right to development, this internal dimension is not contested; the debate concerns the external dimension (development as a human right imposing obligations on states other than one's home state) and as an entitlement between states.

5. The seminal text is that of the World Conference on Human Rights, Vienna Declaration and Programme of Action, A/CONF.157/23, July 12, 1993, par. 5.

6. Cf. ICJ, Case of Military and Paramilitary Activities in and against Nicaragua (Nicaragua v. US), Merits, ICJ Rep. 1986, 218–20.

7. See, e.g., Human Rights Committee, General Comment No. 29, Article 4: Derogations during a state of emergency (2001). Reprinted in "Compilation of General Comments and General Recommendations Adopted by Human Rights Treaty Bodies," HRI/GEN/1/Rev.7 (2004), 184, par. 11.

8. See "Compilation of General Comments," par. 13–15.

9. This does not, however, imply that states cannot use the limitations clauses contained in the rights guaranteed. Cf., e.g., the permissible limitations of the free exercise of religion pursuant to article 18.2, ICCPR.

10. This provision applies not only to fragile states but to all states, because of the open-ended nature of most of the rights contained in the ICESCR (e.g., the "right to health" under article 12 is, in reality, a right "to the highest attainable standards of health.").

11. ICESCR Committee, General Comment No. 3 (The nature of states parties' obligations, article 2, par. 1, of the Covenant) (1990), par. 9. Reprinted in "Compilation of General Comments," 15.

12. "Compilation of General Comments," par. 10.

13. Ibid., par. 13.

14. See, e.g., U.N. Millennium Declaration, A/RES/55/2, September 8, 2000, par. 9 and 24, and World Summit Declaration, A/RES/60/1, September 16, 2005, par. 119 and 134; Comm'n Hum. Rts. Res. 2005/32 ("Democracy and the Rule of Law"), April 19, 2005 (adopted by 46 votes to none, with 7 abstentions).

15. General Comment No. 29, Article 4. "Compilation of General Comments," par. 2.

16. Comm'n Hum. Rts Res. 2005/68, April 19, 2005 ("The role of good governance in the promotion and protection of human rights"), par. 1 (adopted without a vote).

17. World Summit Outcome, A/RES/60/1, September 16, 2005, par. 24.b.

18. GA Res. 41/128, December 4, 1986, article 2.2.

19. U.N. Millennium Declaration, A/RES/52/2, September 8, 2000, par. 25 and par. I 6 ("more inclusive political process").

20. A/RES/60/1, September 16, 2005, par. 135.

21. Resolution 2005/29 ("Strengthening of popular participation, equity, social justice and non-discrimination as essential foundations of democracy"), April 19, 2005 (adopted by 28 votes to 14, with 11 abstentions), par. 8–10.

22. See identical article 1, ICCPR and ICESCR, as well as principle 5 of the Declaration on Principles of International Law, Friendly Relations and Co-operation

Among States in Accordance with the Charter of the United Nations, U.N. General Assembly Res. 2625 (25), October 24, 1970 ("Friendly Relations Declaration").

23. Allen Buchanan introduces and defends this norm as a "natural duty of justice" (2004, 85–86).

24. This does not mean that anyone is entitled to an equal amount of any good of some moral relevance. But each justification given for an unequal distribution of any morally relevant good must be compatible with the equal moral worth of all humans. Clear cases of violation of this requirement are racist or sexist justifications for unequal access to fundamental liberties, to public participation, to education and basic health care, or to the opportunity structures of labor markets. We call an unequal treatment "discriminatory" if it expresses disrespect for the equal moral worth of any person irrespective of gender, race, religion, sexual orientation, etc.

25. Martha Nussbaum (2006, 284–85) emphasizes this relation with regard to her capabilities approach that she takes to be a species of the human rights approach. At the same time, the capabilities approach can be seen as one—but not the only— possible interpretation of the idea of basic interests.

26. Even authors who deny that there is a global scope of distributive justice do accept such a global scope with regard to basic human rights (see Nagel 2005).

27. Allen Buchanan therefore distinguishes between a weak—"Hobbesian"—and a strong—"Fullerian"—interpretation of the rule of law (Buchanan 2004, 459–60).

28. SC Res. 733 (1992) (Somalia), and SC Res. 918 (1994) (Rwanda).

29. SC 814 (1993) (Haiti, still with reference to transboundary effects [refugees]); SC 1132 (1997) (Sierra Leone).

30. See A/RES/60/1, September 16, 2005, par. 138.

31. This terminology follows the distinction introduced by the International Commission on Intervention and State Security (ICISS), The Responsibility to Protect, 2001. Accessed June 26, 2008, www.iciss.ca/pdf/Commission-Report.pdf.

32. According to the ICESCR Committee, "[i]t is particularly incumbent upon those States which are in a position to assist others in this regard" ("Compilation of General Comments," par. 13). It thus evades language that suggests an obligation. For a position in favor of such transnational human rights obligations, see Skogly and Gibney (2002).

33. Article 48, ILC Draft Articles on State Responsibility, Annex to A/RES/56/83, December 12, 2001.

34. See International Law Commission (ILC), Draft Articles on State Responsibility with Commentaries, A/50/10 and Corr. 1 (2001), commentary on article 54, 139, par. 6.

35. Human Rights Committee, General Comment No. 26 (Continuity of Human Rights Obligations) (1997), reprinted in "Compilation of General Comments and General Recommendations Adopted by Human Rights Treaty Bodies," HRI/GEN/1/Rev.7, 2004, 172, par. 4.

36. This conclusion does not conflict with our prior finding that there is no legal right or duty of nonstate actors to help a state discharge its good governance obligations, because it applies to the factual situation where a nonstate actor voluntarily exercises governance functions. It is all the more important if it turns out that there is a moral duty of such an actor to undertake governance functions.

37. See, in particular, the "Norms on the Responsibility of Transnational Corporations and Other Business Enterprises with Regard to Human Rights" drafted by the U.N. Sub-Commission for the Protection and Promotion of Human Rights, U.N. Doc. E/CN.4/Sub.2/2003/12/Rev.2, and their rejection by the Commission on Human Rights through Dec. 2004/116 of April 20, 2004, par. c (recommendation to ECOSOC to "affirm that [the document containing the Norms] . . . has no legal standing."

REFERENCES

Alston, Philip. 2007. *Human Rights, Intervention, and the Use of Force*. Oxford: Oxford University Press.

Amerasinghe, Chittharanjan F. 2006. "The Conundrum of Recourse to Force—to Protect Persons." *International Organizations Law Review* 3:7–53.

Bothe, Michael, Mary Ellen O'Connell, and Natalino Ronzetti, eds. 2005. *Redefining Sovereignty: The Use of Force After the Cold War*. Ardsley, N.Y.: Transnational Publishers.

Buchanan, Allen. 2004. *Justice, Legitimacy, and Self-Determination: Moral Foundations for International Law*. Oxford: Oxford University Press.

Bühring, Ferry, and Nina Hüfken. 2008. "Menschenrechtsstandards für Governance in schwachen und zerfallen(d)en Staaten." In *Transdisziplinäre Governance-Forschung: Gemeinsam hinter den Staat blicken*, edited by Ulrike Höppner, Matthias Kötter, and Sybille de la Rosa, 187–208. Baden-Baden: Nomos.

Cassese, Antonio. 1999. "A Follow-Up: Forcible Humanitarian Countermeasures and Opinio Necessitatis." *European Journal of International Law* 10, no. 4:791–99.

Christiano, Thomas. 1996. *The Rule of the Many*. Boulder, Colo.: Westview Press.

Doehring, Karl. 2004. *Völkerrecht*. 2nd edition. Munich: C.H. Beck.

Dworkin, Ronald. 1978. *Taking Rights Seriously*. Cambridge, Mass.: Harvard University Press.

Eide, Asbjørn. 1989. "Realization of Social and Economic Rights and the Minimum Threshold Approach." *Human Rights Law Journal* 10:35–51.

Feinberg, Joel. 1980. "The Nature and Value of Rights." In *Rights, Justice, and the Bounds of Liberty*, edited by Joel Feinberg, 143–58. Princeton: Princeton University Press.

Forst, Rainer. 1999. "The Basic Right to Justification: Towards a Constructivist Conception of Human Rights." *Constellations* 6:35–60.

Fraser, Nancy. 2005. "Re-framing Justice in a Globalizing World." *New Left Review* 36:69–88.

Gert, Bernard. 1998. *Morality: Its Nature and Justification*. New York: Oxford University Press.

Goodin, Robert. 1988. "What Is So Special About Our Fellow Countrymen?" *Ethics* 98:663–86.

Habermas, Jürgen. 1998. *Between Facts and Norms: Contributions to a Discourse Theory of Law and Democracy*. Cambridge, Mass.: MIT Press.

Hamm, Brigitte I. 2001. "A Human Rights Approach to Development." *Human Rights Quarterly* 23:1005–31.

Herdegen, Matthias. 1989. "Zur Geschäftsführung ohne Auftrag (negotiorum gestio) im Völkerrecht." In *Staat und Völkerrechtsordnung. Festschrift für Karl Doehring*, edited by Kay Hailbronner, Georg Ress, and Thorsten Stein, 303–21. Berlin: Springer.

Holsti, Kalevi. 1996. *The State, the War, and the State of War*. Cambridge, Mass.: Cambridge University Press.

Keohane, Robert O. 2007. "Governance and Legitimacy." Keynote Speech Held at the Opening Conference of the Research Center (SFB) 700 (with Comments by Fritz W. Scharpf), SFB-Governance Lecture Series, no. 1, Berlin.

Kingsbury, Benedict. 1998. "Sovereignty and Inequality." *European Journal of International Law* 9, no. 4:599–625.

Kirkemann Hansen, Jakob, and Hans-Otto Sano. 2006. "The Implications and Value Added of a Rights-Based Approach." In *Development as a Human Right: Legal, Political, and Economic Dimensions*, edited by Bård A. Andreassen and Stephen P. Marks, 36–56. Cambridge, Mass.: Harvard University Press.

Krasner, Stephen D., ed. 2001. *Problematic Sovereignty: Contested Rules and Political Possibilities*. New York: Columbia University Press.

Ladwig, Bernd. 2000. "Militärische Interventionen zwischen Moralismus und Legalismus." *Deutsche Zeitschrift für Philosophie* 48, no. 1:133–47.

Lauterpacht, Eli. 1997. "Sovereignty—Myth or Reality?" *International Affairs* 73, no. 1:137–50.

Mellema, Gregory. 1997. *Collective Responsibility*. Amsterdam: Rodopi.

Nagel, Thomas. 2005. "The Problem of Global Justice." *Philosophy and Public Affairs* 34:147–75.

Nowak, Manfred. 2005. *U.N. Covenant on Civil and Political Rights: CCPR Commentary*. 2nd ed. Kehl: N.P. Engel.

Nussbaum, Martha C. 2006. *Frontiers of Justice: Disability, Nationality, Species Membership*. Cambridge, Mass.: Harvard University Press.

O'Neill, Onora. 1996. *Towards Justice and Virtue: A Constructive Account of Practical Reasoning*. Cambridge: Cambridge University Press.

Randeria, Shalini. 2003. "Globalization of Law: Environmental Justice, World Bank, NGOs, and the Cunning State in India." *Current Sociology* 51, nos. 3–4:305–28.

Rawls, John. 1993. *Political Liberalism*. New York: Columbia University Press.

Rudolf, Beate. 2000. *Die thematischen Mechanismen und Arbeitsgruppen der UN-Menschenrechtskommission*. Berlin: Springer.

———. 2006. "Is 'Good Governance' a Norm of Public International Law?" In *Völkerrecht als Wertordnung—Common Values in International Law. Essays in Honour of Christian Tomuschat*, edited by Pierre-Marie Dupuy, Bardo Faßbender, Malcolm N. Shaw, and Karl-Peter Sommermann, 1007–28. Kehl: N.P. Engel.

———. 2008. "The Relation of the Right to Development to Existing Substantive Treaty Regimes." In *Implementing the Right to Development: The Role of International Law*, edited by Stephen P. Marks, 105–16. Geneva: Friedrich-Ebert-Stiftung.

Schlothfeldt, Stephan. 2007. "Wer ist angesichts der Weltarmut wozu verpflichtet?" In *Weltarmut und Ethik*, edited by Barbara Bleisch and Peter Schaber, 77–94. Paderborn: Mentis.

Schrijver, Nico. 1999. "The Changing Nature of State Sovereignty." *British Yearbook of International Law* 70:65–98.

Sen, Amartya. 1981. *Poverty and Famines: An Essay on Entitlement and Deprivation*. New York: Oxford University Press.

———. 1999. *Development as Freedom*. New York: Knopf.

Shue, Henry. 1980. *Basic Rights, Subsistence, Affluence, and U.S. Foreign Policy*. Princeton: Princeton University Press.

———. 1988. "Mediating Duties." *Ethics* 98:687–704.

———. 1996. *Basic Rights: Subsistence, Affluence, and U.S. Foreign Policy*. 2nd ed. Princeton: Princeton University Press.

Simma, Bruno. 1998. "'Die vergessenen Rechte': Bemühungen zur Stärkung des VN-Sozialpakts." In *Verfassung, Theorie und Praxis des Sozialstaats, Festschrift für Hans Zacher*, edited by Franz Ruland, Bernd Baron von Maydell, and Hans-Jürgen Papier, 867–82. Heidelberg: C.F. Müller.

———, ed. 2002. *The Charter of the United Nations: A Commentary*, vol. 1. 2nd ed. Munich and Oxford: CH. Beck and Oxford University Press.

Stahn, Carsten. 2007. "Responsibility to Protect: Political Rhetoric or Emerging Legal Norm?" *American Journal of International Law* 101, no. 1:99–120.

Tomuschat, Christian. 2003a. "How the Classical Concept of Sovereignty Has Evolved." In *The International and the National: Essays in Honour of Vojin Dimitrijevic*, edited by M. D. Dilas and V. Deric, 21–32. Belgrade: Belgrade Centre of Human Rights.

———. 2003b. "The Applicability of Human Rights Law to Insurgent Movements." In *Krisensicherung und humanitärer Schutz. Festschrift für Dieter Fleck*, edited by Horst Fischer, 573–91. Berlin: Berliner Wissenschafts-Verlag.

UNDP. 1990. "Human Development Report." Accessed June 23, 2008. http://hdr .undp.org/en/reports/global/hdr1990/.

Williams, Bernard. 2005. *In the Beginning Was the Deed: Realism and Moralism in Political Argument*. Princeton: Princeton University Press.

9

State Building or New Modes of Governance?

The Effects of International Involvement in Areas

of Limited Statehood

Ulrich Schneckener

S INCE THE BEGINNING OF THE TWENTY-FIRST century, state building has become (again) one of the key tasks for the international community.[1] In contrast to earlier historical periods, state building does not address the establishment of new states, but the shaping and strengthening of the state's capacities to fulfill basic functions and to respond to the needs of its citizens, be it in the area of internal and external security, the delivery of basic public services, the quality of public administration, or the rule of law. Here, international involvement and interventions by external actors differ to a great extent regarding missions, mandates, and resources. They range from aid and assistance work to the deployment of international troops and the establishment of transitional administrations. Since the mid-1990s, the international community, mainly under the auspices of the United Nations, has conducted the most complex and costly civil-military state-building operations in Cambodia, Bosnia, Kosovo, Sierra Leone, Liberia, Ivory Coast, Democratic Republic of the Congo, Timor-Leste, Afghanistan, and Haiti. Iraq may be added to this list; however, it is a special case because of the U.S.-led military invasion and occupation. In all these cases external actors interfered deeply with state sovereignty, by temporarily taking over a number of governance functions, including the provision of domestic security, the organization and monitoring of elections, and the setting up of rules and institutions. In other words, external actors stepped in with their own civilian and military personnel where—because of violent conflicts—state structures were lacking. This type of quasi-protectorates does not only entail a number of risks for the interveners but also requires a reliable provision of personnel and financial resources by the international community.

Moreover, the real challenge for international state builders is to prevent or to stop processes of state failure in many parts of the world. Depending on the criteria, indicators, and data used to "measure" statehood, about forty to sixty states worldwide are labeled as weak, failing, or failed, including such diverging cases as Colombia, Zimbabwe, Algeria, Yemen, Pakistan, Sri Lanka, and the Philippines.[2] Some observers even pose the question as to whether the OECD country Mexico has to be labeled as a fragile state because of the brutal drug war that has cost thousands of lives. The demand for state building efforts, therefore, exceeds supply, which simply means that the "Kosovo model" cannot be universalized—neither on empirical nor on normative grounds. The debate in academia about concepts such as "neotrusteeships" (Fearon and Laitin 2004) or "shared sovereignty" (Krasner 2004) is missing the point and can be regarded as an expression of Western hubris. Indeed, the overall goal of external state builders, mainly shaped by the industrialized countries, to establish and support sustainable state structures, market democracies, and viable civil societies has proven to be extremely ambitious and is accompanied by a number of dilemmas, inconsistencies, and problems. Despite all efforts, in many instances the result of these activities has not been consolidating statehood, but the creation of a variety of governance arrangements linking local and external actors as well as different levels of interaction and policy making.

The main argument here is therefore that the international involvement does not achieve state building, based on a particular approach or strategic orientation, but in fact different forms of governance, which shape the politics and expectations of both external and local actors and which over time foster the transformation of statehood in many parts of the world. A key aspect of this transformation is a process of transnationalization and blurring of borders that opens new opportunities mainly for local elites but does not necessarily lead to the strengthening of state structures and institutions. The article will make this point by addressing first the various strategies and approaches adopted explicitly or implicitly by external state builders and their (most often unintended) effects on the ground. These strategies are based on diverging world views and conceptions of the "good political order." In most instances, external actors pursue these strategies in parallel and, occasionally, in direct competition for resources and political attention. In any case, the necessity, but also the difficulties for coordination, cooperation, and effectiveness are increased. Second, the focus will be on "new" modes of governance that are neither anticipated nor addressed by the state-building strategies. These modes are described and analyzed by using the concepts of multilevel governance, transnational governance and nodal governance.

Multilevel governance refers to the fact that each and every state-building activity involves various levels of policy making that are not independent from each other but follow different rules and logics. In particular, the gap and the inconsistencies between "headquarter level" and "field level" are a permanent concern in international state building. Transnational and nodal governance refer to specific forms of collaboration of external and local actors as well as of state and nonstate actors at the "field level." These *sui generis* arrangements usually emerged without prior planning or design but during the course of an international involvement. They have not been the goal of state-building missions and activities, but they serve particular interests of external and local actors and may take over a number of governance functions, at least for a certain period of time. These modes range from coordination mechanisms to bodies for implementing policies to joint decision-making. While transnational governance emphasizes the involvement and embeddedness of external actors in local affairs (see Schneckener and Zürcher 2007; Johnston 2006), the concept of nodal governance can be used in order to describe the shifting networks of collaboration and the pluricentric power structure in areas of limited statehood (see Shearing and Wood 2003; Wood and Dupont 2006; Burris, Drakos, and Shearing 2005). The assumption is that these arrangements—although initially set up as temporary measures—normally last much longer than most external actors anticipate. Moreover, they usually develop their own political dynamics and gain a certain degree of autonomy from the original mandate and the political masters in faraway capitals or headquarters. They do not only open new opportunities for new actors, but often also for the "old" elites who are well experienced in dealing with fragile statehood. Therefore, in conclusion, external actors have to acknowledge that their involvement does foster the ongoing process of transforming statehood in postcolonial and postconflict settings. This implies that state builders need to learn to cope with counterproductive, unintended effects and understand better the underlying logic of the modes of governance they introduce to areas of limited statehood.

Strategies of State Building

State building aims at strengthening state structures and institutions as well as the capacities for the state apparatus to govern. International state-building activities, mainly undertaken by international organizations, transnational NGOs, or third-party states, may therefore aim at stabilizing and strengthening existing structures; reforming and transforming existing structures; as well as, if necessary, rebuilding and establishing structures that were either absent before or did not exist in this form. The latter variant is primarily related to postconflict societies in which most state institutions have broken down in the course of a violent conflict. However, also in many other cases of fragile statehood the establishment of new institutions (e.g., an independent judiciary) may be necessary. Against this background international state building is conducted in very different forms since external actors— implicitly or explicitly—pursue different practices, agendas, and overall strategic considerations. The assumptions underlying these approaches differ considerably when it comes to the role of the state, the behavior of local actors, the root causes of fragile statehood, the priorities for state building, the required resources, the time-frame allotted to state-building projects and programs as well as the ways of external involvement in local structures. In brief, these "strategies" that are often not clearly defined and articulated by external actors result from diverging philosophies about the "good" political order. They can roughly be attributed to international relations theories (see table 9.1).

Conceptually speaking, these strategies are not mutually exclusive but are rather complementary; to a certain extent they are even interdependent. In practice these approaches are usually pursued simultaneously, albeit with different emphases, depending on the case at hand. At the same time, however, proponents of these strategies compete for scarce resources of bilateral and multilateral donors and political attention. Therefore, these strategies cannot be neatly attributed to external actors or specific state-building operations. As a rule, most international organizations, multilateral donors, and

TABLE 9.1 State-Building Strategies

Strategy	Priorities (examples)	IR-Theory
Liberalization First	Democratization, economic reform, privatization, integration into the world economy	Liberal approaches, democratic peace theory
Security First	Strengthening the state's monopoly on force, strengthening the security apparatus, security sector reform	Realist approaches
Institutionalization First	Strengthening political and administrative institutions, promoting the rule of law	Institutionalist approaches
Civil Society First	Strengthening social cohesion, enhancing political participation, supporting NGOs, associations, parties	Social-constructivist approaches, norm diffusion

governments often unconsciously draw on various approaches at the same time, because internally each strategy has its advocates in different administrative units such as ministries, departments, or—as in the case of the United Nations—specialized agencies. More often than not different actors within an international bureaucracy or a government with diverging strategic preferences and diverging policy backgrounds compete for limited resources. This functional differentiation gives rise to intrainstitutional competition over resources and policies, and explains the frequently lamented lack of coherence. It is, hence, decisive whether and to what extent external actors are capable of combining the respective advantages of the various strategies, and to what extent they are able to capitalize on the interdependencies that exist between the different measures. In general, four ideal-type strategic orientations or paradigms can be distinguished.

Liberalization First

This strategy constitutes the dominant paradigm in development policy, even though individual actors such as the United States, the World Bank, the IMF, regional development banks, the European Union, and bilateral donors emphasize different aspects when it comes to practical implementation. First and foremost, Liberalization First is about the promotion of political and economic liberties; the strategy aims at democratization and the establishment of market economies (the so-called Washington Consensus). In IR-theoretical terms, this approach comes closest to the liberal assumption, which sees democratic market economies as guarantors of peace and stability—in their internal affairs as well as their external relations. This hypothesis is derived from the democratic peace theory, according to which democracies are less war prone than nondemocracies, and above all do not wage war against each other. Moreover, this approach is informed by assumptions about the pacifying effects of free trade and economic interdependence ("peace by trade") (see Oneal and Russet 1999; David 1999). International relations literature also provides the label "Neo-Wilsonianism," following President Wilson's idea of a liberal international order guaranteeing peace and security (Paris 2004, 40–54).

Advocates of this strategy believe that weak states suffer from a lack of transparent, democratic governance structures and from a lack of economic freedom, which is reflected in pervasive rent seeking, limited access to international markets, technological backwardness, and a low investment rate. Post-conflict cases are therefore regarded and treated as special cases of transformation societies that are transitioning from authoritarian rule to democracy. Consequently, the focus of this state-building strategy is on holding free and fair elections, guaranteeing political liberties and protecting private property, and promoting good governance in terms of effective public administration and comprehensive economic reforms. The latter includes privatization and market liberalization in order to facilitate economic integration into global markets. The state is seen as a guarantor of basic liberties. According to pure theory, it is supposed to confine itself to providing a reliable legal framework within which the market economy can thrive freely. With the adoption of the Millennium Development Goals in 2000, the Liberalization First approach has been broadened and altered to put more emphasis on the welfare aspect of liberalization (Post-Washington Consensus). Particular attention was devoted to poverty reduction and the establishment of effective educational and public health systems. This volte-face was triggered by the realization on the part of large donors that meeting basic human needs is a crucial precondition for realizing civil and economic liberties.

A prominent example for Liberalization First—at least on a conceptual level—is the Bush administration's foreign policy doctrine developed after September 11, 2001, whose centerpiece is the promotion of freedom and democracy around the world. In the same vein, the National Security Strategy of March 2006 considers the creation and promotion of "effective democracies" to be crucial for countering a number of security challenges.[3] Hence, the former secretary of state, Condoleezza Rice, underlined the need for "transformational diplomacy" aimed at the establishment and consolidation of democratic, well-governed states that are responsive to the needs of their citizens and act responsible in the international system.[4]

The Liberalization First program, however, systematically underestimates the destabilizing effects often associated with rapid democratization and the liberalization of markets ("shock therapy"). First, it is in the very nature of elections and electoral campaigns to reinforce polarization and tensions between segments of the society; this applies to postconflict situations in particular as well as to latent conflicts. Considering the almost inevitable unequal distribution of resources, the ruling elite usually enjoys exclusive access to the state media and has manifold opportunities of manipulation; hence, it is usually the power holders who benefit from such processes, because they can clothe their actions in the cloak of democratic legitimacy. In postconflict societies this often reinforces the political cleavages and configurations of power that emerged from the conflict, thus empowering those policy makers who were responsible for the escalation of violence in the first place. The 1996 elections in Bosnia from which ethnonationalist parties emerged as dominant forces provide a virtually paradigmatic example. Under such circumstances moderate forces or new groupings do not really have a chance to influence the contours of the postconflict order.

Second, the economic aspects of Liberalization First—that is, economic reform aimed at privatization and deregulation—usually serve the interests of the economic elite such as clans or oligarchs, thus deepening the socioeconomic divide. Privatization processes in particular are usually associated with corruption and forms of organized crime. This significantly hampers the establishment of tax-funded public institutions devoted to the common good. These effects are reinforced by liberalization efforts' tendency toward deinstitutionalization. Existing institutions and structures are deemed ineffective; they are called into question or even eliminated by donors—see for example the structural adjustment programs adopted by the international financial institutions in the 1980s and early 1990s. The U.S.-led Coalition Provisional Authority (CPA, 2003–4) in Iraq provided a textbook example of the destabilizing effects of Liberalization First. The CPA clearly prioritized rapid democratization and market liberalization over security and rule of law.[5]

Security First

Advocates of this approach, which is derived from realist thinking in international relations, propagate a less ambitious approach. In their view, external actors should focus on guaranteeing physical security, in particular on the (re-)establishment and strengthening of the state's monopoly on the use of force (Marten 2004; Ottaway and Mair 2004; Rubin 2008). According to Etzioni (2007), external actors should in particular avoid any kind of social engineering, be it democratization or nation building efforts, for both normative and empirical reasons. Instead, the Security First agenda is premised on the assumption that if the state is unable to perform the essential task of providing physical security, sustainable development in other areas of governance is impossible ("no development without security"). The primary focus is thus on the internal and external protective as well as coercive dimension of state sovereignty. Therefore, the demobilization—or at least containment—of armed nonstate actors, security sector reform, training of the armed forces, of border troops, the police and the judiciary (in particular with a view to improving the ability of prosecution agencies to effectively combat violence), the transformation of war economies into economies of peace, the fight against crime, and the strengthening of the state's ability to control its territory and its borders are considered critical to any statebuilding effort. Moreover, in the case of postconflict societies, separating the warring parties and eliminating the intrastate security dilemma are considered essential first steps in order to prevent the state from relapsing into conflict. In the case of ethnonational conflicts that have already escalated, some authors therefore support partitioning territories and redrawing borders that may even include territorial secession, in order to permanently separate the warring factions (Kaufmann 1998). Traditional United Nations peacekeeping missions epitomized the Security First approach, because they aimed primarily at stabilizing the situation by separating the belligerent parties ("trip-wire" function) and by monitoring a cease-fire or a peace agreement. Yet, this approach is no longer compatible with the needs of today's multi-dimensional U.N. missions. Generally, the Security First strategy is primarily about security sector reform, programs for the containment of small arms and light weapons (SALW) proliferation, the disarmament, demobilization, and reintegration of former combatants (DDR programs) as well as counter-terrorism and countercrime programs.[6]

The Security First approach, which is more stability than reform oriented, entails the risk of degrading unintentionally into a de facto Security Only approach and ultimately strengthening status quo forces. Although it can hardly be disputed that the provision of physical security is vital to the suc-cess of all other state-building activities, focusing on the state security appa-ratus often leads to the establishment and strengthening of authoritarian or semiauthoritarian structures, which in turn would prove counterproductive in other areas of state building. Under certain circumstances the ruling elites obtain internationally funded and more effective instruments of political power which allow them to block or reverse reforms, repress oppositional forces, or even marginalize certain parts of the population, which in the me-dium term should prove destabilizing and may cause rebellion. Moreover, in some cases governments and state security forces, both supported by inter-national state builders, felt encouraged to escalate festering or acute conflicts with armed rivals and rebels—as happened in the early 2000s in the context of U.S.-funded and -trained antiterror units in Yemen or the Philippines. In general, after September 11, the Security First approach became closely associated with the agenda of the "Global War on Terror" and the notion of "terrorism" used by particular authoritarian regimes that led to a number of severe human rights violations.

Institutionalization First

The primary focus of this strategy is on strengthening legitimate and effec-tive institutions on the national as well as local level in order to enable these to deliver essential services. This approach is partly a reaction to the various failures of the Liberalization First strategy. Despite their common dedication to the ideal of a democratic market economy, the two approaches differ with regard to the means of implementation. In particular for state building in postconflict societies, the formula "institutionalization before liberalization" is deemed appropriate (Paris 2004, 179–211). The basic assumption made by adherents of this strategy, such as Fukuyama (2004), is that knowledge about organizational structures, public administration, and the creation of institutions is transferable while other aspects—sociocultural factors (such as social norms) in particular—can hardly be influenced by external actors. Proponents of the Institutionalization First approach share a belief in the socializing effects of political institutions that—in the medium and long term—contribute to alter the behavior of local actors and further processes of collective learning, which in turn promote respect for public institutions thereby strengthening their capacity to govern effectively. Their activities are therefore primarily directed at establishing and consolidating political institutions (parliaments, councils), promoting the rule of law (establishing constitutional courts, for instance), strengthening and reforming public administration (in particular tax, customs and fiscal authorities), and fighting corruption. Another core task is the creation of institutions and procedures for conflict management and dispute settlement, such as ombudsman offices, committees, arbitration panels, "councils of elders," and traditional courts.

The legitimacy of such measures is crucial to the involvement of all relevant societal groups in these institutions. Institutionalization First is thus compatible with informal or formalized power-sharing models, which place a premium on the inclusion of all relevant actors, not least to prevent cleavages between minorities and the rest of the population. All-party governments, proportional representation, quotas that ensure a fair distribution of offices as well as veto rights are common measures to ensure equal representation (Reilly 2001; Schneckener 2002; O'Flynn and Russell 2005; Jarstad 2008). Other methods for political decision making that do not necessarily correspond to democratic standards, but are nevertheless accepted as legitimate by the local population, are traditional forms of rule, neopatrimonial structures (patron-client relations), and procedures aimed at co-opting and consulting societal groups. This approach is in line with the promotion or revitalization of existing institutions influenced by local traditions inasmuch as these contribute to the consolidation of statehood. Hence, proponents of this concept are not only skeptical regarding rapid economic liberalization but also regarding the imposition of the classical model of a majority democracy (Westminster style), in particular in the context of multiethnic societies. In practice, bi- and multilateral donors pursue this approach especially with a view to reforming public administration and promoting the rule of law.

Since the Institutionalization First approach is emphasizing the need to create or enhance institutional capacity, the strategy tends to privilege actors whose main objective is to secure their power basis and pursue their particularistic interests, rather than to consolidate statehood in the long run. The elite-oriented, top-down perspective of this approach favors such tendencies. In particular the necessity inherent in this strategy to (temporarily) draw on pre- or nondemocratic procedures and institutions, respectively, may undermine or entirely frustrate the long-term goal of democratization. The unintended result of this strategy could, thus, ultimately be the consolidation of authoritarian or clientelistic structures, whose representatives reject any type of reform-oriented policy by making reference to tradition, ethnicity, or religious beliefs, and who continue to pursue their policies behind institutional "facades"—see, for instance, the latest developments in Sudan, Zimbabwe, or Kenya despite official power sharing or grand coalition arrangements between the "old" regime and opposition parties. Correspondingly, the gap between legally formalized procedures and factual politics would widen. In the long run, this would harm the legitimacy of externally induced institutionalization and would exacerbate the population's alienation from the state's institutions.

Civil Society First

This approach, which figures prominently in the literature on peace research and development policy, puts civil society at the center of state-building efforts. In contrast to the three previous strategies, this approach emphasizes the need for bottom-up processes (Harvey 1998; Debiel and Sticht 2005; Van Tongeren et al. 2005). It acts on the assumption that the state and its institutions must develop at the grassroots level and must be sustained by society as a whole. This approach is thus primarily about the development of a political culture and political norms that are supported by a broad majority. Yet this is exactly what is often lacking in weak states. Usually the gap between the ruling elites, the state apparatus, and fragmented societal actors looms large. Adherents of the Civil Society First concept, therefore, believe it to be of prime importance to strengthen social cohesion, to improve opportunities for political participation, to support disadvantaged and marginalized groups, as well as to promote the development of a (critical) public. They admonish governments to respect basic civil liberties and human rights such as freedom of the press and free speech rights, freedom of assembly, and freedom of association. Moreover, they implement projects in the field of women's and children's rights, education, culture, and social work. Their objective is the mobilization of civil society forces (empowerment).

In comparison to the other strategies, this approach places a stronger emphasis on enhancing the state's input legitimacy; it views the state primarily as a forum for participatory bargaining processes and discourses shaped by different segments of the society. In the case of postconflict countries the promotion of civil society by external actors typically includes the delivery of basic humanitarian services, psychological support (such as providing trauma therapy to victims of war), the repatriation of refugees and displaced persons, the reintegration of child soldiers, methods of nonviolent conflict management as well as national reconciliation (victim-offender mediation, for instance). In practice, this usually entails supporting human rights groups, women's associations and peace activists, churches, journalists, political parties, unions, and local communities (Fischer 2006). More often than not the creation of such NGOs is induced by external actors; some NGOs are local spin-offs of international NGOs or activist networks that have specialized in particular issue areas. Hence, in contrast to the other strategies presented in this chapter, advocates of the Civil Society First approach give more importance to the promotion of complementary or alternative structures sustained by nonstate actors, even as temporary solutions until effective state structures are (back) in place to deliver services to large parts of the population.

Proponents of Civil Society First assume that state building is often doomed to failure because of insufficient civil society mobilization. However, this perspective ignores that most fragile states grapple with the weakness of public institutions vis-à-vis private and societal actors. Frequently in these cases, state authority is undermined by nonstate actors who increasingly assume its tasks and functions. Supporting NGOs and other civil society actors in a situation of obvious state weakness risks strengthening just those parallel structures, thereby impeding the development of legitimate statehood. In addition, there are several fundamental difficulties with the implicit normative premises associated with the term civil society. One problem is the identification of actors that constitute "civil society" in any given case. Is the "West" trying to impose its own standards on non-Western societies? This approach thus has an inherent tendency to go beyond a transformation of statehood and aims at a comprehensive restructuring of society. This will inevitably increase external interference into local structures and will require a greater investment of resources as well as raise serious questions of legitimacy. For example, evidence abounds that NGOs—in particular, those that are externally funded—can only to a very limited extent be regarded as authentic civil society actors. More often than not local populations perceive NGOs as "foreign elements" whose services are generally accepted but who are not regarded as legitimate representatives of local communities but as "alien" forces. Equally problematic is the orientation of most NGOs toward particularistic interests instead of the common good and their prevalent subordination to the objectives of external donors. Other issues are the imperative of fundraising, which dominates many activities, and the financial attractiveness of the salaries NGOs offer. They are usually higher than salaries offered by the state, which leads to a corresponding brain drain of local employees out of the public sector. Finally, there often exists a barrier to civil society engagement because of the bureaucratic and intransparent structures within NGOs. These effects are particularly striking in the case of postconflict societies in which NGOs virtually mushroom—see Bosnia after 1996, Kosovo after 1999 or Afghanistan after 2002.[7]

In summary, one may conclude that Liberalization First and Civil Society First adopt a holistic perspective, which dictates a comprehensive (maximalist) agenda. Both approaches, therefore, intrude deeply into existing state and societal structures. Accordingly, it does not come as surprise that the danger of unintended consequences and negative side-effects is extremely high. The other strategies, by contrast, can be reduced to a rather modest if not minimalist agenda and are more focused and less intrusive. Security First and Institutionalization First can, thus, be assumed to be more susceptible to "second-best solutions" and suboptimal results, respectively, while the other two strategies, due to their normative maximalist agendas, will be less amenable to compromise solutions. On the contrary, experience has shown that Liberalization First and Civil Society First tend to successively broaden their agenda in the face of emerging problems, thereby adjusting to the actual complexity of political and socioeconomic processes step by step. As a result, despite their explicit objective—namely, achieving market liberalization and democratization or strengthening civil society—priorities in the state-building process shift or become blurred. The more modest variants of Security First or Institutionalization First may reduce the likelihood of a clash regarding state-building goals. Moreover, the sequencing of measures these approaches propose seems less complicated and more apt to be implemented, not least because of the relatively narrow confines of these measures. On the flipside, however, these approaches risk to fall short of what may be necessary to consolidate statehood by focusing exclusively on the state's core functions. These rest on rather shaky foundations if the economic and social environment continues to be highly unstable. Moreover, their top-down orientation favors elite interests but does not foster societal change. As a matter of fact, the risk of "mission creep" inheres in these two strategies. The more demanding the approaches to security sector reform or to strengthening the rule of law, the greater the likelihood that broader issues such as democratization and strengthening civil society will become salient. Hence, despite their initial intention, in practice, missions with a rather modest mandate (e.g., the so-called light footprint approach for Afghanistan in 2002) were quickly extended in scope, due to the realization that the security situation, the stability of political institutions, the quality of public administration and rule of law, as well as economic development all depend on each other.

Multilevel Governance

All strategies have in common that they do not systematically reflect the challenges of multilevel and multiagency politics. They are by and large based on the assumption that external actors intervene and build up local capacities—regarding market economy and democracy, security, rule of law, or civil society. When the mission is accomplished the tasks and responsibilities will simply be handed over to the "educated" and "trained" locals. This rather paternalistic and static model, however, underestimates the dynamics of interaction, not only between locals and externals, but also among locals and among externals. International state building implies de facto multilevel governance. Analytically, at least four different levels of interaction can be distinguished—all of which have an impact on the conduct and the result of state-building strategies and activities. First, we have the interaction among local actors, in particular between (former or actual) parties to a violent conflict; second, the relationship between local and external actors; third, the interaction among the different external actors in the field, comprising international donors, diplomats, military, and NGOs; and finally, the layer of national capitals or headquarters of international organizations where coordination, policy planning, and decision making has to take place between ministries, departments, or, in the case of international organizations or multilateral formats, between member states.

This multilevel architecture constitutes a complex system in which actual or suspected policy decisions and actions at one level will shape the expectations, the behavior and the actions of actors at other levels. Some of these effects may be intended or at least anticipated, most often, however, they are neither. For external state builders, therefore, the multiple coordination challenge would already be enormous—even if the major players, such as international organizations and bilateral donors, would apply by and large the same doctrine which, as we have seen, is usually not the case. In addition, the operative logic and constraints under which external actors have to work in the field differs greatly from those in their respective capital or headquarter. One most notable result are serious tensions and even mistrust between those, be it military or civilian personnel, who encounter directly the difficulties at the field level and those who have to muster the necessary resources and political commitments for state building in national or international bureaucracies.

Against this background, multilevel governance meets at least two sets of challenges: the first is related to the decision making and policy planning of the external state builders (headquarter level); the second points to the typical dilemmas and difficult choices external actors face vis-à-vis local actors (field level). First of all, external actors are often driven by a number of concerns that have nothing do with the situation on the ground, as the second set of challenges will show. This refers to the headquarter level and the interaction between various external state builders, since experience shows that misperception and mistakes made on this level can hardly be corrected in the field and will significantly increase the likelihood of unintended consequences. The success and failure of state-building activities therefore crucially depends on external actors' response to the following issues.

Political Attention

To what extent is the international community prepared and able to maintain a political interest in state building over a longer period of time? As a rule, international attention is highest when violence has escalated or a humanitarian disaster that affects regional and international security is impending. As soon as the crisis has seemingly eased off, the topic disappears from the international agenda (such as the U.N. Security Council's), not least because other crises have already taken its place and require the international community's undivided attention. Almost all major state-building operations—let alone other, less spectacular activities—suffer from this effect. The decline or lack of international attention goes hand in hand with the dwindling interest of the donor countries' publics in the situation, which dilutes the prospects of mobilizing sufficient financial and human resources for the international community's engagement.

Strategic Planning, Operative Planning, and Resource Allocation

Another fundamental issue is the question of systematic state-building strategies and the difficulties external actors face in planning specific measures and providing adequate resources. In practice, plans are devised and structures are created in an ad hoc manner; international organizations must ask their members to provide the requisite resources and personnel on a case-by-case basis. In the past it has frequently proven difficult to secure continuous and sufficient support for international state-building measures. It is difficult to assess in advance how much funding will be available, which complicates the strategic and operative planning of civilian as well as military interventions. Moreover, states sometimes do not actually make available the resources they have pledged. Governments and international organizations frequently lack the necessary planning capacity as well as cross-departmental structures and concepts, which would not only accelerate the political decision-making process, but also contribute to the creation of systematic state building know-how.

Coordination and Coherence

Considering the multitude of external actors and the various layers of decision-making involved in state-building efforts, problems of coordination and coherence almost inevitably arise. Usually each actor pursues its own conception of state building, which is partly influenced by the nature of its mandate and has its own view regarding how measures should be rank-ordered, what objectives should be pursued in the short- to medium-run, and how these objectives are to be attained. In particular some international

NGOs and national development agencies compete over scarce resources, influence, and competencies. At the same time most of these actors, for reasons of prestige, seek to retain a certain measure of autonomy and control over their activities, which makes coordination—not to mention coherence—almost impossible.

Legitimacy

Legitimacy is a resource that is coveted by external actors, in particular democratically elected governments, who often face a dilemma. On the one hand, external actors must respond to expectations and demands of the local population affected by state failure, particular local groups or the ruling elite; on the other hand, however, in order to mobilize the necessary resources (i.e., their taxpayers' money), their action must be considered legitimate by their own constituencies at home. At the same time, the input and output dimensions of legitimacy are critical, because depending on the case at hand, the performance of external actors is measured against one or the other dimension. Differences arise depending on whether the actor is answerable to the local population or its own public. Moreover, there sometimes is a trade-off between the two dimensions: the objective of so-called local ownership (input legitimacy), for instance, may hamper effective decision-making and the implementation of political measures and, thus, lead to suboptimal, unintended outcomes (output legitimacy). Furthermore, external governments that seek the support of their national constituencies for state-building measures tend to tailor their mandate in a manner that frequently proves ineffective, and ultimately neither produces a satisfactory outcome in the field nor satisfies their own public. The promotion of NGOs and of particular values or blueprints of statehood may please the external actors' own constituencies, but may lead to considerable problems of legitimacy in the field and, thereby, triggering unintended consequences.

The legitimacy issue already illustrates the gap of values and interests that often characterizes the difficult relationship of external state-builders and local actors. In a number of cases, the typical dilemmas at the field level, five of which are explored here, have been investigated, in particular with regard to peace agreements and transitional administrations (Cousens and Kumar 2001, Stedman, Rothchild, and Cousens 2002, Caplan 2005, Paris and Sisk 2008). First, each and every intervention affects directly or indirectly local power structures. In most instances, this is intended since external actors deliberately support particular groups and try to marginalize others. However, local actors, in particular political leaders, usually anticipate these changes and act accordingly, often by exploiting tensions and increasing the potential for the use of violence. In extreme cases, external actors may themselves become targets of violent acts and here they are left with a number of bad options: external actors may be forced to protect themselves, which makes it difficult to engage actively with local partners and civil society; they may strike back militarily, which increases the risk of civilian casualties and affects the legitimacy of the whole state-building undertaking; or they may leave the country and thereby loose any credibility vis-à-vis the locals. Second, as studies on financial, development, or humanitarian aid have shown, state building may foster rent-seeking behavior and aid dependency of large segments of the society.

Third, attaching political and economic conditionality to aid and assistance, which is to some degree part of any state-building strategy (but especially in the case of Liberalization First and Civil Society First), usually leads to supporting good performers instead of bad or poor performers. The latter, however, are often the true troublemakers; many postconflict countries remain at the risk of state failure because of particular spoiler groups that feel neglected from external aid, but still have the potential to destabilize the situation on the ground. Fourth, the notion of "local ownership" has proven to be rather ambivalent. On the one hand, external actors want to reestablish or to assure local ownership of the political decision making process in order to force groups and leaders to take responsibility for certain actions. On the other hand, quite often local actors show no interest in acting responsible and making compromises, if necessary, but rather expect the international community to do the (unpopular) work and even blame it for ineffective governance. Therefore, on several occasions neither difficult decisions are taken nor necessary measures are implemented by the local leaders; both are basically left to external state builders despite their intentions to foster local ownership.

Fifth, dealing with actual or potential spoilers, especially with armed nonstate actors, also leads to a number of dilemmas (Stedman 1997; Schneckener 2006a, 2009). They often harm any kind of state-building process since they frequently profit from state fragility and failure. In order to make some progress, external actors are sometimes forced to integrate some of them into the evolving political structures, which grant them privileges and liberties that, in turn, they can use to undermine the process of stabilizing and reforming state structures. In addition, the handling of para- or quasi-state structures, established, for example, by warlords, clan chiefs, big men, or rebel groups, is a particularly tricky issue (see Afghanistan, DR Congo, and Somalia). These have frequently replaced or coexist with state structures, and although they may offer a minimum of stability at the local level, they ultimately prevent the establishment of sustainable state structures—financed, implemented, or monitored by the international community. More often than not these para-state structures are detached from the central government and own a local monopoly of force, sometimes defined in territorial, sometimes in functional terms, hence competing with the central government's attempt to project a monopoly on the use of force. The question arises as to whether such structures, which in individual cases may have a stabilizing effect, can be used as an interim solution or as building blocks in the (re-)establishment of statehood; or whether such a strategy will ultimately prevent the creation of an effective statehood because it strengthens militant actors and adversely affects the prospects of sustainable development (see in particular Mehler 2004). These typical dilemmas are compounded by the temporally limited engagement of external actors. Local elites are well aware of the fact that the internationals will leave one day and, hence, adjust their own policies accordingly. In particular those who do not have an interest in changing the status quo and try to defend their privileges will pursue a "filibuster strategy," for instance by remaining aloof, engaging in noncommittal reform debates, establishing bureaucratic hurdles, or by demonstrating indifference. They simply know that time is on their side.

Transnational and Nodal Governance

In order to respond to these problems and dilemmas, new modes of governance usually emerge at the field level, which have so far attracted less attention in the state- and peace-building literature. These modes of governance are neither anticipated nor designed by capitals and headquarters since they are not reflected by the state-building strategies. The main reason for this deficit is that external state builders often underestimate the fact that they interfere in a specific local "order" from which particular segments of the populations—not just armed groups—benefit. Contrary to the underlying assumption of most state-building strategies, there is no "tabula rasa" situation or "power vacuum," not even in the immediate aftermath of a civil war. But the truth is, there is always somebody who "governs" or, at least, who pretends to do so, be it a president, national government, general, dominant party, ethnic group, local warlord, tribe, clan, and so on. Therefore, external actors have to find arrangements with these (potential) "rulers" who, as for example in Afghanistan or in Somalia, may vary from region to region, from province to province, and village to village. The alternative is that external actors try to build alliances with nonruling groups and so-called change agents in order to challenge established or reestablished local power structures. In both cases, external state builders need to engage with local actors by using a number of informal or formalized arrangements at a national, regional, or communal level. These arrangements—although initially set up as temporary measures—often last much longer than anticipated, sometimes over years and even decades. They usually emerge in an ad hoc fashion, for instance in the context of coordination or decision-making bodies, in which both international and local actors are represented. Partly, however, these arrangements are only by-products or unintended consequences of the interaction of various actors—a case in point is the ambivalent cooperation of the U.S. Army with former warlords in Afghanistan as well as the support for local Sunni militias in Iraq.

Prominent examples are formalized mixed international-domestic bodies in Bosnia, Kosovo, and Afghanistan, which have been set up deliberately in order to channel money and policies. To take three examples from Afghanistan. In the northeast of the country, the German government set up so-called provisional development funds, which are administered jointly by German and Afghan representatives at the provincial level. In mid-2005, the U.N. mission in Afghanistan (UNAMA) established in the province Paktia, in collaboration with the provincial government and the Zadran tribes, the "Zadran Arc Stabilisation Initiative," which was supported inter alia by USAID, the U.S.-led Provincial Reconstruction Team (PRT), and international NGOs in order to allow for reconstruction work in an area rife with tribal insurgency. Since 2004 the NGO Tribal Liaison Office, originally initiated by SwissPeace, has opened a number of offices throughout southeast Afghan provinces, mainly supported by Western foundations and foreign ministries, which served as a consultation mechanism with *shuras*, elders, tribal leaders, and others in order to gain acceptance for development projects, to offer facilitation in cases of conflict, and to build local capacities (Karokhail and Schmeidl 2006).

Generally, these new forms of governance are labeled transnational governance since they involve a cross-border element due to the presence of foreign actors. They comprise both external and local as well as nonstate and state actors; and they are largely characterized by efforts of information exchange, mutual understanding, and horizontal coordination. Additionally, the concept of nodal governance, originally developed in studies on networked governance, can be applied since the term refers to a situation where no single source of power exists and where governance takes place within a "shifting networks of alliances rather than as a product of the realization of governing interests" (Johnston 2006, 34). Moreover, these arrangements function as "nodes" in the sense that they work as institutional settings with a set of methods, a particular way of thinking (mentality), and resources aiming at mobilizing "the knowledge and capacities of members to manage the course of events" (Burris, Drakos, and Shearing 2005, 33). This does not imply that all participants act on equal footing in such arrangements. Indeed, most often some actors are more dominant and powerful than others, because of the access of resources (including local knowledge), and will certainly shape the rules and the outcome of the interaction. However, the notion of command and control is much more contested than in hierarchical and formalized bureaucratic structures. For instance, the external actor, be the U.N., the U.S. government, an international NGO, or a private enterprise, may play either a superior role (at least temporarily), be one player among many, or act merely as an observer or mediator loosely attached to a network of locals who intervenes only in the event of a crisis. However, transnational and nodal governance also implies a sharing of costs and responsibilities that usually generates tensions and disappointments, in particular between international actors who invest resources for state building and local elites who want to secure their dominant position in state and society.

As the examples show, the degree of formalization and institutionalization varies—in some bodies, for instance, international and local representatives meet regularly and interact on the basis of an agreement (e.g., memorandum of understanding), which clearly determines the responsibilities and functions of each actor. Other arrangements only exist in the form of unwritten rules and occasional contacts among varying participants. Some of these forms of governance have proved to be extremely functional and long standing (as in Bosnia or Kosovo), and may even work as functional equivalents of statehood since they are able to deliver a number of services to the population (e.g., provision of security, development aid, preparation and organization of elections, rule of law). In contrast, a number of arrangements turn out to be rather transient phenomena that vanish as soon as the situation changes and various actors seek new opportunities. This seems to be the case in a number of Afghan provinces and districts, where local authorities, former warlords, tribal and village militias, the Afghan army, and international troops build fragile counter-insurgency coalitions against the Taliban.

As a rule, one can argue that the more local state actors are involved, the more formalized and structured these "nodes" become. Furthermore, state actors often try to win influence and control vis-à-vis societal groups by using these forms of governance. This indirect approach by a national government can be studied in cases of a rather weak administration, as in Afghanistan, but also in countries like Pakistan with an apparently strong state apparatus, which nevertheless lacks the knowledge and the capabilities to control and to govern effectively in peripheral regions (e.g., Tribal Areas, Khyber Pakhtunkhwa, or Balochistan) or in urban environments such as Karachi (Wilke 2009). Under these circumstances, therefore, state actors have to rely on the collaboration with others and may engage in transnational arrangements, set up and shaped by external actors, in order to win back "lost territory" or, at least, to learn more about the activities of relevant nonstate actors.

In general, transnational and nodal forms of governance do not figure prominently in official statements issued by external state builders. At best, such formats are seen as less-than-ideal solutions and transitional bodies on the path to strengthening the state's institutions and capacities. However, these modes have far-reaching effects that are too often underestimated by those who intervene in areas of limited statehood. By their engagement, external actors become inevitably embedded in local politics. They get dragged further and further into locally driven practices and power politics, rooted in tradition, culture, and history, which are both difficult to read and to change by outsiders. Such practices and mechanisms typically include forms of patronage and clientelism, power sharing and co-optation, as well as the mobilization of traditional structures and informal ways of self-organization (i.e., clan structures, ethnic networks, kinship). Most of these mechanisms fuel the vested interests of local elites, but do not necessarily lead to a market democracy or a civil society as initially envisaged by external state builders. Moreover, the modes of governance introduced by outsiders will often be instrumentalized and eventually manipulated by dominant local elites for their own interests. From the point of view of elites, these arrangements offer new opportunities for strengthening their position and for acquiring "political rents." They gain access to resources and capacities that generally improves their position within their own networks and with regard to possible rivals or opponents. Via transnational and nodal governance they also have the opportunity to expand their networks, in particular across borders, and to connect themselves with political and economic centers outside the country. In other words, ruling elites—well experienced in dealing with "fragility"—try to use these modes in order to readjust or transform their traditional clientistic, neopatrimonial, or semiauthoritarian politics.

Thus, in the course of the intervention, external actors become part of the local landscape that may change their role and, probably, their identity. In practice, the transnational and nodal governance arrangements are subject to the inherent dynamic of a process, which can hardly be in control of external actors, let alone those who are based in distant capitals and headquarters. True, in cases of comprehensive state-building operations, international actors may be in the position to shape the rules of the game; however, it proved to be an illusion to assume that they are in command and control. As Bosnia, Kosovo, or Timor-Leste show, this applies even in cases of formalized interim administration where external actors, based on a U.N. mandate, enjoy executive functions. Thus, the often used language of "local ownership," "transfer of responsibility," or "exit" is misleading, since it is based on the false assumption that external actors are in the position of de facto rulers who have simply to hand over their tasks to the locals when the state-building "job" is done. This rather mechanistic logic still dominates the thinking and planning of most Western interveners, in particular when military or police personnel is deployed, and does not at all reflect the dynamic of the whole process.

Conclusions

It seems to be plausible to assume that the various arrangements characterized by multilevel, transnational and nodal governance will shape the politics of state building and the kind of statehood far more than all the concepts, programs, and strategies written and discussed in national and international bureaucracies. The ultimate outcome of many interventions is therefore not the establishment of self-sustaining and viable state structures, but an open-ended international involvement by different modes of governance, which often prove to be instrumental for the status quo interests of local elites and, therefore, lead to the unintentional stabilization of existing power structures.

Furthermore, the new modes of governance that are introduced by the influx of state actors, international organizations, financial institutions, NGOs, or private companies do foster the ongoing process of transforming statehood in many postcolonial and postconflict settings. Since the late 1970s, this transformation has been under way and is characterized by processes of transnationalization, privatization, and commercialization of state functions, including the provision of security. Transnational ties and networks as well as the privatization of services are therefore by no means new for most countries in Latin America, Africa, as well as in Central, South, and Southeast Asia. However, because of a number of state-building activities by the international community at the turn of the twenty-first century, these developments were enforced. Even the most remote and peripheral areas such as regions in Afghanistan, Pakistan (e.g. Tribal Areas, Balochistan), Indonesia (e.g., Aceh), Sudan (e.g., Dafur), Yemen, Somalia, DR Congo, or West Africa became more and more penetrated by external actors, most often accompanied by local agents of the central government. As can be illustrated by the provision of security, this engagement does often not lead to the strengthening of the state's monopoly of the use of force or the rule of law, but to transnational and nodal security governance, involving in particular private and commercial security providers, in the form of foreign firms, mercenaries, or local militias (Chojnacki and Branovic 2007). As the examples of Afghanistan, Iraq, and DR Congo show, international state building works here as a "market opener" for private businesses that are hired in order to protect both external actors as well as local elites.

However, despite all these short- and long-term effects, the alternative not to engage in regions of violent conflict and state failure is neither realistic nor desirable. The option of disengagement or nonintervention would simply imply to leave developments and events in many parts of the world as they are, and to risk a further decline of state capacities and the increase of conflict potentials. The consequences would be an increasing number of costly humanitarian crises as well as socioeconomic, ecological, and security problems, which usually spread across borders and have severe destabilizing transnational effects. Moreover, fragile statehood not only fuels these problems, but makes it much more difficult to address them effectively at the international level. In other words, the phenomenon of fragile statehood underlines the necessity of regional or global governance initiatives, but, at the same time, undermines the application and effectiveness of international norms and regimes.

Thus, the key question for state builders is not how to avoid counter-productive effects but to learn to cope with them and to better understand the underlying logic of the modes of governance they introduce in areas of limited statehood, be it intended or unintended. For this end, there are a number of requirements external actors have to meet. First and foremost, they should see themselves not as "external" to local developments, but as an integral part of the process and its dynamics. In other words, they do not simply assist and support state structures that exist autonomously; instead, via the different modes of governance, they become directly or indirectly part of these structures. This also implies that any kind of short-term or "quick impact" approach is self-betrayal.

Second, the international community could aim at reducing the complexity of the multilevel architecture of most state-building undertakings by cutting down the number of actors and levels involved. This implies an element of hierarchy and prioritization in order to steer the state-building process in a more focused manner. Such an approach, in order to be successful, presupposes that external actors have to become more aware and self-reflective about their own strategic orientation, which is often only stated implicitly. Moreover, intervening states and international organizations have to do their homework more carefully at the level of capitals and headquarters before they commit themselves to comprehensive state-building operations. They need to focus their activities, because the more maximalist the state-building agenda gets, the more external actors will necessarily be involved. Therefore, more modesty concerning achievable objectives is needed. And they should ask themselves whether they are willing and able to mobilize the required resources or whether they will only run into a capacity-expectation gap vis-à-vis the local population, which causes frustrations and fuels unintended effects, including the return to social uprisings or violent conflicts.

Third, external actors should be more aware about the use, effects, potential, and limits of transnational and nodal governance arrangements that often came into being without prior planning or conceptualization. They need to make more strategic use of these kinds of arrangements and integrate them more consciously and deliberately into their state-building approaches. At the same time, they should make use of the flexibility of these arrangements and be prepared to adapt them according to the situation and the shifting patterns of power. In particular, external actors have to assess regularly how their presence and actions within such arrangements influence the perception, behavior, and decisions of local actors, most notably of political leaders and their constituencies. They also need to acknowledge that, inevitably, some local actors will feel excluded by these arrangements and may spoil the process.

Fourth, external actors have to be more open and flexible to the outcome of their undertaking. They need to be prepared to change their policies, if necessary even radically, and not to stick to a certain path, blueprint, or strategy, once drafted and decided in distant headquarters, in fear of losing credibility vis-à-vis local actors or the public back home. And finally, external actors should not underestimate the capacities of various segments of the society who have learned to live with the lack of resources and state structures. In order to recognize who would be affected by what, external actors need to know more about these social practices and mechanisms, which in many countries assure an environment of "fragile stability." External actors need to be far more receptive and adaptive toward indigenous politics, including traditional rule, clientelism, patronage, co-optation and family- or clan-based organization—even if they do not fit into the ideas of a market democracy, the state's monopoly of the use of force, the rule of law, or a vibrant civil society.

Notes

1. This development has been reflected by a growing body of literature. See in particular Rotberg (2003; 2004), Fukuyama (2004), Paris (2004), Caplan (2005), Chesterman (2005), Chesterman, Ignatieff, and Thakur (2005), Schneckener (2006b), Call and Wyeth (2008), and Paris and Sisk (2008).

2. One of the most politically influential rankings is the Failed States Index (since 2005) of the magazine *Foreign Policy* in cooperation with the Fund for Peace. For a critical analysis of different rankings and indices on statehood, see Schneckener (2007). See also Risse, chapter 1.

3. See The White House, National Security Strategy of the United States of America, March 2006, chap. 4–7. http://georgewbush-whitehouse.archives.gov/nsc /nss/2006/.

4. See former Secretary of State Rice's speech on "Transformational Diplomacy," Georgetown University, Washington, D.C., January 18, 2006. This position was endorsed in the final report of the *Princeton Project on National Security*, in which the authors state: "We must develop a much more sophisticated strategy of creating the deeper preconditions for successful liberal democracy—preconditions that extend far

beyond the simple holding of elections. The United States should assist and encourage Popular, Accountable, and Rights-regarding (PAR) governments worldwide" (Ikenberry and Slaughter 2006, 6).

5. On the one hand, it has become clear from the CPA's decisions regarding the De-Baathification of the state apparatus (order 1 and 5) and regarding the dissolution of remainders of the Iraqi army (order 2) that it consciously pursues deinstitutionalization (including the layoffs of half a million civil servants) in order to pave the way for (alleged) democratization. On the other hand, the CPA ordered a shock treatment for the Iraqi economy, which had been centrally planned to date. This included tax cuts (order 37) and the creation of favorable conditions for foreign investors (order 39). As early as May 2003, shortly after the official cessation of hostilities, the head of the CPA, Bremer, had declared Iraq "open for business."

6. For international concepts and guidelines, see for example United Nations Development Program (UNDP), Security Sector Reform and Transitional Justice: A Crisis Post-Conflict Programmatic Approach, March 2003; OECD/DAC, Security System Reform and Governance, DAC Guidelines and Reference Series, Paris: OECD, 2005.

7. As early as 1998 more than four hundred NGOs were active in Bosnia, the overwhelming majority of which were dependent on international funding. See Belloni 2001; Chandler 2004.

REFERENCES

Belloni, Roberto. 2001. "Civil Society and Peacebuilding in Bosnia and Herzegovina." *Journal of Peace Research* 38, no. 2:163–80.

Burris, Scott, Peter Drakos, and Clifford Shearing. 2005. "Nodal Governance." *Australian Journal of Legal Philosophy* 30:30–58.

Call, Charles T., and Vanessa Wyeth, eds. 2008. *Building States to Build Peace*. Boulder, Colo.: Lynne Rienner.

Caplan, Richard. 2005. *International Governance of War-Torn Territories*. Oxford: Oxford University Press.

Chandler, David. 2004. "Democratization in Bosnia: The Limits of Civil Society Building Strategies." In *Civil Society in Democratization*, edited by Peter Burnell and Peter Calvert, 225–49. Portland, Ore.: Frank Cass.

Chesterman, Simon. 2005. *You, the People: The United Nations, Transitional Administration, and State-Building*. Oxford: Oxford University Press.

Chesterman, Simon, Michael Ignatieff, and Ramesh Thakur, eds. 2005. *Making States Work: State Failure and the Crisis of Governance*. Tokyo: United Nations University Press.

Chojnacki, Sven, and Zeljko Branovic. 2007. "Räume strategischer (Un-)Sicherheit. Ein Markt für nicht-staatliche Gewaltakteure und Gelegenheiten für Formen von Sicherheits-Governance." In *Regieren ohne Staat? Governance in Räumen begrenzter Staatlichkeit*, edited by Thomas Risse and Ursula Lehmkuhl, 181–204. Baden-Baden: Nomos.

Cousens, Elizabeth M. and Chetan Kumar, eds. 2001. *Peacebuilding as Politics: Cultivating Peace in Fragile Societies*. Boulder, Colo.: Lynne Rienner.

David, Charles P. 1999. "Does Trade Promote Peace? Liberal (Mis)steps in the Peace Process." *Security Dialogue* 30, no. 1:25–41.

Debiel, Tobias, and Monika Sticht. 2005. "Towards a New Profile? Development, Humanitarian, and Conflict-Resolution NGOs in the Age of Globalization." Report no. 79. Duisburg: Institute for Development and Peace.

Etzioni, Amitai. 2007. *Security First: For a Muscular, Moral Foreign Policy*. New Haven, Conn.: Yale University Press.

Fearon, James, and David Laitin. 2004. "Neotrusteeships and the Problem of Weak States." *International Security* 28, no. 4:5–43.

Fischer, Martina, ed. 2006. *Peacebuilding and Civil Society in Bosnia-Herzegovina: Ten Years After Dayton*. Berlin: Lit Verlag.

Fukuyama, Francis. 2004. *State Building: Governance and World Order in the Twenty-first Century*. Ithaca, N.Y.: Cornell University Press.

Harvey, Paul. 1998. "Rehabilitation in Complex Political Emergencies: Is Rebuilding Civil Society the Answer?" *Disasters* 22, no. 3:200–217.

Ikenberry, John G., and Anne-Marie Slaughter. 2006. "Forging a World of Liberty Under Law: U.S. National Security in the Twenty-first Century." Princeton Project Paper, Princeton University. Accessed December 1, 2010. www.princeton.edu/~ppns/report/FinalReport.pdf.

Jarstad, Anna K. 2008. "Power-Sharing: Former Enemies in Joint Government." In *From War to Democracy: Dilemmas of Peacebuilding*, edited by Anna K. Jarstad and Timothy D. Sisk, 105–33. Cambridge: Cambridge University Press.

Johnston, Les. 2006. "Transnational Security Governance." In *Democracy, Society, and the Governance of Security*, edited by Jennifer Wood and Benoit Dupont, 33–51. Cambridge: Cambridge University Press.

Karokhail, Masood, and Susanne Schmeidl. 2006. "Integration of Traditional Structures Into the State-Building Process: Lessons from the Tribal Liaison Office in Loya Paktia." *Publication Series on Promoting Democracy Under Conditions of State Fragility*, no. 1:59–79.

Kaufmann, Chaim. 1998. "When All Else Fails: Ethnic Population Transfers and Partitions in the Twentieth Century." *International Security* 23, no. 2:120–56.

Krasner, Stephen. 2004. "Sharing Sovereignty: New Institutions for Collapsed and Failing States." *International Security* 29, no. 2:85–120.

Marten, Kimberly Zisk. 2004. *Enforcing the Peace: Learning from the Imperial Past*. New York: Columbia University Press.

Mehler, Andreas. 2004. "Oligopolies of Violence in Africa South of the Sahara." *Nord-Süd aktuell* 18, no. 3:539–48.

O'Flynn, Ian, and David Russell, eds. 2005. *Power Sharing: New Challenges for Divided Societies*. London: Pluto Press.

Oneal, John R., and Bruce Russet. 1999. "Assessing the Liberal Peace with Alternative Specifications: Trade Still Reduces Conflict." *Journal of Peace Research* 36, no. 4:423–42.

Ottaway, Marina, and Stefan Mair. 2004. "States at Risk and Failed States: Putting Security First." Policy Outlook, Carnegie Endowment for International Peace, Washington, D.C.

Paris, Roland. 2004. *At War's End: Building Peace After Civil Conflict*. Cambridge: Cambridge University Press.

Paris, Roland, and Timothy Sisk, eds. 2008. *The Dilemmas of State-Building: Confronting the Contradictions of Postwar Peace Operations*. London: Routledge.

Reilly, Benjamin. 2001. *Democracy in Divided Societies: Electoral Engineering for Conflict Management*. Cambridge: Cambridge University Press.

Rotberg, Robert, ed. 2003. *State Failure and State Weakness in a Time of Terror*. Washington, D.C.: Brookings Institution Press.

——, ed. 2004. *When States Fail: Causes and Consequences*. Princeton: Princeton University Press.

Rubin, Barnett R. 2008. "The Politics of Security in Postconflict State-Building." In *Building States to Build Peace*, edited by Charles Call and Vanessa Wyeth, 25–47. Boulder, Colo.: Lynne Rienner.

Schneckener, Ulrich. 2002. "Making Power-Sharing Work: Successes and Failures in Ethnic Conflict Regulation." *Journal of Peace Research* 38, no. 3:203–28.

——. 2006a. "Fragile Statehood, Armed Non-State Actors, and Security Governance." In *Private Actors and Security Governance*, edited by Alan Bryden and Marina Caparini, 23–40. Berlin: Lit Verlag.

——, ed. 2006b. *Fragile Staatlichkeit. "States at Risk" zwischen Stabilität und Scheitern*. Baden-Baden: Nomos.

——. 2007. "Internationales State-building. Dilemmata, Strategien und Anforderungen an die deutsche Politik." Stiftung Wissenschaft und Politik, S 10/07, Berlin, May.

——. 2009. "Spoilers or Governance Actors? Engaging Armed Non-States Groups in Areas of Limited Statehood." SFB-Governance Working Paper Series, No. 21. Berlin, October.

Schneckener, Ulrich, and Christoph Zürcher. 2007. "Transnational Security Governance in fragilen Staaten. Oder: Geht Sicherheit ohne Staat?" In *Regieren ohne Staat? Governance in Räumen begrenzter Staatlichkeit*, edited by Thomas Risse and Ursula Lehmkuhl, 205–22. Baden-Baden: Nomos.

Shearing, Clifford, and Jennifer Wood. 2003. "Nodal Governance, Democracy, and the New 'Denizens.'" *Journal of Law and Society* 30, no. 3.

Stedman, Stephen. 1997. "Spoiler Problems in Peace Processes." *International Security* 22, no. 2:5–53.

Stedman, Stephen J., Donald Rothchild, Elizabeth M. Cousens, eds. 2002. *Ending Civil Wars: The Implementation of Peace Agreements*. Boulder, Colo.: Lynne Rienner.

Van Tongeren, Paul, Malin Brenk, Marte Hellema, and Juliette Verhoeven, eds. 2005. *People Building Peace II: Successful Stories of Civil Society*. Boulder, Colo.: Lynne Rienner.

Wilke, Boris. 2009. "Governance und Gewalt. Eine Untersuchung zur Krise des Regierens in Pakistan am Fall Belutschistans." SFB-Governance Working Paper Series, No. 22. Berlin, December.

Wood, Jennifer, and Benoit Dupont. 2006. "Introduction: Understanding the Governance of Security." In *Democracy, Society, and the Governance of Security*, edited by Jennifer Wood and Benoit Dupont, 1–11. Cambridge: Cambridge University Press.

10

Applying the Governance Concept
to Areas of Limited Statehood

Implications for International Foreign and Security Policy

LARS BROZUS

FROM A GLOBAL AS WELL AS A HISTORICAL PERSPECTIVE the modern nation-state is the exception rather than the rule.[1] Outside of the developed world, areas of limited statehood dominate the picture. This chapter discusses the implications of applying particular Western-style governance concepts to areas of limited statehood. I show how systematic research on governance in areas of limited statehood helps to clarify positions in the political debate about the transferability of concepts: Do they travel? And what are the results?

Current debates in international foreign and security policy tend to picture areas of limited statehood as presenting threats to the so-called developed world. Most of the scenarios refer to threats resulting from destabilization because of conflicts spilling over from areas of limited statehood. Terrorism, organized crime, or mass movements of people are frequently noted in this context. To confront these challenges powerful actors like the United States (2002, 2006) or the European Union (2003) have developed security strategies that focus on failed and failing states, a subcategory of areas of limited statehood. International interventions and state-building projects are policy options under consideration to counter these challenges. While most international interventions are mandated restrictively, some aim at establishing new institutions and even new forms of governance, as in Bosnia, Kosovo, Afghanistan, and Iraq. Thus, concepts of governance become an important part of state-building strategies. However, too often the implications of applying the fundamentally Western concept of governance to areas of limited statehood remain unclear. Available evidence points to massive discrepancies between the expectations of the intervening international community, which is there to help but not to stay, and the local population, resulting in frustration for both. Consequently, international state-building strategies in areas of limited statehood aiming at establishing good or better governance should be adapted.

In the first part of the chapter I outline current debates that perceive areas of limited statehood primarily as a threat to international foreign and security policy. To counter these threats state-building strategies are designed that aim at establishing modern statehood. This ideal type statehood has been deduced from the image of the so-called Western nation-state, particularly the developed welfare state in continental Europe in the 1960s and 1970s. Consequently, state-building strategies tend to sell a comprehensive "governance package" while often disregarding local forms of governance that remain notably resistant against sociopolitical change.

The second part of this chapter discusses the implications of research on governance in areas of limited statehood for international politics against the background of normative considerations and empirical findings. The results suggest that international state-building projects should be limited in scope while giving more consideration to providing basic governance services like security or welfare.

In the third part of the chapter, I discuss some of the pitfalls for international state-building projects. As the sometimes paradoxical effects of these projects begin to show, systematic research on governance in areas of limited statehood becomes ever more important. Finally, I conclude by discussing how "governance-shaping," rather than state building, may be a more promising road toward creating self-supporting political entities.

Areas of Limited Statehood

Limited statehood can be defined as the persistent absence of a monopoly on legitimate force, severely restricting the implementation of political decisions by a government (Risse and Lehmkuhl 2006; Risse 2007a). Areas of limited statehood consist of territorial, social, and functional spaces lacking certain features of "modern" forms of governance that characterize the political process in the developed or OECD world. Essentially, areas of limited statehood lack effective domestic sovereignty (Krasner 2004). In extreme cases, as in Somalia, it is missing completely. Somalia has not had an effective government that is capable of delivering basic governance services for more than twenty years. A large part of the international state system can be categorized as areas of—more or less—limited statehood. On a continuum with the end points completely consolidated—statehood on the one end and completely limited statehood on the other—failing and failed states are the most prominent subcategory close to the latter end point.

It is important to note that certain features of limited statehood are common throughout the international state system. Almost no government can at all times enforce political decisions in all parts of its territory or in all policy areas. Even in the OECD world we find areas of limited statehood. We may distinguish between limited and consolidated statehood by measuring the scope and intensity of deficient domestic sovereignty: The more a government fails to enforce political decisions over time and in many different policy areas, the more limited statehood appears. Another key difference between limited and consolidated statehood concerns the provision of basic governance services. In areas of consolidated statehood, nonstate actors may contribute to rule setting and rule enforcement in various policy areas, thus complementing governmental action. In areas of limited statehood, nonstate actors do not complement but substitute governmental service provision. For example, if private NGOs do not provide health care for children in Somalia, then it is not provided at all.

In the context of globalization and securitization processes, areas of limited statehood are increasingly linked to global scenarios of threats and dangers. Within the security strategies of the United States (2006, 2010) and the European Union (2003), areas of limited statehood occupy a prominent place. The U.S. Security Strategies describe regional conflicts that may produce failed states as a major challenge that has to be faced:

> Regional conflicts can arise from a wide variety of causes, including poor governance, external aggression, competing claims, internal revolt, tribal rivalries, and ethnic or religious hatreds. If left unaddressed, however, these different causes lead to the same ends: failed states, humanitarian disasters, and ungoverned areas that can become safe havens for terrorists.
>
> (National Security Strategy of the United States of America 2006, 15)

"Failing states breed conflict and endanger regional and global security" (National Security Strategy of the United States of America 2010, 8). The E.U. regards state failure as a key threat and states that

> [b]ad governance—corruption, abuse of power, weak institutions and lack of accountability—and civil conflict corrode States from within. In some cases, this has brought about the collapse of State institutions. Somalia, Liberia and Afghanistan under the Taliban are the best known recent examples. Collapse of the State can be associated with obvious threats, such as organised crime or terrorism. State failure is an alarming phenomenon that undermines global governance, and adds to regional instability.
>
> (European Security Strategy 2003, 4)

International politics focuses more and more on areas of limited statehood because the probability of violent conflict with potentially destabilizing consequences is perceived as being highest here. In contrast to traditional foreign policy and security strategies that were obsessed with powerful enemies, now failed and failing states—the powerless—are placed at the center of threat analysis. Because of political instability, they provide breeding grounds for the emergence of threats that may have regionally and even internationally destabilizing effects. Consequently, strategies and instruments are developed to deal with these dangers (Schneckener 2005, 2006, 2007; see Schneckener's chapter in this volume). The main threats, according to these analyses of areas of limited statehood, are linked to security issues (Mützelburg 2007, 288):

- Violent conflicts triggering humanitarian disasters and mass movements of refugees and migrants with locally, regionally, and internationally destabilizing effects. This in turn increases the risk that OECD countries are affected by the consequences of these conflicts. At the same time public pressure to end them mounts on the members of the international community, especially those having the capacities to conduct international interventions.[2]
- Organized crime, using areas of limited statehood for transit and supply.
- Terrorist groups that use areas of limited statehood for recruitment, recreation, and training.

To counter these threats, the creation of robust governance and government structures is proposed: "It is about the political and economic reconstruction (and sometimes the construction) of devastated states, the state building in postconflict situations" (Mützelburg 2007, 289).[3] The programmatic objective of these internationally orchestrated efforts is the establishment of modern OECD style statehood.[4] Modern statehood refers to a robust state with a legitimate government and effective domestic sovereignty that is capable of providing basic governance services. Basic governance services comprise the provision of collective goods in the policy areas of security, political authority, and welfare. This objective is to be achieved through the commitment of the international community, which—in exceptional cases—can take on the form of a military intervention (see Krasner 2004; with regard to Africa, see Reno 1997).

Failed and failing states like Afghanistan, Somalia, and post-Saddam Iraq show that in some cases threats to international foreign and security policy actually can be traced back to areas of limited statehood. Therefore, for example, the intervention of the international community in Afghanistan is regarded as a test case for its ability to establish structures and processes that permanently prevent the use of Afghan territory as a "recruitment, training, and recreation space" for terrorist groups as well as organized crime (Risse 2007b)—that is, to succeed in building a modern state. However, doubts about the actual extent of the threat and the empirical relevance of the underlying assumptions and observations are also expressed. Schlichte points out that it is by no means clear that state failure automatically leads to increasing international security threats. Furthermore, "the number of domestic wars, in the debate often linked to state failure, . . . has declined massively since the early 1990s" (Schlichte 2005, 74). In addition, external interventions often miss their goal and generate rather counterproductive results, doing more harm than good (Broszka 2006; Fukuyama 2004).

Implications of Research on Governance in Areas of Limited Statehood

How can effective and legitimate governance be made sustainable in areas of limited statehood? Which political problems emerge under these conditions? In this section, I illuminate different aspects of current research on governance in areas of limited statehood and address the various normative issues in the context of the increasing number of international interventions. The empirical aim is to contribute to a better understanding of the diversity of existing forms of governance outside of the OECD world.

In contrast to the vast knowledge about modern forms of governance in areas of consolidated statehood, research about governance in areas of limited statehood tends to suffer from lacking theoretical concepts and empirical evidence. The systematic and rigorous study of structures and processes of governance in the absence of consolidated statehood constitutes an important desideratum of the academic discipline of International Relations. This is all the more remarkable as modern forms of governance like the Western nation-state are the exception rather than the rule (Leibfried and Zürn 2005). Historically and geographically much more common are "traditional" forms of governance. Furthermore, processes of globalization and denationalization attach an ever greater importance to political structures and processes in the non-OECD world with respect to consequences for the international community. While the political importance of this part of the world increases significantly, the knowledge about actors, forms and objectives of governance remains marginal.

The resulting consequences for international politics toward areas of limited statehood have so far not been sufficiently addressed. The available evidence suggests that local and regional forms of governance are considerably more persistent than presumed by modernization and development theories (Menzel 1992). A brief glance at the history of decolonization supports this point: some fifty years ago the independence of Ghana initiated a phase of accelerated decolonization. Many observers expected that decolonization would lead to the universal modernization of traditional forms of governance. Essentially, two political alternatives were available during the East-West confrontation. Both represented modern, nontraditional forms of political rule: liberalism and democracy on the one side, socialist, state-directed economies on the other. The assumption of many modernization theorists was that regardless of which camp the new members of the international community would adhere to, a modernization process of their political as well as economic and social systems would inevitably follow.

Today, it is obvious that political modernization did not occur as expected (Berman 2007; Fukuyama 2004). Not only do traditional forms of governance continue to exist, but quite often attempts at modernization resulted in dead ends, leading sometimes to territorial disintegration instead of better governance. In extreme cases even a return to seemingly outdated forms of political authority occurred, such as the establishment of a theocratic regime in Iran after 1979. Breaking with the modernization policies of the shah's regime, the new theocratic elite proclaimed a programmatic shift away from secular models of society and politics. This dual development—no comprehensive political modernization and no universal convergence of the forms of governance (which for a brief moment after the end of the East-West confrontation was expected again by some observers; cf. Fukuyama 1989) on the one hand, occasional relapses into (even pre-) traditional forms of political authority on the other—clarifies the importance of analyzing governance in areas of limited statehood both for political science as well as practical politics.

The question of normative standards for governance in failing and failed states is highly relevant for the debate on the right—or the duty—to intervene in cases of flagrant human rights violations (RTP or Responsibility to Protect; see the International Commission on Intervention and State Sovereignty 2001). When are interventions justifiable? What is their goal? Who should consider intervention? Ladwig (2007) examines the principles of legitimate international interventions in areas of limited statehood and discusses seven moral preconditions (see also chapter by Ladwig and Rudolf in this volume). He claims that only the protection of basic human rights can justify an external intervention. It is important to note that only states that are willing to invest the necessary efforts and resources should consider interventions. They have to be committed strictly to international law. The aim of the operation can only be the (re-) construction of local democratic authorities.[5] Once this is achieved, the intervention must end because of the people's right to self-determination: "The assumption that it would be possible to leave ruins of statehood quickly after a military intervention is normatively and de facto erroneous. The responsibility to provide immediate relief is instantly followed by the responsibility for the development of a viable order. If possible this should be a legitimate order which has to be supported by the people living in it" (Ladwig 2007, 371).

Another interesting aspect of Ladwig's remarks concerns the need for a positive correlation between the extent of the human rights violations and the scale of the international intervention that inevitably results in at least transitional heteronomy. Thus, only massive and continuing human rights violations can justify a full-scale international intervention. Minor violations should of course not be ignored, but cannot be used as an excuse for a lasting occupation.

A lot can be learned about governance in areas of limited statehood by historical comparisons since striking similarities exist regarding fundamental structures and processes: the absence of effective domestic sovereignty, the blurred distinction between public and private spheres, and the participation of both private and public actors in governance. Analyzing governance under these conditions points to the microtechniques of power. It can deepen our understanding of current forms of governance in areas of limited statehood. For instance, the participation of private actors in the provision of governance services in colonial North America seems to have been the rule rather than the exception: "In many cases where the local administration neglected its duties, other institutions and actors who were not a part of the official colonial administration took over responsibilities or were entrusted directly by the crown with these tasks" (Lehmkuhl 2007, 114; see chapter by Conrad and Stange in this volume).

Research conducted by Chojnacki and Branovic (2007) illustrates how important historical research can be for current debates (see also chapter by Chojnacki and Branovic in this volume). They investigate areas of "strategic (in-) security." These areas are characterized by two features:

(1) Security is not a public good but rather a privatized and scarce commodity.
(2) Instead of a state monopoly on legitimate force, a "force oligopoly" (Debiel et al. 2005, 6) exists in which several actors compete with each other, often using violence.

These two features are also characteristic of the colonial past of North America. Given the weakness of the colonial authorities, citizens repeatedly resorted to self-help measures to enhance their security, such as sending out punitive expeditions against pirates. In some cases, which were probably not intentional, these actions helped to shape a political community that could enter into political competition with the colonial authorities and even the home country.

Chojnacki and Branovic make two more points: first, force oligopolists in areas of limited statehood act according to perceived opportunity structures; and second, local forms of security provision such as village militias tend to be temporary phenomena. This has implications for state-building strategies in areas of limited statehood: If "changing geographical and economic opportunity structures [can influence] force oligopolists to prefer the provision of security over the use of violence against the population" (Chojnacki and Branovic 2007, 199), it seems obvious that intervening actors should try to influence these opportunity calculations thereby meeting Ladwig's postulate for intervention (protection of basic human rights). This could include, for example, offering less compromised force oligopolists political and material incentives if they enter into nonviolent political competition.[6]

Besides constraining political authority and supplying basic security, another fundamental governance service is the provision of public goods in the policy area of welfare. Börzel et al. (2007) investigate companies that provide governance services in health care by financing HIV/AIDS programs in South Africa. No effective state regulation used to exist in this policy area, thus putting at risk the trained workforce of multinational companies, for example in the automotive industry. State regulation was finally initiated because of the initiative of these companies. So contrary to common assumptions, under certain conditions companies may participate in the production of public goods, even if state regulation does not require them to do so (see also the chapter by Börzel at el. in this volume, focusing on environmental protection). Therefore, the conditions under which companies are willing to take on corresponding commitments are an important factor for the provision of governance services. According to Börzel et al. (2007), universally accepted international standards played a crucial role in this respect in South Africa. Correspondingly, multilateral frameworks seem better suited than bilateral agreements to have an impact on state regulation. Apart from the participation of companies in the provision of public goods in the health sector, this has further implications:

> If it is indeed so that there was a spill-over of entrepreneurial self-regulation into state regulation leading to the establishment of government regulatory capacity, then the role of multinational corporations in the globalization process appears in a slightly different light. Their transnational economic activities need not necessarily lead to a race to the bottom, but given certain conditions may also result in a race to the top.
>
> (Börzel et al. 2007, 289)

State Building in Areas of Limited Statehood

Empirically, the number of international interventions has increased substantially since the 1990s. Some of these interventions are long-term state-building missions with the aim of creating modern statehood, such as in Bosnia-Herzegovina, Kosovo, Afghanistan, and Iraq. Their objective is to establish structures and processes of governance that allow for a comprehensive modernization of state and society. But are these feasible goals? Is the transfer of modern forms of governance to areas of limited statehood possible? The starting point for answering these questions is the issue of "transferability" (Risse and Lehmkuhl 2007) of modern forms of governance. If governance in the OECD world, as Börzel (2007) points out, depends on a modern "core of statehood," including effective domestic sovereignty and institutionalized checks and balances, transferability would in many cases not be possible. After all, it is the ineffectiveness of domestic sovereignty resulting in the poor provision of governance services that defines areas of limited statehood. The crux of the governance problem in areas of limited statehood is the weakness of state institutions that are unwilling or unable to provide basic governance services and collective goods in the policy areas of security, political authority, and welfare (Fukuyama 2004; Risse 2007a; Zürcher 2007), as described here:

- Security is systematically becoming scarce and increasingly privatized. Thus, security becomes a product allowing private actors profitable trading. Security is provided more and more to the highest bidder and less and less to the general public (Chojnacki and Branovic 2007; see chapter by Chojnacki and Branovic in this volume). Even state actors serving in the security sector such as the police or the military sometimes participate in the (re)commodification of security (Braig and Stanley 2007).
- Political authority is not constrained reliably (Risse 2007a; Boomgaarden 2007). Institutionally unlimited political authority allows for political arbitrariness that in turn may provoke the establishment of parallel or shadow structures of political authority.
- Welfare benefits are not sufficiently provided (Beisheim et al. 2007; Börzel et al. 2007). Education, health, and social security are only selectively available for privileged groups of the population and in preferred regions. The distribution of scarce public goods on the ground of intransparent criteria very likely promotes corruption.

If the weakness of state institutions constitutes the core problem of governance in areas of limited statehood, the obvious counter-strategy would be to strengthen these institutions. Thus, Fukuyama (2004) argues that the empowerment of state institutions that are capable of providing basic governance services is the central task when it comes to state building. The international community has tried to achieve this through various attempts such as in Bosnia, Kosovo, or Afghanistan. However, external interference has resulted in very mixed and sometimes even paradoxical experiences (Schneckener and Zürcher 2007; see Schneckener's chapter in this volume).

In the area of security there are mixed experiences with the so-called security sector reform. In general, a post–civil war situation is the starting point for these reforms. Disarmament, demobilization, and reintegration (DDR) of former combatants into civilian life are the major goals. But even under near-perfect conditions (undisputed territory with a comparatively small population, the consent of the population to external intervention, no relevant interests of third parties) as in the case of RAMSI—the international mission for state building in the Solomon Islands (Regional Assistance Mission to Solomon Islands; led by Australia)—the intervening powers may be confronted with serious and persistent problems (Fukuyama 2008; Hameiri 2007; Wainwright and Harris 2005).

Regarding political authority, elections are the international community's favorite criterion for a successful political transformation process. Elections are expected to establish legitimate rulers and thus to increase the likelihood of effective domestic sovereignty. They may create problems, however, if voters express primordial ties rather than political choices. An indispensable prerequisite for the general recognition of the results of elections that may cause a genuine change in the domestic balance of political power seems to be a minimum of trust in the neutrality of state institutions. If this confidence or trust does not exist, elections are often no more than expressions of ethnic, religious, or cultural ties to certain collectives. In other words, elections produce the intended results most likely if a certain sense of political community exists beyond the most basic units of society like families or groups. The various recent elections in Iraq or Afghanistan drive this point home: basically, these were "censuses" tracking the ethnic, religious, and cultural composition of the country. Political preferences beyond these affiliations were not expressed (Diamond 2005, 18–20; Mansfield and Snyder 2005).

In the area of welfare, the international community's strategies range from the radical privatization in Iraq after the U.S.-led intervention to "soft" privatization, as in Kosovo under the auspices of the European Union and to substitution programs for drug cultivation (Afghanistan). Again, specific problems abound starting with the problem of awarding contracts (to which extent should they be given to local or international companies, to which extent should public institutions remain responsible for the provision of basic governance services and collective goods, etc.), to having difficulties finding uncompromised investors (Fukuyama 2004).

Another important factor for the fundamental task of external state building refers to changing attitudes toward foreign powers: the interventionists are quickly confronted with the problem that they are not perceived as a helping force but rather as occupying powers. Even in the globalized world of the twenty-first century, the demand for self-determination and self-government bears considerable mobilizing power. The wars in former Yugoslavia and in some parts of the former Soviet Union clearly demonstrate the impressive power of concepts such as nation and ethnicity. Thus, even in the "age of globalization," self-government seems to remain a central goal of political collectives. Occupying powers are not welcome and are only tolerated until basic governance services, namely security, are provided with a sufficient degree of reliability (Rotberg 2007, 61).

Interestingly, the requested self-government does not have to comply with OECD standards. Even if it appears likely that the provision of governance services by the political collective demanding self-government will be a good deal worse than their provision by the international community, the desire for self-government continuously expresses itself. In Kosovo, the Albanian political collective vigorously strived for self-government. The withdrawal of the international community, which had assumed governmental powers in 1999 and provided basic governance services since then, makes a decline in quantity and quality of these services very likely (Tansey 2007).

- Regarding security: Until independence, both international as well as local contingents formed the police forces of Kosovo. The handover of responsibility to domestic forces risks increased uncertainty for the population since—despite all the progress regarding police training—part of the Kosovo Police still seems vulnerable to political, ethnic, and criminal instrumentalization.
- Regarding political authority: The international presence also helped to create political institutions in Kosovo that guaranteed basic checks and balances. To what extent this will continue without the full-fledged "shadow of the international community" remains to be seen.

Despite these significant risks, the desire for self-government among the Albanians in Kosovo remained unbroken and despite serious doubts about the ability of Kosovo for effective self-government, Kosovo's independence was finally granted in 2008—though not undisputed.[7]

In addition to "the occupier's problem," there exists a second pitfall: the provision of basic governance services by international actors may be counterproductive for the goal of establishing self-supporting governance. This contradicts any well-meant reconstruction efforts, as the international administration in Kosovo exemplifies: "The very presence of international administrators in Kosovo, as in other cases of international governance, has contributed to some of the capacity problems, with international staff assuming control to achieve essential outcomes, but thereby reducing the potential for domestic capacity building" (Tansey 2007, 143; see also Schlichte and Veit 2006; and Zürcher 2007). This in turn increases the likelihood of parallel nonstate structures to be perceived by parts of the political collective as a potentially useful counterweight to (central) state control in order to avert arbitrariness. Since the international community has to leave sooner or later, the governance services they provide are not sufficiently reliable. Planning for the period after the international presence and recruiting allies for the protection of one's own interests becomes a rational strategy. As long as parallel nonstate structures can successfully claim legitimacy, and as long as these structures are able to deliver a minimum of basic governance services at the local or regional level, it will be difficult for (central) state actors to gain sufficient legitimacy to permanently eliminate these structures (Keohane 2007). Thus, international co-governance can be self-defeating.

Given the mixed experience with international state building missions it comes as no surprise that it is principally contested whether external interventions can successfully establish modern statehood.[8] Trutz von Trotha (2005), for instance, argues that in many cases the "rise of the local" counters efforts to strengthen centralized political control, the model of political regulation common to most OECD countries. Menkhaus (2007), too, emphasizes the significance of local governance arrangements, labeling them "ad hoc governance." This form of governance presents an often delicate balance between locally relevant political actors who would be threatened by the establishment of functioning institutions beyond their influence. Accordingly, they have no interest in contributing to more robust centralized government institutions and may undermine attempts to establish them (Zürcher 2007). Thus, in areas of limited statehood we often find a variety of governance configurations including multilevel governance, multiactor governance, and nonhierarchical modes of governance along with governance by, with, or without government (Czempiel and Rosenau 1992).

Conclusions: Governance Shaping Instead of State Building?

Whether areas of limited statehood actually pose a major threat to international politics remains a contested topic. Not disputed is the fact that in many cases basic governance services in these areas are provided insufficiently. The United Nation's Economic Commission for Africa (ECA) report "Relevance of African Traditional Institutions of Governance" confirms this point: "Public-service delivery in Africa is generally poor. An ECA study . . . reveals that less than 31 per cent of the population of the countries in the survey sample expressed satisfaction with the service-delivery of their local governments" (ECA 2007, 22). Poverty, hunger, and violence remain typical phenomena of failing and failed states. Therefore, the international community will have to stay engaged. But what is the best strategy for doing so?

Despite the limited success of even the best attempts to establish modern forms of governance in areas of limited statehood, resignation is in no way appropriate. Even under conditions of a complete destruction of statehood, certain basic governance services may still be delivered. Menkhaus shows that a dysfunctional central government must not lead to anomy or anarchy. In Somalia a variety of forms of governance deliver basic governance services at the local level:

> Communities that have been cut off from an effective state authority—whether out of governmental indifference to marginal frontier territories, or because of protracted warfare, or because of local and external vested interests in perpetuating conditions of state failure—consistently seek to devise arrangements to provide for themselves the core functions that the missing state is supposed to assume, especially basic security.
>
> (Menkhaus 2007, 75)

The examples given in this chapter support this thesis. Accordingly, the question of whether the model state of the OECD can be universalized would be considerably less relevant (Berman 2007). This in turn would reduce the pressure on both the international community and the population in areas of limited statehood to implement the complete "modernization package" (Risse and Lehmkuhl 2007, 8) that comes along with OECD-style statehood, thus greatly reducing excessive demands and frustration for both. Moreover, international interventions should be much more modest in their approach to state-building projects. To be successful, they require patience and perseverance. The right to self-determination and self-government has to be respected at all times to avoid entrapment leading to a stranded occupation.

A de-Westernized governance concept can help to understand why even under conditions of limited statehood some basic governance services typically attributed to the state (security, political authority, and basic welfare) may be delivered. The challenge for international politics, therefore, may be one of governance shaping, not of state building. Influencing local forms of governance in order to make them more effective and reliable seems more promising than designing institutions for failed and failing states. For instance, research on governance in areas of limited statehood suggests that the potential of local forms of governance should be explored more systematically. The empowerment of traditional institutions can be an important element in the attempt to establish better forms of governance. Traditional governance institutions may serve as transfer mechanisms that provide legitimacy to governmental decisions. Some African countries already have begun to install adjunct parliamentarian bodies consisting of traditional authorities, thus formally incorporating them into the political process (the House of Chiefs in Ghana or Botswana; cf. ECA 2007, 23). This could be an interesting example that should be monitored closely by the international community.

The more precise and detailed our knowledge of the existing forms of governance in areas of limited statehood is, the higher the probability of successful action should be. The reliability and durability of international commitments thus could benefit from a better understanding of governance in areas of limited statehood. This applies to the normative justification of political strategies that may be crucial for their public acceptance; it is also important for the evaluation of the success of these strategies. International interventions are a huge liability not only for foreign and security policy, but also for domestic politics, as the case of Iraq clearly demonstrates. Despite extensive planning and good intentions, the risks of externally supported state building remain immense. The motivation of the international community to start new state-building projects has certainly not grown after recent experiences.

Notes

1. I am indebted to Marianne Beisheim, Ursula Lehmkuhl, and Thomas Risse for comments on an earlier version of this chapter.

2. Empirically it can be shown that public pressure actually translates into action by the international community. Thus, the number of international interventions in

areas of limited statehood has increased significantly since the 1990s (Brzoska 2006; Fukuyama 2004). Zangl and Zürn (2003, 258–68) elaborate on the relevant changes in the domestic and international political constellation.

3. All translations from German in this chapter are mine.

4. How to achieve this objective is the subject of intense debate. Nation versus state building is a central concept in this debate (Hippler 2004; Zürcher 2007). Schneckener (2006, 33–35) distinguishes conceptually between state and nation building. For the remainder of this paper I will use the term state building.

5. The (re-) construction of democratic authorities must be the goal of interventionists. An intervention justified by the protection of basic human rights ending in the installation of a new tyranny would be absurd. But should the demos decide freely against certain features of democracy, the interventionists would have to respect its right to self-determination and accordingly leave before turning into an occupying power (Ladwig 2007, 370–71).

6. See the discussion on the integration of so-called moderate Taliban into the political system of Afghanistan (Ruttig 2007). For the basic problem of involving former force oligopolists into political structures and strategies for handling conflicts in this process see Buckley-Zistel (2006).

7. However, an international presence will continue to exist in Kosovo. See Bradley and Knaus (2004), Etzioni (2007), and Tansey (2007, 143): "With limited domestic capacity in many of its core political and security institutions, as well as questionable commitment in some quarters to genuinely impartial decision-making, Kosovo faces obstacles in both providing effective governance and ensuring adequate citizen security and rights protection."

8. Fukuyama (2004) mirrors this debate by stressing the important aspect of local demand for modernization and reform. If this demand is not strong enough the likelihood increases that reforms are not sustainable: "Well-meaning developed countries have tried a variety of strategies for stimulating such local demand, from loan conditionality to outright military occupation. The record, however, if we look at it honestly, is not an impressive one, and in many cases our interventions have actually made things worse" (Fukuyama 2004, 30).

References

Beisheim, Marianne, Andrea Liese, and Cornelia Ulbert, 2007. "Erfolgsbedingungen transnationaler Partnerschaften. Hypothesen und erste Ergebnisse." In *Regieren ohne Staat? Governance in Räumen begrenzter Staatlichkeit*, edited by Thomas Risse and Ursula Lehmkuhl, 247–71. Baden-Baden: Nomos.

Berman, Sheri. 2007. "Lessons from Europe." *Journal of Democracy* 18, no.1:28–41.

Boomgarden, Georg. 2007. "Governance in Räumen begrenzter Staatlichkeit aus außenpolitischer Perspektive." SFB-Governance Lecture Series 2, Berlin.

Börzel, Tanja A. 2007. "Regieren ohne den Schatten der Hierarchie. Ein modernisierungstheoretischer Fehlschluss?" In *Regieren ohne Staat? Governance in Räumen begrenzter Staatlichkeit*, edited by Thomas Risse and Ursula Lehmkuhl, 41–63. Baden-Baden: Nomos.

Börzel, Tanja A., Adrienne Héritier, and Anna Kristin Müller-Debus. 2007. "Der Regulierungsbeitrag von Großunternehmen im Kampf gegen HIV/AIDS in Süd-Afrika." In *Regieren ohne Staat? Governance in Räumen begrenzter Staatlichkeit*, edited by Thomas Risse and Ursula Lehmkuhl, 272–91. Baden-Baden: Nomos.

Bradley, John, and Gerald Knaus. 2004. "Towards a Kosovo Development Plan: The State of the Kosovo Economy and Possible Ways Forward." ESPIG Policy Paper 1, Pristina.

Braig, Marianne, and Ruth Stanley. 2007. "Die Polizei—(k)ein Freund und Helfer? Die Governance der öffentlichen Sicherheit in Buenos Aires und Mexiko Stadt." In *Regieren ohne Staat? Governance in Räumen begrenzter Staatlichkeit*, edited by Thomas Risse and Ursula Lehmkuhl, 223–44. Baden-Baden: Nomos.

Brzoska, Michael. 2006. "Friedensmissionen. Erfolg und Scheitern." *Blätter für deutsche und internationale Politik* 12:1491–98.

Buckley-Zistel, Susanne. 2006. "In-Between War and Peace: Identities, Boundaries, and Change After Violent Conflict." *Millennium—Journal of International Studies* 35, no. 1:3–21.

Chojnacki, Sven, and Zeljko Branovic. 2007. "Räume strategischer (Un-) Sicherheit: Ein Markt für nichtstaatliche Gewaltakteure und Gelegenheiten für Formen von Sicherheits-Governance." In *Regieren ohne Staat? Governance in Räumen begrenzter Staatlichkeit*, edited by Thomas Risse and Ursula Lehmkuhl, 183–206. Baden-Baden: Nomos.

Czempiel, Ernst-Otto, and James N. Rosenau. 1992. *Governance Without Government: Order and Change in World Politics*. Cambridge: Cambridge University Press.

Debiel, Thomas, Stephan Klingebiel, Andreas Mehler, and Ulrich Schneckener. 2005. "Zwischen Ignorieren und Intervenieren. Strategien und Dilemmata externer Akteure in fragilen Staaten." Stiftung Entwicklung und Frieden Policy Paper 23, Bonn.

Diamond, Larry. 2005. "Building Democracy After Conflict: Lessons from Iraq." *Journal of Democracy* 16, no. 1:9–23.

Economic Commission for Africa. 2007. "Relevance of African Traditional Institutions of Governance." Addis Ababa, Ethiopia, August.

Etzioni, Amitai. 2007. "The Lessons of Kosovo." *National Interest*. http://national interest.org/commentary/the-lessons-of-kosovo-1524.

European Security Strategy. 2003. "A Secure Europe in a Better World." Brussels, December 12.

Fukuyama, Francis. 1989. "The End of History?" *National Interest* (Summer): 3–18.

——. 2004. "The Imperative of State-Building." *Journal of Democracy* 15, no. 2: 17–31.

——. 2008. "State-Building in the Solomon Islands." Accessed July 9, 2008. www .sais-jhu.edu/faculty/fukuyama/Solomons.doc.

Gunaratra, Rohan. 2002. *Inside Al Qaeda: Global Network of Terror*. New York: Columbia University Press.

Hameiri, Shahar. 2007. "The Trouble with RAMSI: Reexamining the Roots of Conflict in Solomon Islands." *Contemporary Pacific* 19, no. 2:409–41.

Hippler, Jochen, ed. 2004. *Nation-Building. Ein Schlüsselkonzept für friedliche Konfliktbearbeitung?* Bonn: Dietz.

International Commission on Intervention and State Sovereignty. 2001. "The Responsibility to Protect: Report of the International Commission on Intervention and State Sovereignty." Ottawa.

Keohane, Robert O. 2007. "Governance and Legitimacy." SFB-Governance Lecture Series 1, Berlin.

Krasner, Stephen D. 2004. "Governance Failures and Alternatives to Sovereignty." CDDRL Working Paper 1, Stanford.

Ladwig, Bernd. 2007. "Gebotene Fremdbestimmung? Normative Überlegungen zum Umgang mit zerfallen(d)er Staatlichkeit." In *Regieren ohne Staat? Governance in Räumen begrenzter Staatlichkeit*, edited by Thomas Risse and Ursula Lehmkuhl, 354–73. Baden-Baden: Nomos.

Lehmkuhl, Ursula. 2007. "Regieren im kolonialen Amerika: Colonial Governance und koloniale Gouvernementalité in französischen und englischen Siedlungskolonien." In *Regieren ohne Staat? Governance in Räumen begrenzter Staatlichkeit*, edited by Thomas Risse and Ursula Lehmkuhl, 111–33. Baden-Baden: Nomos.

Leibfried, Stephan, and Michael Zürn. 2005. *Transformations of the State?* Cambridge: Cambridge University Press.

Mansfield, Edward D., and Jack Snyder. 2005. "Prone to Violence." *National Interest*. http://nationalinterest.org/article/prone-to-violence-596.

Menkhaus, Ken. 2007. "Governance Without Government in Somalia: Spoilers, State Building, and the Politics of Coping." *International Security* 31, no. 3:74–106.

Menzel, Ulrich. 1992. *Das Ende der Dritten Welt und das Scheitern der großen Theorie*. Frankfurt/Main: Suhrkamp.

Mützelburg, Bernd. 2007. "Zerfallende Staaten. Herausforderungen an die nationale und multilaterale Politik." In *Staatszerfall und Governance*, vol. 7 of *Schriften zur Governance-Forschung*, edited by Marianne Beisheim and Gunnar Folke Schuppert, 287–92. Baden-Baden: Nomos.

National Security Strategy of the United States of America. 2006. Washington, D.C.: The White House.

——. 2010. Washington, D.C.: The White House.

Reno, William. 1997. "Welthandel, Warlords und die Wiedererfindung des afrikanischen Staates." *WeltTrends* 5, no. 14:8–29.

Risse, Thomas. 2007a. "Regieren in Räumen begrenzter Staatlichkeit." SFB-Governance Working Paper 5, Berlin.

——. 2007b. "Was in Afghanistan auf dem Spiel steht." *Internationale Politik* 62, no. 4:106–108.

Risse, Thomas, and Ursula Lehmkuhl. 2006. "Governance in Areas of Limited State-hood: New Modes of Governance?" Research Program of the Research Center (SFB) 700. SFB-Governance Working Paper 1, Berlin.

——. 2007. "Governance in Räumen begrenzter Staatlichkeit. Anmerkungen zu kon-zeptionellen Problemen der gegenwärtigen Governance-Diskussion." In *Staats-zerfall und Governance*, vol. 7 of *Schriften zur Governance-Forschung*, edited by Marianne Beisheim and Gunnar Folke Schuppert, 144–59. Baden-Baden: Nomos.

Rotberg, Robert I. 2007. "The Failure and Collapse of Nation States." In *Staatszerfall und Governance*, vol. 7 of *Schriften zur Governance-Forschung*, edited by Marianne Beisheim and Gunnar Folke Schuppert, 59–97. Baden-Baden: Nomos.

Ruttig, Thomas 2007: Die Taleban nach Mulla Dadullah. Ihre Strukturen, ihr Pro-gramm—und ob man mit ihnen reden kann (SWP-Aktuell 31), Berlin.

Schlichte, Klaus. 2005. "Gibt es überhaupt 'Staatszerfall'? Anmerkungen zu einer aus-ufernden Debatte." *Berliner Debatte Initial* 16, no. 4:74–84.

Schlichte, Klaus, and Alexander Veit. 2006. "Uganda und Kongo-Kinshasa. Gespon-serte Herrschaft." *Die Gazette* 11:32–35.

Schneckener, Ulrich. 2005. "Fragile Staatlichkeit als globales Sicherheitsrisiko." *Aus Politik und Zeitgeschichte* 28/29:26–31.

——. 2006. "States at Risk. Zur Analyse fragiler Staatlichkeit." In *Fragile Staatlich-keit. "States at Risk" zwischen Stabilität und Scheitern*, edited by Ulrich Schneckener, 9–40. Baden-Baden: Nomos.

——. 2007. "Fragile Staatlichkeit und State-building. Begriffe, Konzepte und Analy-serahmen." In *Staatszerfall und Governance*, vol. 7 of *Schriften zur Governance-Forschung*, edited by Marianne Beisheim and Gunnar Folke Schuppert, 98–121. Baden-Baden: Nomos.

Schneckener, Ulrich, and Christoph Zürcher. 2007. "Transnational Security Gover-nance in fragilen Staaten. Oder: Geht Sicherheit ohne Staat?" In *Regieren ohne Staat? Governance in Räumen begrenzter Staatlichkeit*, edited by Thomas Risse and Ursula Lehmkuhl, 205–22. Baden-Baden: Nomos.

Tansey, Oisín. 2007. "Democratization Without a State: Democratic Regime-building in Kosovo." *Democratization* 14, no. 1:129–50.

Trotha, Trutz von. 2005. "Der Aufstieg des Lokalen." *Aus Politik und Zeitgeschichte* 28/29:32–38.

Wainwright, Elsina, and Murray Harris. 2005. "Lektionen aus dem Südpazifik." *Inter-nationale Politik* 60, no. 9:54–61.

Zangl, Bernhard, and Michael Zürn. 2003. *Frieden und Krieg. Sicherheit in der natio-nalen und postnationalen Konstellation*. Frankfurt: Suhrkamp.

Zürcher, Christoph. 2007. "When Governance Meets Troubled States." In *Staatszer-fall und Governance*, vol. 7 of *Schriften zur Governance-Forschung*, edited by Mari-anne Beisheim and Gunnar Folke Schuppert, 11–27. Baden-Baden: Nomos.

MARIANNE BEISHEIM is senior research associate at the SWP German Institute for International and Security Affairs, Berlin.

TANJA A. BÖRZEL is professor of European integration at the Otto Suhr Institute of Political Science, Freie Universität Berlin.

ZELJKO BRANOVIC is research associate at the Research Center Governance in Areas of Limited Statehood, Freie Universität Berlin.

LARS BROZUS is senior research associate at the SWP German Institute for International and Security Affairs, Berlin.

SVEN CHOJNACKI is professor of comparative politics and peace research at the Otto Suhr Institute of Political Science, Freie Universität Berlin.

SEBASTIAN CONRAD is professor of modern history at the Department of History, Freie Universität Berlin.

LAURA VON DANIELS is research associate at the Hertie School of Governance and at the Research Center Governance in Areas of Limited Statehood, Berlin.

HENRIK ENDERLEIN is professor of international political economy at the Hertie School of Governance, Berlin.

ADRIENNE HÉRITIER is professor of public policy at the European University Institute, Florence, Italy.

NICOLE KRANZ is research associate at the Center for Transnational Relations, Foreign, and Security Policy, Otto Suhr Institute of Political Science, Freie Universität Berlin.

BERND LADWIG is professor of modern political theory at the Otto Suhr Institute of Political Science, Freie Universität Berlin.

ANDREA LIESE is professor of international organizations and public policy at the Faculty of Economics and Social Sciences, University of Potsdam, Potsdam.

THOMAS RISSE is professor of international politics at the Otto Suhr Institute of Political Science, Freie Universität Berlin and coordinator of the Research Center Governance in Areas of Limited Statehood.

BEATE RUDOLF is professor of law and director of the German Institute for Human Rights, Berlin.

ULRICH SCHNECKENER is professor of international relations and peace and conflict studies at the School of Social Science, University of Osnabrück, Osnabrück.

GUNNAR FOLKE SCHUPPERT is professor of governance and head of the Rule of Law Center at the Social Science Research Center Berlin (WZB).

MARION STANGE was research associate at the Research Center Governance in Areas of Limited Statehood and is now program director at the Alexander von Humboldt Foundation.

CHRISTIAN THAUER is postdoctoral fellow at the Center for Transnational Relations, Foreign and Security Policy, Otto Suhr Institute of Political Science, Freie Universität Berlin.

CHRISTOPH TREBESCH is research associate at the Hertie School of Governance and at the Research Center Governance in Areas of Limited Statehood, Berlin.

GPSR Authorized Representative: Easy Access System Europe, Mustamäe tee
50, 10621 Tallinn, Estonia, gpsr.requests@easproject.com